ANY FOOD IS A "DIET" FOOD— WHEN IT'S PREPARED PROPERLY! . . .

. . . and by eating the foods you like, you avoid the boredom of ordinary diets while reducing safely and permanently. FAMILY CIRCLE LOW-CALORIE COOKING will show you how to

- Choose meats that are kind to both waistline and budget

- Make skinny versions of your favorite Italian recipes

- Enjoy refreshing salads which are healthful and hearty

- Brighten up plain foods with wine and spices

- Use culinary imagination to turn vegetables into treats

- Entertain lavishly with calorie-shy party dishes

- Enhance your meals with rich, slimming sauces

- Trim the calorie counts of dozens of forbidden desserts and much, much more!

FAMILY CIRCLE cookbooks
published by BALLANTINE BOOKS

Family Circle®

Creative
Low-Calorie
Cooking

by Barbara Gibbons

BALLANTINE BOOKS • NEW YORK

Library of Congress Catalog Card Number: 73-77971

ISBN 0-345-25940-8

This edition published by arrangement with The Family Circle, Inc., an Iowa Corporation.

Manufactured in the United States of America

First Ballantine Books Edition: August 1978
Second Edition: March 1979
First Canadian Printing: August 1978

Edited by Nancy A. Hecht

Art director: Philip Sykes
Art assistant: Marsha Camera

Photographs by George Nordhausen

Contents

Foreword

Back when I weighed 200-and-plenty, I had only two kinds of recipes: Before and After. My Before Recipes (before I went on yet another diet) consisted of fatty high-calorie foods that simply tilted the scale in the wrong direction. My After Recipes (or more appropriately, during) were broiled-in-the nude foods—totally unappetizing and emotionally devastating.

Since then, I've given up Before-and-After Cooking. Now I weigh 125 and I have scores of recipes I enjoy, most of which only seem fattening!

There's no secret to my success story and there's no starvation either. It was really a matter of learning how to duplicate the taste and texture of my favorite foods, without the unneeded extra calories.

I hope the recipes in this book become favorites of yours . . . they provide an enjoyable, positive way to lose weight and to keep you from ever having to go on a diet again!

—Barbara Gibbons

A Letter from the Editor

Two years ago, I received a letter from a housewife in New Jersey which said in part: "I just can't diet. It wasn't until I started to 'decalorize' all my family's favorite foods that I succeeded in bringing my weight from 208 to 125 . . . without dieting."

That letter marked the beginning of a whole new career for its writer, Barbara Gibbons. Out of it grew *Family Circle's* popular monthly column, *Creative Low-Calorie Cooking*—and this book, with over 300 of Barbara's best recipes and calorie tips. But that isn't all. Since the appearance of the column, United Features signed Barbara up for a syndicated feature, and her three-times-a-week column, *The Slim Gourmet,* now is carried by more than 100 newspapers.

Creative Low-Calorie Cooking combines several ingredients important to all of us—whether we're on a diet or simply looking for good recipes that help feed our families more nutritiously.

In a day of fast foods and sporadic meals, it's delightful to find recipes that will fit into anyone's time schedule without sacrificing health. Each recipe in this book is designed with this thought in mind.

Some of the recipes incorporate low-calorie products. Others take advantage of some special cooking and 'de-calorizing' techniques designed to take the excess fats, starches and sugars out of foods. These cooking techniques and 'de-calorizing' tips are common sense suggestions such as the following: Instead of cooking hamburgers in a skillet with oil broil the hamburgers on a rack in a broiler pan. That way, all the fat drips down into the pan, away from the meat.

I think you as a homemaker, wife, working mother, husband, single girl, gourmet cook, or someone who just enjoys good food, will find *Creative Low-Calorie Cooking* a kitchen helpmate you can't do without!

—Arthur Hettich
Editor
Family Circle Magazine

How to Succeed as a Creative Low-Calorie Cook

Dieting is negative. It stresses what you can't do and can't have. But Creative Low-Calorie Cooking is a positive approach that puts you back in the kitchen, using all your culinary cleverness to weed away the extra calories in the foods you love. And it's one lose-weight method that can really work, even for diet dropouts!

You don't give up fattening foods, you just make them less fattening, or non-fattening. And slowly, but surely, the extra pounds disappear.

It's the one method, perhaps the only method for the woman who enjoys good food and loves to cook. She's the one who finds dieting doubly difficult, because a strict food regimen deprives her not only of the food she loves, but her cooking hobby as well. So why not put all that "culinary creativity" to work . . . in your favor instead of against you.

Stay Slim Forever, the Easy Way

This isn't a "quick weight loss diet" (which is inevitably followed by an even-quicker weight gain). Differing from dangerous fad diets and unbalanced crash programs, Creative Low-Calorie Cooking is a healthy, nutritionally-sound approach, a whole new way of cooking and eating that can keep you happily slender for the rest of your life!

Everyone Benefits

Learning to cook the low-calorie way keeps overweight from becoming hereditary in your family. By trimming the empty-caloried sugars and starches from foods, you leave room in your children's menu for nutritionally meaningful snacks. Your husband's health will probably benefit, too, by the elimination of excess fat (particularly saturated animal fats) from his food. Cutting down on fat is one of the major recommendations of the American Heart Association.

The Basic Recipe

1. Eat what you want, but never a high-calorie food when there's a lower-calorie version available. For example, eat ice milk instead of ice cream, part skim cheese instead of whole milk cheese, low-calorie sodas, jams and salad dressings in lieu of the higher-calorie ones. This principle applies to every meal, every day and includes special occasions.

2. Count every last calorie because every one counts. There's no such thing as a calorie difference too slight to bother with. Over the years even the slightest calorie difference can add up to several dress sizes.

3. Eat a well-balanced diet that includes all the basics. This is a lifelong program, not a crash diet, so you can't afford to short-change nutrition.

4. Make a game of low-calorie cooking . . . it's fun to cheat your cookbook out of extra calories.

5. This program starts immediately . . . no waiting for Monday morning or after George's birthday. Forget the "stuff today, starve tomorrow" syndrome.

Getting Started

Here's what you'll need:
Calorie Charts and Guides:

These are your "scorecards." Nobody has yet come up with a better and simpler way to keep track of food intake, so take the time to become a calorie expert. After a few weeks of conscientious calorie-counting, you'll be armed for life with a tip-of-the-tongue count for 90% of the foods you eat.

Since this is a major overhaul of your cooking habits, a simple counter or the chart in your cookbook won't do. You'll need several, by different publishers, to research all your special favorites. You can start with the one beginning on page 314. It gives calorie counts for over 600 foods. Also include one of the brand-name calorie guides that list products, mixes and convenience foods by brand name. The U.S. Department of Agriculture publishes a 189-page handbook, *The Composition of Foods,* which includes calorie counts as well as other nutritional information—it's a worthwhile $2 investment you can make by sending your order to the Superintendent of Documents, Washington, D.C. 20402.

Your own "Weights & Measures" Department

Invest in an accurate set of measures and a postal scale. Most dieters have no idea how minuscule a 3- or 4-ounce serving of meat is, or a one-eighth cut of pie! After one week of weighing and measuring your food, you'll develop a reasonably accurate "eye" and won't have to bother.

The Proper Equipment

A nonstick skillet is an absolute necessity, along with a rack-equipped broiling pan so meats don't simmer in their own fat.

Your Research Library

Become a collector of low-calorie cookbooks. Borrow them first from your public library to see which ones you like. Cookbooks for diabetics and heart patients are full of good hints, too. And most makers of low-calorie foods publish recipe booklets that are yours for the writing.

Go on a Supermarket Calorie Hunt

It's one of the most fascinating ways to plunge into your program. There are hundreds of low-calorie foods and lower-calorie versions of fattening foods to choose from . . . and they're all not necessarily grouped together in the diet-foods section. Most low-fat or fat-free, sugar-reduced or sugar-free items are less fattening than the conventional product, but check the label carefully to be sure.

Make it a resolution to buy and try all the low-calorie, low-fat and low-sugar products you can. Give each one a fair trial—resolve to finish the package before making a determination. If you can't go "cold turkey" into a low-calorie product, try "weaning" yourself by mixing it half-and-half with the regular product—sugar-free maple syrup and regular syrup; diet French dressing and regular dressing.

Go After the Big Three:
Starches, Sweets and Fats

Starchy Foods

They're a double threat to the would-be skinny. They don't do their dirty work alone; they usually team up with fats or sugars as their ally—bread and butter, cake with icing, buttered rice, spaghetti with meatballs.

Try to limit yourself to two slices of bread a day . . . the ones you can't do without. Some people must have a sandwich for lunch, while others can't face dinner without breaking bread.

Make bread calories less potent and more profitable by choosing one of the lower-calorie or protein-enriched breads in your supermarket. Gluten bread, for example, is very much like ordinary white bread, yet it's only 35 calories per slice (compared with 65 for ordinary bread). Protein-enriched breads made from part soy flour are between 40 and 50 calories a slice.

There are protein-enriched pastas on the market today, too, made partly from soy flour. They aren't much lower in calories, but the protein content makes them more filling and more nutritious.

If you'd like to try making home-baked, protein-enriched goodies, experiment with low-fat soy flour, often available in the health-food section of your supermarket or in a health-food store. One cupful is 368 calories compared with 422 for all-purpose wheat flour. Try mixing it equally with wheat-flour for lower-calorie, protein-enriched baked goods.

Sweets

Throwing out your sugar bowl is one of the most effective ways to cut calories dramatically. If you can't satisfy your sweet tooth with fruit, by all means make use of today's modern sugar substitutes. Virtually all of the sugar substitutes on the market today are based on saccharin, the sweetener that has been used by countless diabetics for more than 60 years. But today's saccharin-based sugar substitutes have been modernized.

They come in tablet, liquid and powdered concentrates, as well as granulated types that you can use spoon-for-spoon in place of sugar.

You can cook with today's sugar substitutes, too. Use them as an adjunct to sugar in any recipe except those that depend on sugar for bulk (confectioners' icing or chocolate fudge, for example). The best way to have fun experimenting is to substitute half of the sugar called for in a recipe with its equivalent in sugar substitutes; consult the label for how much to use.

There are 16 calories in 1 teaspoon of sugar, 49 in 1 tablespoon and 791 in a cupful, so acquiring a "taste" (or at least a tolerance) for sugar substitutes is well worth it!

• Saccharin-based sweeteners tend to lose some of their sweetening power with extended cooking, so add them *last,* when possible . . . stir sweetener into a pudding recipe *after* it's removed from the heat, for example.

• Increasing the amount of vanilla in a recipe tends to enhance the impression of sweetness.

• You can minimize the need for sweetness by cutting back on "sour" or "bitter" flavors . . . use a little less lemon or chocolate than your recipe calls for and you won't need as much sugar or sweetener.

• Sweetness needs a pinch of salt for accent, even artificially-sweetened foods! The reason some packaged dietetic products seem bland is because the manufacturer is trying to meet the needs of the salt-free dieter too. Try adding a pinch of salt to diet chocolate pudding mix (unless you're on a salt-free diet) and taste the difference!

Following is a table of equivalents that applies to most sweeteners. Use this table as a guide when reworking many of your favorite sugar-laden recipes. Since individual brands may vary, however, be sure to always consult the label before substituting a sweetener for sugar. And, if you're on a sugar-free diet, be sure to seek your doctor's advice about which and how much are safe for you to use.

Table of Equivalents

Note: If you're on a sugar-free diet, be sure to seek your doctor's advice about which sugar substitute to use and how much is safe for you to use.

Sugar	¼ Grain Tablets
1 teaspoon	1
1 tablespoon	2½
¼ cup	12
½ cup	24
¾ cup	36
1 cup	48

There are also ½ grain saccharin tablets, each equal to 2 teaspoons sugar.

Sugar	Granulated Concentrate
1 teaspoon	¹⁄₁₀ teaspoon
1 tablespoon	¼ teaspoon
¼ cup	1⅕ teaspoons
½ cup	2⅖ teaspoons
¾ cup	3⅗ teaspoons
1 cup	5 teaspoons

There are also non-concentrated sugar replacements with the same volume as sugar and can be used spoon-for-spoon and cup-for-cup in place of sugar.

Sugar	Liquid
1 teaspoon	6 drops
1 tablespoon	¼ teaspoon
¼ cup	1 teaspoon
½ cup	2 teaspoons
¾ cup	1 tablespoon
1 cup	4 teaspoons

Getting the Fat Out

Most fats average around 100 calories a tablespoon, whether it's vegetable oil, butter, margarine or the fat attached to a steak.

Switching from whole milk to skim milk cuts your milk calories in half. In between these two are fortified low-fat milks that seem so rich and creamy because they've got extra milk solids—not fats.

Butterfat makes the difference in ice cream, too— the richest ice cream is twice as fattening as the leanest ice milk.

Diet margarine is exactly half the calories of butter or regular margarine.

Reducing the Calorie Count of Meats

In recent years, the popularity of high-protein reducing diets has led many people to conclude that the more meat you eat, the thinner you get. This is not necessarily the case, especially if you enjoy sausage, hamburger or well-marbled steaks. In fact, most Americans eat more meat than they need, if government dietary allowances are followed. Two 3-ounce servings per day is enough to satisfy your entire protein requirement per day. (Use a postal scale and a spoonful of hamburger to see how little meat that really is!)

But we Americans are meat-eaters because we like

it. To enjoy a beefed-up menu without a beefy figure, take every fat-trimming shortcut there is.

When you Shop

Choose meat carefully and select only the leanest cuts. Have fat shorn off by the butcher, or trim it yourself before cooking. Don't buy regular hamburger or any of the other prepackaged ground meats. Have lean cuts ground to order. The fat saving is considerable.

When you Cook

Always bake or broil on a rack, so melting fats can escape.

For range-top cooking, a nonstick skillet and one tablespoon of oil is all you need for the leanest meats. Fattier meats like hamburger or lamb chops don't even need that—they can sauté in their own fat. Or better yet, broil them.

Overcooking, not lack of fat, robs meat of moistness—so invest in a meat thermometer.

When you slow-simmer meats in a sauce or a stew, prebrown them under the broiler instead of in the pot. Prepare the meat a day ahead and refrigerate it overnight. The chilling brings the fat to the surface where it hardens. Before reheating the meat, lift off the hard fat . . . You've just saved yourself all those extra calories. Remember, fat adds only calories to savory stew—not flavor. Add the vegetables and slow simmer until they're tender. Thicken the sauce and you're on your way to a flavorful, figure-conscious dinner.

When you Serve

Decide in advance what constitutes a proper meat serving and prepare only that much. Or, to save some kitchen time, prepare just enough for two same-size meals. Freeze one and serve the other.

Let Variety Be Your Spice

Beef, lamb, pork and ham are comparatively high-calorie main courses compared with veal, poultry, liver and seafood. Try this technique for cutting calories: Every time you buy a pound of high-calorie meats, buy an equal amount of the lower-calorie group. For example, for every pound of hamburger, buy an equal amount of chicken; for every pound of pork chops, buy its equivalent in scallops or liver. This self-enforced widening of your main-course repertoire can cut your family's calorie intake dramatically.

Does the Substitution Game Pay Off?

Let's look at the daily menu for two imaginary neighbors, Mary and Margaret, both 35 years old and 5′ 5″ tall. On the left is what Mary eats on a typical day. Margaret follows the same menu and eats just as much, but she substitutes the lower-calorie versions of Mary's foods. After a period of time, with no difference in their activity, Mary will probably weigh close to 200 pounds and still be gaining weight, while Margaret remains a trim 125.

MARY'S MENU

Breakfast	Calories
½ grapefruit with 1 teaspoon sugar	63
2 slices toast with 2 tablespoons strawberry jam	250
2 eggs fried in 2 tablespoons butter or margarine	260

MARGARET'S MENU

	Calories
½ grapefruit with low-calorie sugar substitute	48
2 slices protein-bread toast with 2 tablespoons low-sugar imitation strawberry jam	132
2 eggs fried in non-stick skillet	162

Lunch

Tuna salad sandwich (3 ounces oil-pack tuna, 2 tablespoons mayonnaise or salad dressing, 2 slices bread) **510**

1 bottle or can (12 ounces) cola beverage **145**

½ cup cherry-flavor gelatin with 2 tablespoons whipped cream **125**

Tuna salad sandwich (3 ounces water-pack tuna, 2 tablespoons low-calorie mayonnaise, 2 slices protein bread) **281**

1 bottle or can (12 ounces) low-sugar cola beverage **2**

½ cup low-calorie, cherry-flavor gelatin, 2 tablespoons low-calorie whipped topping **24**

Mid-afternoon

Chocolate Sundae (½ cup ice cream, 2 tablespoons chocolate sauce, 2 tablespoons whipped cream) **308**

Chocolate Sundae (1½ cups ice milk, 2 tablespoons low-sugar chocolate sauce, 2 tablespoons low-calorie whipped topping) **152**

6 P.M.

Vodka and Bitter Lemon Mixer **228**

Vodka and sugar-free citrus flavor carbonated beverage **103**

Dinner

½ cup fruit cocktail **98**

Green salad (½ small head iceberg lettuce, 2 tablespoons French dressing) **145**

Broiled Hamburger with Mushroom Sauce (6 ounces ground beef, ⅓ cup canned mushroom gravy) **438**

½ cup cooked carrots with ½ tablespoon butter or margarine **73**

½ cup calories reduced fruit cocktail **60**

Green salad (¼ small head iceberg lettuce, 2 tablespoons low-calorie French dressing) **33**

Broiled Hamburger with Mushroom Sauce (6 ounces lean ground round, ⅓ cup canned mushroom gravy) **348**

½ cup cooked green beans with tablespoon butter or margarine   65

1 medium-size baked potato with 2 tablespoons sour cream   140

Strawberry Shortcake (1/16 packaged 10-inch sponge cake, ½ cup frozen strawberries in syrup, 2 tablespoons whipped cream)   325

½ cup cooked carrots with ½ tablespoon diet margarine   48

½ cup cooked green beans with ½ tablespoon diet margarine   40

1 medium-size baked potato with 2 tablespoons plain yogurt   106

Strawberry Parfait (½ cup fresh or frozen unsweetened strawberries sweetened with low-calorie sugar substitute, 2 tablespoons low-calorie whipped topping)   191

All Day
6 cups of coffee (each with 2 tablespoons sugar and 2 tablespoons light cream)   756

6 cups of coffee (each with 2 tablespoons skim milk and low-calorie sugar substitute)   104

Total   3,701   1,834

Family Circle
Creative Low-Calorie Cooking

Chapter 1

Wake Up to Breakfast

Despite a constant barrage of nutrition talk about the benefits of better breakfasts, many Americans miss the message! Some would-be skinnies still think that skipping meals is the best way to slim down. Cutting calories is great, but taking them from the top is self-defeating.

Breakfast can be Spartan or substantial, leisurely or on-the-run . . . just as long as it's *rich in protein*. Protein is the food that stays with you, pumping you full of bright-eyed bushy-tailed bounce until lunchtime. Low-calorie foods that are rich in protein include eggs, cottage cheese, lean meats, fish and poultry. There are also many no-time-for-breakfast foods that are protein-enriched—breads, cereals, breakfasts-for-drinking, and meal-in-a-can drinks or puddings.

And when Sunday rolls around it's time to bring on our low-calorie pancakes and bacon . . . they'd do any "pancake house" proud!

Recipes for Pancake Lovers

About Pancake Mixes

If you like the convenience of packaged mixes, here are some facts you'll want to know:

1

• Buckwheat pancake mix is your best buy in calories and protein. One ounce of dry mix is 93 calories and 10.5 percent protein—compared with 101 calories and 8.6 percent protein for most packaged plain and buttermilk pancake mixes.

• In the health-food store or section of your supermarket, look for high-protein soy flour pancake mix. It's convenient to use and close to 14 percent protein.

Dos and Don'ts for Pancake Cooks

• *Don't* add fat or oil to the recipe . . . or the skillet. Butter, margarine, shortening, bacon grease and vegetable oil range between 100 and 125 calories an unnecessary tablespoon!

• *Do* use a nonstick skillet or griddle, one with a Teflon-type coating or an old-fashioned soapstone griddle. Be sure your griddle is properly seasoned.

• *Do* have your griddle whistle-clean. If you make pancakes often, reserve a nonstick skillet especially for that purpose.

• *Don't* have your griddle over-hot. Once the surface reaches the dancing-water stage, lower the heat to prevent sticking and to keep the pan from smoking.

• *Do* use one of the convenient spray-on or wipe-on lecithin coatings for fat-free frying. Lecithin is a natural food product that adds no flavor or calories yet permits you to cook "fried" foods with no fat.

• *Don't* make your pancakes overlarge; they'll be troublesome to turn. Besides, four small ones are psychologically more satisfying than two big ones.

• *Do* "pad" your pancakes with blueberries, apple slices, pineapple tidbits or other unsugared fruit. Fruit adds more bulk than calories!

GERMAN PANCAKE WITH PEACHES

Bake at 425° for 20 minutes.
Makes 6 servings at 211 calories each.

1 cup sifted all-purpose
flour
½ teaspoon baking
powder
½ teaspoon salt
1 cup skim milk

5 eggs
1 tablespoon vegetable
oil
1 can (1 pound) diet-
pack sliced peaches,
drained

1. Sift flour, baking powder and salt into a mixing bowl. Beat in milk, using a rotary beater, then the eggs, one at a time.
2. Heat the oil in a large (9-inch) skillet with an oven-proof handle. Pour in the batter all at once. Cook 1 minute over medium heat.
3. Bake in hot oven (425°) 20 minutes, or until pancake is browned and puffy. Top with drained, sliced peaches; serve at once.

FOR UNDER-400-CALORIE BREAKFAST: 1 wedge of German Pancake topped with peaches, 2 ounces "Mock Bacon," ½ grapefruit, black coffee.

BLUEBERRY HOTCAKES

Makes 24 three-inch pancakes at 30 calories each.

1 cup all-purpose flour,
sifted
2 teaspoons baking
powder
4 teaspoons sugar
½ teaspoon salt

1 egg
1 cup skim milk
⅔ cup fresh or frozen
unsweetened
blueberries

1. Sift flour, baking powder, sugar and salt into a mixing bowl. Combine egg and milk; add to flour mix-

ture. Stir only until ingredients are moistened. Batter will be lumpy. Fold in blueberries.

2. Heat a nonstick skillet or griddle until a drop of water dances on the surface. Use a measuring tablespoon to drop level tablespoons of batter on heated griddle. Bake over low heat until the surfaces of the pancakes are bubbled. Turn and bake other side.

YOGURT PANCAKES

Makes 25 three-inch pancakes at 30 calories each.

1¼ cups sifted all-
   purpose flour
½ teaspoon salt
1 teaspoon baking soda
Pinch of baking
   powder

1 egg yolk, slightly
   beaten
1 container (8 ounces)
   plain yogurt
¼ cup skim milk
2 egg whites

1. Sift flour, salt, baking soda and baking powder into a mixing bowl.
2. Combine egg yolk, yogurt and skim milk; add to flour mixture. Stir only until the ingredients are moistened. The batter will be lumpy.
3. Beat egg whites until stiff but not dry; fold into batter.
4. Heat a nonstick skillet or griddle until a drop of water dances on the surface. Use a measuring tablespoon to drop level tablespoons of the batter on the heated griddle. Bake over low heat until the surfaces of the pancakes are bubbled. Turn and bake other side until lightly browned. Serve immediately.

APPLE-YOGURT PANCAKES: Stir ½ cup thinly sliced apples into batter. Bake as above. Sprinkle pancakes with cinnamon and sugar substitute before serving. Makes 25 three-inch pancakes at 31 calories each.

FOR UNDER-400-CALORIE BREAKFAST: 5 Apple-Yogurt Pancakes topped with more plain yogurt; 3

slices "Baked Bacon," 5 ounces grapefruit juice and black coffee.

LOW-CALORIE WHEAT CAKES

Makes 26 three-inch pancakes at 27 calories each.

1¼ cups sifted all-purpose flour	½ teaspoon salt
2½ teaspoons baking powder	1 egg, slightly beaten 1¼ cups skim milk

1. Sift flour, baking powder and salt into a mixing bowl.

2. Combine egg and milk; add to flour mixture. Stir only until ingredients are moistened. Batter will be lumpy.

3. Heat a nonstick skillet or griddle until a drop of water dances on the surface. Use a measuring tablespoon to drop level tablespoons of the batter on heated griddle. Bake over low heat until the surfaces of the pancakes are bubbled. Turn and bake other side.

WHOLE WHEAT CAKES: Substitute whole wheat flour (unsifted) for the all-purpose flour. Makes 20 three-inch pancakes at 35 calories each.

FOR UNDER-400-CALORIE BREAKFAST: 5 Wheat Cakes with 1 ounce Low-Calorie Maple Syrup, 2 ounces broiled beef sausage, 5 ounces orange juice and black coffee.

COTTAGE-STYLE PANCAKES

Makes 24 pancakes (about 3½ inches) at 33 calories each.

2 eggs	1 cup sifted all-purpose flour
1 cup low-fat cottage cheese	½ teaspoon baking soda
⅔ cup skim milk	½ teaspoon salt

1. Place the eggs, cottage cheese and skim milk in container of electric blender. Whirl at high speed until mixture is creamy. Scrape down sides of container.

2. Add flour, baking soda and salt to mixture in container. Whirl only until creamy and blended.

3. Heat a nonstick skillet or griddle until a drop of water dances on the surface. Pour batter on the heated griddle to make pancakes about 3½ inches in diameter. Bake over low heat until the surfaces of the pancakes are bubbled. Turn and bake other side.

BLUEBERRY PANCAKES: Fold ½ cup fresh or frozen (unsweetened) blueberries in batter. Bake as directed above. Makes two dozen 3½-inch pancakes at 34 calories each.

FOR UNDER-400-CALORIE BREAKFAST: 4 Cottage-Style Pancakes with 1 ounce Low-Calorie Maple Syrup, broiled orange sections, 3 slices beef bacon, coffee with skim milk and sugar substitute.

PROTEIN PANCAKES

Makes 32 three-inch pancakes at 29 calories each.

¾ cup sifted all-purpose flour
⅓ cup sifted low-fat soy flour
2½ teaspoons baking powder
½ teaspoon salt
1 egg, slightly beaten
1⅓ cups skim milk

1. Sift flour, soy flour, baking powder and salt into mixing bowl.

2. Combine egg and milk; add to flour mixture. Stir only until ingredients are moistened. Batter will be lumpy.

3. Heat a nonstick skillet or griddle until a drop of water dances on the surface. Use a measuring tablespoon to drop level tablespoons of batter on heated griddle. Bake over low heat until the surfaces of the pancakes are bubbled. Turn and bake other side.

BACON-CRISP PROTEIN PANCAKES: Sprinkle the surface of each pancake with 1 teaspoon of bacon-flavored soy protein before turning. This adds 10 calories per pancake.

FOR UNDER-300-CALORIE BREAKFAST: 4 Bacon-Crisp Protein Pancakes, 1 ounce Low-Calorie Honey Syrup, ½ grapefruit and black coffee.

SLIM CHEESE BLINTZES

Makes 8 blintzes at 55 calories each.

BLINTZES

1 egg yolk
½ cup skim milk
6 tablespoons sifted
    all-purpose flour
Pinch of salt
1 teaspoon vegetable
    oil

FILLING

¾ cup low-fat cottage
    cheese
1 egg white
Pinch of salt
Sugar substitute to
    equal 2 teaspoons
    sugar
½ teaspoon vanilla
½ teaspoon ground
    cinnamon

1. Combine yolk, milk, flour and salt; beat until smooth.

2. Brush bottom of 6-inch nonstick skillet or crepe pan with oil. Heat over medium heat.

3. Use a measuring tablespoon to spoon about 1½ tablespoons of batter into the heated skillet. Cook one side only, over medium heat. When underside is lightly browned, turn out onto a plate. Continue as above; put pieces of wax paper between the prepared blintzes.

4. Combine cottage cheese, egg white, salt, sugar substitute, vanilla and cinnamon. Place filling in centers of prepared blintzes, about a tablespoon each. Fold the sides of the blintzes over to enclose the filling. Place filled blintzes, fold-side down, on a nonstick baking dish or cooky sheet.

5. Bake in moderate oven (350°) 15 minutes. Serve hot.

FOR UNDER-300-CALORIE BREAKFAST: 3 Slim Cheese Blintzes topped with 4 tablespoons warmed, crushed diet-pack pineapple, about 5 ounces of orange-grapefruit juice and coffee with skim milk.

Pared-down Pancake Toppings

Here are some stand-ins for those sugar-packed syrups:

• *Dietetic Maple Syrup*—On your supermarket diet shelf. Only six to 12 calories a tablespoon, instead of 60 or so for conventional pancake syrups.

• *"Diet Half-and-Half"*—Mix up your own low-sugar blend! Combine equal parts of dietetic syrup with real maple syrup for a topping that's only half as fattening as most syrups.

• *Diet Jams and Jellies*—Make a diet-wise pancake spread. The sugarless (dietetic) types are five to 20 calories per tablespoon, compared with 60 calories for regular. The low-sugar types are about 30 calories per tablespoon.

• *Quick Fruit Syrups* are easy to make from sugarless or low-sugar jams and jellies: Simply combine with equal amounts of water and simmer; stir over low heat until melted and simmering. Five to 15 calories per tablespoon.

• *Diet Margarine* is 25 calories a pat (½ tablespoon), half the calories of butter or regular margarine. But why use margarine and syrup?

• *Fresh Fruit*—Serve sliced or crushed strawberries, peaches or blueberries, slightly sugared or pseudo-sweetened. They're the most calorie-wise toppings of all! Or use unsweetened canned or frozen fruit . . . or low-calorie crushed pineapple or applesauce. Or . . . make your own syrup.

LOW-CALORIE MAPLE SYRUP

Makes 1 cup—14 calories per tablespoon.

1 tablespoon
  cornstarch
5 tablespoons sugar
Pinch of salt
	1 cup cold water
	2 teaspoons maple
	  flavoring

1. Combine cornstarch, sugar, salt and water in small saucepan; mix well.

2. Cook the mixture over medium heat, stirring constantly, until syrup thickens and bubbles. Lower heat; simmer 1 minute. Remove from heat; stir in maple flavoring. Cool; use immediately or store in container with tight-fitting lid.

LOW-CALORIE SYRUP WITH HONEY—Substitute ¼ cup honey for the sugar and omit the maple flavoring. Makes 1 cup—18 calories per tablespoon.

TEN-CALORIE MAPLE SYRUP—Reduce sugar to 2½ tablespoons. After removing syrup from heat, stir in sugar substitute to equal 4 tablespoons sugar. Makes 1 cup—10 calories per tablespoon.

SUGARLESS MAPLE SYRUP—Omit sugar in Low-Calorie Maple Syrup. After syrup is cooked, stir in sugar substitute to equal 7 tablespoons of sugar, or sweeten to taste. Makes 1 cup—3 calories per tablespoon.

PINEAPPLE OR ORANGE PANCAKE SAUCE—Substitute unsweetened pineapple or orange juice for the water and reduce the sugar to 2 tablespoons. Makes 1 cup—13 calories per tablespoon.

French Toast

DIETER'S EGG-RICH FRENCH TOAST

Makes 2 slices at 85 calories each.

1 egg	2 slices protein bread
1 tablespoon water	Cinnamon
Pinch of salt	Sugar substitute

1. Beat egg, water and salt together and pour in a shallow dish. Soak the bread in this mixture for several minutes, until completely saturated.
2. Use a spatula to lift the soaked bread from the dish into a cold, nonstick skillet. Cook over low heat until underside is lightly browned. Turn and brown second side. Sprinkle with cinnamon and sugar substitute; serve hot.

BASIC FRENCH TOAST

Makes 8 slices at 78 calories each.

1 teaspoon vegetable oil	½ teaspoon salt
2 large eggs	½ teaspoon vanilla
⅔ cup skim milk	8 slices diet protein bread

1. Wipe a large nonstick skillet with the oil.
2. Beat eggs, milk, salt and vanilla together and pour into a shallow bowl. Dip the bread, a slice at a time, in mixture. Brown the bread on the skillet over a moderate flame, turning once.

PINEAPPLE DANISH TOAST

Makes 4 servings at 129 calories each.

1 egg
Pinch of salt
6 tablespoons
  unsweetened
  pineapple juice
4 slices protein bread
½ cup low-fat cottage
  cheese

4 slices pineapple
  (from 1-pound,
  4-ounce can) packed
  in pineapple juice
Cinnamon
Granulated sugar
  substitute

1. Combine egg, salt and pineapple juice; beat slightly. Dip bread into this mixture.

2. Place the wet bread on a cold, nonstick skillet. Cook slowly over moderate heat until one side is brown. Turn carefully with spatula. Continue to cook until other side is brown.

3. Top each slice of toast with 2 tablespoons cottage cheese and pineapple ring. Broil under high heat until cheese is heated and bubbly. Sprinkle with cinnamon and sugar substitute. Serve immediately.

BREAKFAST "STRAWBERRY SHORTCAKE"

Makes 1 serving at 273 calories.

2 slices Egg-Rich
  French Toast
½ cup low-fat cottage
  cheese

4 tablespoons fresh
  strawberries
Sugar substitute

Prepare the Egg-Rich French Toast (see recipe opposite). Layer two slices of toast with cottage cheese and strawberries sweetened with sugar substitute.

Eggs

Egg-Lover's Calorie Guide

Small	60
Medium	75
Large	80
Extra Large	94
Jumbo	105

Cooking Eggs Without Extra Fat

Use a heavy skillet with a nonstick coating in good condition. Be sure the surface is perfectly clean and smooth. If you're a frequent egg-eater, reserve a skillet just for this purpose. Use one of the spray-on or wipe-on lecithin coatings. (Lecithin is a natural food product that adds no calories yet permits "fried" foods with no fat.)

TO DRY-FRY AN EGG—Spray a small nonstick skillet with lecithin coating. Break egg into the cold skillet. Cook over low heat until white is set. If you like your eggs once over lightly, gently turn the egg over with a nonstick-coated spatula. Continue to cook over low heat until second side is lightly browned.

For sunny-side-up fans, do not turn the egg once the white is set. Simply cover the skillet with a tightly-fitting lid and continue cooking over low heat for a few minutes more.

TO DRY-SCRAMBLE EGGS—Mix 2 eggs with 2 tablespoons of water and a pinch of salt and pepper. Spray a small nonstick skillet with lecithin coating. Pour egg mixture into cold skillet and place over low heat. Cook slowly, lifting mixture around edge as it cooks, just until eggs are set, about 3 minutes. Serve immediately.

FOR A PERFECT OMELET—Spray a large non-stick skillet with lecithin coating. Heat just hot enough so that a drop of water bounces off its bottom, but not sizzling hot. Beat 3 eggs lightly with a fork, just enough to barely mix yolks and whites. Add 3 teaspoons water, and salt and pepper to taste. Pour eggs into skillet, tilting skillet so that eggs cover the bottom. Reduce heat slightly and, with a spatula, lift omelet gently up from the rim and tilt skillet so that uncooked egg runs underneath. When eggs have barely set, raise heat slightly to lightly brown the bottom. Fold the omelet and slip onto a warm plate. This size omelet will serve 2.

CHICKEN SCRAMBLE

Makes 1 serving at 199 calories.

2 eggs	1½ tablespoons water
½ envelope or teaspoon instant chicken broth	1 teaspoon butter or margarine

1. Beat the eggs, water and broth with fork.
2. Melt butter or margarine in a small- or medium-size skillet; pour in egg mixture. Cook slowly, lifting mixture around edge as it cooks, just until eggs are set but still shiny-moist on top.

OVEN-BAKED CHEESE OMELET

Bake at 400° for 20 minutes.
Makes 2 servings at 196 calories each.

2 whole eggs plus 2 egg whites	½ cup uncreamed low-fat cottage cheese
½ teaspoon salt	1 tablespoon vegetable oil

1. Separate eggs. Add salt to the egg whites and beat until stiff peaks form.

2. Combine egg yolks and cottage cheese; stir lightly. Fold in beaten egg whites.

3. Oil the inside of a medium-size skillet with an oven-proof handle (or a shallow baking dish). Add egg mixture and bake in hot oven (400°) 20 minutes, or until omelet is puffy and browned.

SWEET PINEAPPLE OMELET—Add few drops liquid sugar substitute and ½ teaspoon vanilla to egg mixture. Bake as above. Spread ½ cup calories-reduced crushed pineapple over half of omelet. Score down center and fold out onto plate. Sprinkle with cinnamon. Makes 3 servings at 154 calories each.

SLIM SPANISH OMELET

Makes 2 servings at 194 calories each.

½ cup tomato sauce	Pinch of garlic salt
1 teaspoon onion flakes	Pinch of salt
	Pinch of pepper
1 tablespoon dried green pepper flakes	Pinch of cayenne
	4 eggs, slightly beaten

1. Combine tomato sauce with seasonings in a medium-size saucepan. Cook over medium heat until sauce bubbles. Reduce heat; simmer for several minutes while preparing eggs.

2. Spray a large (9-inch) skillet with lecithin coating. Heat just hot enough so that a drop of water bounces off its bottom, but not sizzling hot.

3. Pour in eggs, tilting skillet so that eggs cover the bottom. Reduce heat slightly and, with a spatula, lift omelet gently up from the rim and tilt skillet so that uncooked egg runs underneath.

4. When eggs have barely set, raise heat slightly to lightly brown the bottom. Tilt the pan and, with a

spatula, fold the omelet and slip onto a warm platter. Cover with sauce; serve.

SCRAMBLED EGGS

Makes 2 servings at 190 calories each.

1 teaspoon margarine	½ teaspoon salt
4 eggs	Pinch of pepper
4 tablespoons skim milk	

1. Wipe inside of 8-inch nonstick skillet with margarine; place skillet over moderate heat.
2. Mix eggs, milk, salt and pepper together; pour into skillet. Cook slowly, lifting mixture around edge as it cooks, just until eggs are set, about 3 minutes. Remove from heat; serve immediately.

COTTAGE SCRAMBLE

Makes 4 servings at 189 calories each.

6 eggs	1 cup low-fat cottage cheese
4 tablespoons skim milk	Liquid hot-pepper seasoning,
Pinch of salt	Worcestershire sauce
Pinch of pepper	or curry powder
1 tablespoon butter or margarine	

1. Beat the eggs lightly. Add milk, salt and pepper.
2. Melt butter or margarine in medium-size skillet; pour in egg mixture. Cook slowly, lifting mixture around edge as it cooks, just until eggs are thick.
3. Stir in cottage cheese and seasonings to taste.

ORIENTAL OMELET

Makes 2 servings at 125 calories each.

3 tablespoons onion flakes	bean sprouts, drained
3 tablespoons minced celery	1 envelope or teaspoon instant chicken broth
3 tablespoons minced green pepper	½ cup water
3 tablespoons canned	2 eggs
	Dash of soy sauce

1. Combine onion flakes, celery, pepper, bean sprouts, chicken broth and water in small saucepan. Simmer over medium heat 1 to 2 minutes.
2. Heat small nonstick skillet just hot enough so that a drop of water bounces off its bottom, but not sizzling hot. Beat eggs lightly with a fork, just enough to barely mix yolks and whites; pour eggs into skillet, tilting skillet so that eggs cover the bottom. Top with vegetable mixture.
3. Reduce heat slightly; cook until omelet is browned on the bottom. Tilt the pan and fold omelet; slip onto a platter. Season with soy sauce.

Saving Calories on Breakfast Meats

What would breakfast be without a slice of sausage or bacon? Unfortunately, both pork products are nearly 50 percent fat. Here are ideas for beating the high cost (calorically) of breakfast meat:

• *"Baked" Bacon*—This is an easy how-to for breakfast bacon! Simply spread the strips on a rack in a baking pan and bake in a very hot (450° or more) oven while you're preparing breakfast. No turning, and the fat drains into the pan. Serve it very, *very* crisp—the crispier it is, the fewer calories.

• *Give Sausage a Bath*—Fork-prick breakfast links and drop them in a pot of boiling water. By the time the water is cool, much of the fat will have melted. Then bake or broil (never fry).

• *Buy Beef Bacon*—Exactly like the pork product in flavor but only 113 calories per ounce (uncooked) instead of 189. It's cut from beef short plate. More expensive, but then the lower fat content means more meat.

• *Make Your Own Beef Sausage*—Flavor one pound of fat-trimmed extra lean ground beef round with 1 teaspoon poultry seasoning, plus ½ teaspoon garlic salt and ⅛ teaspoon pepper. Shape into patties and broil. Makes 8 servings at 79 calories each.

• *Or . . . "Mock Bacon!"*—From lean cooked ("boiled") ham, the kind you buy at the deli cold-cut-counter. It has only 68 calories an ounce, a bargain when compared with bacon or sausage. Cut the slices in bacon-wide strips and heat (only till warm) under your broiler.

• *Or Serve Smoked Turkey*, or smoked chicken. It's only 38 calories an ounce. The smoky flavor makes it an ideal breakfast meat; look for it at your cold-cut-counter; warm it under the broiler.

Chapter 2

Satisfying Lunch Ideas

You don't have to give up America's favorite midday meal just because you're watching your weight! Even a sandwich can be "decalorized" if you're a Creative Low-Calorie Cook.

According to most diets, sandwiches just don't exist! That's because most reducing regimes allot 300 calories or less for lunch, while the typical take-it-from-home sandwich is at least that, or more. (A deli "super-sandwich" or a Dagwood concoction on a pair of size nine slabs of bread can easily double or triple that count!) But skimping in the middle doesn't make sense . . . shortchanging on protein, the "meat" of the meal, will only lead to nibbling later on.

The trick is to cut calorie corners each step of the way, without cheating yourself on satisfaction. The recipes and bread suggestions in this chapter show you how to go about it enjoyably—and successfully.

Saving on Bread Calories

Ordinarily ("soft") white bread is about 70 calories a slice, but you can slim a sandwich from the outside-in by switching to a leaner bread. Here are some pointers:

• "Sandwich-thin" bread is only around 55 calories a slice.

18

• "Diet," "protein," or "special formula" breads may be anywhere from 30 to 55 calories a slice, so look for the calorie count printed on the label. Breads made from soy flour have a protein boost. "Gluten" bread, made from low-starch flour, is the slimmest bread of all—only 35 calories a slice.

• Dark breads (rye, pumpernickel, cracked or whole wheat) are leaner in calories than white bread, ounce-for-ounce, but the slices are usually larger. Look for skinny-slice types, or buy it whole and cut it yourself.

• Hard rolls, "Jewish rolls," English muffins, hamburger and hot dog rolls are about 150 calories each, but you can trim them down to about 78 calories by serving your sandwiches open-face on half a roll.

• Serving a sandwich open-face on one slice of bread automatically cuts the bread calories in half.

Calorie-Counting At The "Cold-Cut" Counter

This isn't easy. Three slices of smoked turkey may be only 210 calories . . . but the same amount of Cappicola weighs in at a whopping 423! Most luncheon meats range between 200 and 260 calories for a three-ounce portion (three sandwich-size slices); liverwurst and Braunschweiger are closer to 270, and dry salami is 390.

One of the best bets is poultry-based products—chicken loaf, smoked turkey, turkey breast, smoked chicken—which range from 100 to 140 calories for three ounces.

Most dieters consider all pork products calorie-suspect, but the fact is that ordinary cooked ham ("boiled ham"), at only 198 calories for three ounces, is one of the best sandwich buys around!

At 138 calories for three ounces, lean roast beef, baked ham and roast turkey are good choices. You can tell at a glance if they're lean! Homemade roasts are best of all; you can trim the fat yourself!

For Hamburger and Hot-dog Lovers

The easiest way to "decalorize" a hamburger is to be a fussy shopper who insists on lean ground beef: An ordinary three-ounce broiled hamburger is 245 calories, while an extra-lean burger is only 185!

Frankfurters range between 140 and 168 calories each. Frankfurters with cereal or soy protein are usually lower in fat and calories than those labeled "all beef" or "all meat." Look for the new low-fat hot dogs or "turkey franks" (that's right—they're made from turkey meat).

Making the Most of Cheese

Most sandwich-happy varieties are between 95 and 115 calories an ounce, so choose your cheese zippy sharp instead of mousy meek and you'll get the most flavor at the same calorie rate.

Cheese products labeled "cheese foods" and "cheese spreads" are lower in fat, protein and calories than natural cheeses—80 to 90 calories an ounce.

Instead of cream cheese (55 calories a tablespoon), switch to its part-skim milk taste twin, Neufchâtel cheese (37 calories a tablespoon)—or "farmer cheese," a spreadable relative of cottage cheese. "Farmer cheese" weighs in at only 27 calories a tablespoon.

Those Mayonnaise-y Salads

Eggs, tuna, turkey, crabmeat, chicken—they're all calorie-wise, until they're slathered with mayonnaise at 100 calories a tablespoon! (Mayonnaise-type "salad dressing" is less fattening—65 calories.)

You can add a creamy flavor punch to your salad

spread by mixing it with low-fat cottage cheese (10 calories per tablespoon), plain yogurt (9 calories per tablespoon) or your favorite bottled low-calorie salad dressing (2 to 20 calories). Low-calorie Caesar dressing really turns on egg salad, and a low-calorie cole-slaw-type dressing is great with crabmeat! Look for mayonnaise-type dressings on the diet shelf of your supermarket, but check the label to make sure your choice is low in calories instead of simply salt- or sugar-free!

Make the most of your sandwich spread by adding lots of chopped celery and onions. Every sandwich looks more festive with a crunchy fresh lettuce leaf. Don't forget sliced tomatoes, green pepper strips, dill pickle slices, cucumber chips, carrot sticks and other calorie-shy side snacks.

HOT ROAST BEEF

Makes 2 servings at 210 calories each.

Combine 1 tablespoon flour, 1 envelope or teaspoon instant beef broth and ¾ cup water in a small saucepan. Cook over low heat, stirring constantly, until thickened and bubbly; keep warm. Toast 2 slices thin sandwich bread; cut each in half. Arrange 3 ounces lean roast beef for each sandwich on each slice. Spoon gravy over.

HAM AND LETTUCE

Makes 1 serving at 288 calories.

Spread 1 tablespoon low-calorie mayonnaise and ½ teaspoon prepared mustard on 1 slice thin sandwich bread. Arrange crisp lettuce and 3 ounces thin-sliced cooked ham on top.

HOLLYWOOD BURGER

Makes 1 serving at 228 calories.

Combine 1 tablespoon of minced onion with 3 ounces lean ground beef in a small bowl. Shape into a patty; broil. Toast half a hamburger roll. Serve burger on roll topped with 1 tablespoon Mock Sour Cream.

MOCK SOUR CREAM: Combine ¼ cup buttermilk and 1 cup low-fat cottage cheese in container of electric blender. Whirl at high speed, scraping down sides often, until mixture is smooth. Makes 1 cup at 176 calories.

HAM 'N' EGG SALAD

Makes 1 serving (see below for calorie count).

Combine 2 ounces of lean cooked ham, chopped; 1 hard-cooked egg, chopped; 1 tablespoon minced onion; 1 tablespoon chopped celery and 2 teaspoons low-calorie French dressing in a small bowl. Spread on half a lettuce-lined hard roll for 303 calories. Or for even fewer calories, spread the salad on 1 thin slice sandwich bread (281 calories).

HOT DOG AND SAUERKRAUT

Makes 1 serving at 213 calories.

Pan-broil hot dog. (A nonstick skillet is fine for this.) Toast half a hot dog roll; spread with ½ teaspoon mustard-with-onion. Serve hot dog in half roll topped with 1 tablespoon of well-drained canned sauerkraut.

OPEN-FACE PIZZABURGER

Makes 1 serving at 287 calories.

Shape 2 ounces lean ground beef into a patty; broil. Place on a very thin slice of French bread. Top with 1 ounce part skim mozzarella cheese, 1 tablespoon catsup and ½ teaspoon leaf oregano, crumbled. Put back under broiler, just until top bubbles.

"MINI-HERO"

Makes 1 serving at 261 calories.

Halve a small hard roll; remove all the soft interior, leaving just 2 crusty surfaces. (Save soft crumbs for topping a casserole, if you wish.) Fill with 1 ounce of thin-sliced cooked ham, 1 ounce Swiss cheese, 1 tablespoon shredded lettuce, 1 tablespoon chopped onion and 1 tablespoon of low-calorie Italian dressing.

PINEAPPLE-CHEESE "DOUBLE DANISH"

Makes 1 serving at 173 calories.

Toast 2 slices white gluten bread; spread each with 1 ounce pot cheese. Top each with 2 tablespoons crushed pineapple in pure juice (drained). Sprinkle with cinnamon. Broil until bubbly.

BARBECUED BEEF

Makes 3 servings at 223 calories each.

Barbecue Sauce: Combine 1 cup tomato sauce, 1 teaspoon lemon juice, 1 tablespoon dried onion flakes, dash Worcestershire sauce and a pinch of dry mustard. Bring to boiling; stir in sugar substitute equal to 2 teaspoons sugar. Arrange 3 ounces lean roast beef on each of 3 hamburger roll halves. Spoon the barbecue sauce over roll and beef.

TUNA BUNS

Makes 4 servings at 150 calories each.

Drain a 6½-ounce can of water-packed tuna; combine with ¼ cup of low-calorie mayonnaise. Spread mixture on hamburger rolls. Top with thin slice of dill pickle.

PIMIENTO CHEESE

Makes 1 serving at 210 calories.

Combine 1 tablespoon of chopped pimiento with 2 ounces Neufchâtel cheese. Toast 2 slices white gluten bread. Spread cheese mixture evenly over the toasted slices.

TRIM TUNA SALAD ON RYE

Makes 2 servings at 212 calories each.

Drain a 3½-ounce can water-pack tuna; combine with 2 tablespoons plain yogurt, pinch of dry mustard, pinch of celery salt, 1 teaspoon dried parsley flakes. Line 2 thin slices rye bread with lettuce; spread the tuna mixture evenly over each lettuce-lined slice.

TURKEY TETRAZZINI

Makes 1 serving at 268 calories.

Toast 1 thin slice sandwich bread. Top with 2 ounces turkey loaf. Sprinkle with ½ ounce of shredded Cheddar cheese. Broil until cheese melts. Sprinkle with chopped parsley.

HOT TURKEY

Makes 2 servings at 187 calories each.

Prepare as for Hot Roast Beef sandwich using instant chicken broth instead of beef for gravy and using 3 ounces sliced cooked turkey breast per serving.

Chapter 3

Super Soups

What could be more heart- or tummy-warming to a waistline watcher than a bowl of delicious hot soup— or for that matter, a creamy cool one that fills all those empty little corners. The Creative Low-Calorie Cook's repertoire of soups can start with hearty soups you make ahead in quantity and freeze in solo-size portions for a meal-in-a-hurry. Not gutless little consommés, but big-bowl soups with solid chunks of beef or chicken and a jam-pack of vegetables! So dig out your big stock pot or that old pressure cooker. The long, slow simmering renders nearly all of the fat from the meat into the broth . . . and the chilling sends it all to the surface where you can lift it off before reheating! A hearty, husky soup is one of the best meals around for the dieter—or anyone else, because the vegetable vitamins hang around in the broth! Read on for the beginning of some great moments with soup.

Low-Fat Chunky Soups

Hearty knife-and-fork soups are easy to make, using almost any combination of meats and vegetables. Here's the basic idea:

• Put about 3 pounds of lean beef plus a soupbone, or 2 whole chickens, in a big stockpot. Add 1 tablespoon salt and 3 quarts of cold water. Bring to boiling. Cover; reduce heat and simmer for 2 to 4 hours, or until meat is tender.

• Remove meat and refrigerate broth only. Discard skin and bones from meat; cut meat into hearty chunks, trimming off any remaining fat.

• When broth is chilled, lift off all the fat (it rises to the surface as broth cools). Return broth to the stockpot with cut-up meat. Add a little wine if you like (most of the calories evaporate in the cooking).

• Add 3 cups coarsely cut-up vegetables. (Use low-calorie ones, avoiding beans, corn, peas, potatoes, rice, noodles or barley.) Cover and simmer, over low heat, 20 minutes more. Uncover and serve. Or for make-aheads, do the following:

• Let soup cool. Divide it into lunch-size portions and pour into 12- or 16-ounce paper cups. Freeze until ready to use. To reheat, tear off the paper cup and put frozen soup cube in a saucepan.

• For a hurry-up version of this soup, make use of lean leftover meat, fat-skimmed canned consommé (or instant beef or chicken broth) and canned or frozen vegetables. Heat and serve.

• A good lunch-size serving should offer ½ cup meat, ½ cup vegetables and ¾ to 1 cup of broth . . . all for under 300 calories.

VICHYSSOISE (CREAM OF POTATO SOUP)

Here's a lower calorie version of a fattening favorite.

Makes 8 one-cup servings at 107 calories each.

2 pounds potatoes	4 envelopes or
1 tablespoon diet	teaspoons instant
margarine	chicken broth
2 tablespoons minced	3½ cups boiling water
onion	3⅓ cups skim milk
1 tablespoon finely cut-	½ teaspoon salt
up green onion	Pinch of pepper
	Chives (optional)

1. Cook potatoes in water to cover 30 minutes, or until tender. Drain; peel and mash.

2. Melt margarine in a large saucepan. Add onion and green onion; cook until tender. Dissolve chicken broth in the boiling water; add to onions.

3. Mix skim milk and potatoes. Add to broth. Season with salt and pepper. Cook and stir over medium heat until steaming.

4. Pour about 2 cups at a time into container of electric blender; blend until smooth. Serve hot or cold. Sprinkle with finely chopped chives, if you wish.

TOMATO SOUP ROMANO

Makes 5 one-cup servings at 101 calories each.

1 can (1 pound) tomatoes, cut up and undrained
3 cups water
½ cup finely cut-up celery
2 teaspoons instant minced onion
2 envelopes or teaspoons instant beef broth
2 envelopes or teaspoons instant chicken broth
1 teaspoon seasoned salt
¼ teaspoon pepper
1 cup nonfat dry milk
4 tablespoons grated Romano cheese

1. Combine in 2-quart saucepan tomatoes, water, celery, onion, broths and seasonings. Simmer about 15 minutes, or until tomatoes are heated and celery is tender. Do not boil.

2. Put soup into container of electric blender; blend until smooth, about 1 minute. Add milk. Serve topped with cheese.

MUSHROOM-CLAM CHOWDER

Makes 4 one-cup servings at 133 calories each.

1 can (4 ounces)
mushroom stems
and pieces
2 teaspoons diet
margarine
1 can (7 ounces)
minced clams,
undrained
1 stalk of celery,
minced
1 small onion, minced

4 whole cloves
(or ¼ teaspoon
ground cloves)
1⅓ cups nonfat dry
milk
1 tablespoon
cornstarch
1½ cups water
1 teaspoon salt
Pinch of pepper
Pinch of cayenne
(optional)

1. Drain mushrooms, reserving liquid. Sauté mushrooms in margarine in a heavy nonstick saucepan.

2. Add the mushroom liquid, clams, clam juice, celery, onion and cloves. Cover; simmer 5 minutes. Remove cloves.

3. Mix milk, cornstarch, water and seasonings. Add to saucepan. Heat until steaming but do not boil.

TUNA SKINNY-STRONE SOUP

Makes 5 one-cup servings at 180 calories each.

1 tablespoon diet
margarine
1 small onion, minced
1 stalk of celery,
minced
1 clove of garlic,
minced
1 can (10½ ounces)
condensed chicken
broth, undiluted

2 cans (5½ ounces
each) tomato juice
1 teaspoon basil
¼ teaspoon thyme
1 teaspoon salt
¼ teaspoon pepper
1 package (10 ounces)
frozen mixed
vegetables
2 cans (7 ounces each)
tuna, packed-in-water

1. Melt diet margarine in a saucepan. Add onion, celery and garlic. Cook until soft but not brown.

2. Add broth, tomato juice, basil, thyme, salt and pepper. Bring to boiling; add mixed vegetables. Cover; reduce heat and simmer 10 minutes. Add tuna. Serve hot.

BEEFY TOMATO SOUP

Makes five ½-cup servings at 45 calories each.

1 can (10¾ ounces) condensed tomato soup

1 can (10¾ ounces) water

2 beef-bouillon cubes

Combine the soup, water and bouillon cubes in a small saucepan. Heat to boiling.

GAZPACHO

Makes 6 one-cup servings at 64 calories each.

4 ripe tomatoes
1 medium onion, minced
1 clove of garlic, minced
1 green pepper, coarsely chopped

1 large cucumber, coarsely chopped
1 cup tomato juice
1 tablespoon wine vinegar
2 teaspoons olive oil
2 teaspoons salt
¼ teaspoon pepper

1. Spear tomatoes, one at a time, with a fork and rotate over medium heat for 1 minute. Peel off the skin; chop coarsely.

2. Combine vegetables with the tomato juice, vinegar, oil, salt and pepper.

3. Cover; refrigerate for several hours. The Gazpacho will thicken as it chills. Serve icy cold in small bowls, or in cupped lettuce leaves on salad plates.

POTAGE PURÉE

Makes 7 one-cup servings at 99 calories each.

1 large onion	Generous pinch
1½ pounds potatoes	of pepper
(3)	Pinch of leaf marjoram,
2 carrots	crumbled
1 small turnip	1 can condensed
3 sprigs of parsley	chicken broth and
(3 tablespoons)	enough water to
2 teaspoons salt	make 5 cups

1. Peel onion, potatoes, carrots and turnip. Trim and chop all vegetables.

2. Combine vegetables, seasonings, broth and water in a large kettle or Dutch oven. Bring to boiling. Cover; reduce heat, and simmer 20 minutes, or until vegetables are just tender.

3. Force vegetables and liquid through a sieve, or put everything into container of electric blender; purée for 30 seconds. Reheat to serve.

CALORIE-WISE COMMERCIAL SOUPS

Calorie Range per Cup	
55-66	Beef-Vegetable
5-10	Bouillon (cubes or granulated chicken, beef, onion and vegetable)
10-40	Broth, Beef or Chicken
43-50	Chicken with Rice
15-28	Consommé
37-55	Onion

CUCUMBER COOLER

Makes 4 one-cup servings at 26 calories each.

2 small cucumbers
   (¾ pound),
   chopped (about
   2 cups)
1 teaspoon salt
1 envelope or teaspoon
   instant chicken broth

1 cup boiling water
½ cup skim milk
1 teaspoon lemon
   juice
¼ teaspoon liquid hot-
   pepper seasoning
6 ice cubes

1. Season cucumber with salt; let stand 15 minutes.
2. Dissolve chicken broth in boiling water; chill.
3. Combine cucumber and all remaining ingredients in container of electric blender. Cover; blend until smooth. Garnish each serving with cucumber slice, if you wish.

QUICK LOW-CALORIE MINESTRONE

A low-fat vegetable-happy Italian soup that's easy to make with convenience foods.

Makes 6 servings at 26 calories each.

2 envelopes or
   teaspoons instant
   beef broth
3 cups boiling water
4 ounces (½ an 8-
   ounce package)
   produce department
   vegetables for
   coleslaw
2 tablespoons celery
   flakes

1 tablespoon parsley
   flakes
1 medium-size onion,
   chopped (½ cup)
1 can (1 pound)
   Italian plum
   tomatoes, chopped
1 bay leaf
1 teaspoon leaf
   oregano, crumbled
½ teaspoon salt
⅛ teaspoon pepper

1. Dissolve instant beef broth in boiling water. Add coleslaw vegetables, celery flakes, parsley flakes, onion, tomatoes, bay leaf, oregano, salt and pepper.

2. Cover; simmer until vegetables are tender, 15 minutes.

Chapter 4

Salads and Dressings

Almost every dieter looks to salad as an understanding partner in the great calorie countdown. But all too often, this look is only superficial—and ends with an unadorned, emotionally uninspired clump of lettuce leaves and fresh fruit. Who said salad has to be such plain-Jane punishment? Certainly not the Creative Low-Calorie Cook who knows better because she's learned that appeal doesn't have to mean added pounds.

In this chapter we take a good long look at salad and all its flavorful possibilities. There are salads that are lightly tossed together with a cup of creativity but only a teaspoon of calories. There are gelatin salads so packed with fruits and vegetables that they belie their weight-watching intent, as well as many meal-in-one salads and make-ahead dressings that you'll want on hand whenever temptation might gnaw at your will-power.

Tossed Salad

CLEREMONT SALAD

Makes 24 servings at 40 calories each.

1 large head of
cabbage (about
2 pounds)
3 medium-size
cucumbers
2 medium-size carrots
2 medium-size green
peppers
1 large red onion,
sliced in rings

1½ cups cider or wine
vinegar
⅔ cup water or club
soda
¼ cup vegetable oil
4 tablespoons salt
2 tablespoons liquid
sugar substitute

1. Shred cabbage; pare and slice cucumbers and carrots. Halve the green peppers; remove seeds and slice. Toss the cabbage, cucumbers, carrots, green pepper and onion together in a large heavy crock or bowl.

2. Combine the vinegar with water or club soda, oil, salt and sugar substitute. Pour over vegetables.

3. Cover; chill 1 to 3 days, or until vegetables are well marinated.

CAESAR SALAD

Makes 10 servings at 52 calories each.

2 slices diet white
bread
1 tablespoon vegetable
or olive oil
½ teaspoon garlic salt
1 head romaine lettuce
(1 pound)
2 eggs
4 tablespoons lemon
juice

¼ teaspoon dry
mustard
2 tablespoons grated
Parmesan cheese
1 teaspoon salt
¼ teaspoon pepper
4 anchovy fillets,
finely chopped
(1 teaspoon)
OR: 1 teaspoon
Worcestershire sauce

1. Toast the bread; cut into cubes. Combine with oil and garlic salt in 2-cup jar with screw top. Cover; shake until croutons are well-coated.

2. Tear lettuce into bite-size pieces. Bring water to boiling in a small saucepan; add eggs; reduce heat and simmer 1 minute. Remove from heat; drain. Break eggs over lettuce; toss.

3. Mix the lemon juice, with the dry mustard, Parmesan cheese, salt, pepper and anchovy fillets in covered container. Shake until mixed.

4. Pour dressing over lettuce; toss lightly. Add crouton-oil mixture; toss again.

FOR EASY CAESAR SALAD: Toss the greens and croutons with bottled low-calorie Caesar dressing (about 8 calories a teaspoon).

WALDORF SALAD

Makes 4 half-cup servings at 42 calories each.

1 cup diced celery
1 tablespoon seedless
  raisins
1 medium-size apple,
  diced (1 cup)

2 tablespoons low-
  calorie mayonnaise
  or plain yogurt
4 lettuce leaves

1. Toss all the ingredients except lettuce in medium-size bowl; chill.

2. When ready to serve, wash and dry lettuce leaves and arrange on individual salad plates. Spoon apple mixture into leaves.

CONFETTI POTATO SALAD

Makes 12 one-cup servings at 103 calories each.

6 medium-size pota-
toes, pared and
diced
4 tablespoons lemon
juice
2 medium-size onions,
sliced in rings
6 eggs, hard-cooked,
shelled and diced
1 medium-size green
pepper, halved,

seeded and diced
(½ cup)
4 tablespoons diced
pimiento
4 tablespoons low-
calorie mayonnaise
1 tablespoon salt
Pinch of pepper
Watercress or parsley
for garnish

1. Put the potatoes in salted water to cover in sauce-pan; add 2 tablespoons of the lemon juice. Bring to boiling and cook 15 minutes, or until just tender. Drain; cool.

2. Gently toss onions, eggs, green pepper and pi-miento in large serving bowl. Add potatoes, remaining 2 tablespoons of lemon juice, mayonnaise, salt and pepper; mix well. Cover; chill several hours.

3. When ready to serve, garnish with watercress, parsley sprigs or tomato wedges, if you wish.

CUCUMBER SALAD

Makes 3 servings at 48 calories each.

½ cup plain yogurt
2 tablespoons lemon
juice
½ teaspoon salt

1 teaspoon sugar
2 medium-size
cucumbers

1. Combine the yogurt, lemon juice, salt and sugar in medium-size bowl.

2. Pare cucumbers; cut into paper-thin slices. Toss with dressing. Cover; chill several hours.

Coleslaw

COLESLAW WITH PINEAPPLE

Makes 6 servings at 64 calories each.

1 small head cabbage
  (about 1 pound)
2 medium-size carrots
1 can (8 ounces)
  crushed pineapple
  packed-in-juice,
  drained
1 container (8 ounces)
  plain yogurt
2 tablespoons cider
  vinegar
1 teaspoon garlic salt
⅛ teaspoon pepper

1. Shred cabbage; pare and chop carrots.
2. Mix the drained pineapple, yogurt and vinegar in large bowl; salt and pepper to taste.
3. Combine the dressing with cabbage and carrots. Cover; chill several hours.

SOUR CREAM COLESLAW

Makes 6 servings at 60 calories each.

1 medium-size head
  cabbage (2 pounds)
½ cup low-calorie
  mayonnaise
¼ cup plain yogurt
2 tablespoons half-and-
  half sour cream
Liquid sugar substitute
  to equal 2
  tablespoons
1½ tablespoons cider
  vinegar
1 teaspoon salt
¼ teaspoon pepper

1. Shred cabbage. Combine all remaining ingredients in large bowl; fold in cabbage.
2. Cover; chill several hours.

RED COLESLAW

Makes 6 servings at 45 calories each.

1 medium-size head
  red cabbage
1 medium-size onion,
  minced
1 medium-size green
  pepper, halved,
  seeded and chopped
  (½ cup)

1 medium-size carrot,
  pared and chopped
½ cup plain yogurt
3 tablespoons lemon
  juice
1½ teaspoons salt
¼ teaspoon instant
  garlic powder
¼ teaspoon pepper

1. Toss vegetables together in large bowl.
2. Combine all remaining ingredients; fold into the vegetables. Cover; chill.

YOGURT COLESLAW

Makes 4 servings at 33 calories each.

½ cup plain yogurt
1 teaspoon cider
  vinegar
2 teaspoons sugar
1 teaspoon celery seeds

½ teaspoon salt
⅛ teaspoon pepper
2 cups finely shredded
  cabbage

1. Combine yogurt, vinegar, sugar and celery seeds in a medium-size bowl; salt and pepper to taste.
2. Add the cabbage; mix until well blended. Cover; chill several hours or overnight.

Hearty Meal-Size Salads

TUNA-CAPER SALAD

Makes 4 servings at 130 calories each.

½ head lettuce
½ pound fresh
  spinach
1 medium-size carrot,
  pared and thinly
  sliced
½ cup thinly sliced
  radishes
1 cup diced celery

2 tablespoons sliced
  green onions
1 tablespoon chopped
  parsley
1 can (7 ounces) tuna,
  packed-in-water
1 tablespoon capers
½ cup Tomato Juice
  Dressing

1. Wash, drain and dry lettuce and spinach; tear into bite-size pieces. Toss with carrots, radishes, celery, onions and parsley in a large salad bowl.

2. Drain and flake tuna; add to salad bowl; add capers. Salt and pepper to taste; toss gently. Moisten with ½ cup Tomato Juice Dressing; toss again.

TOMATO JUICE DRESSING

Makes ¾ cup at 14 calories per tablespoon.

⅔ cup tomato juice
3 tablespoons cider
  vinegar
1 envelope old-

fashioned French
dressing mix
French dressing mix

Combine ingredients in covered jar; shake until well mixed. Chill; shake again before using.

POLYNESIAN CHICKEN SALAD

Makes 4 servings at 205 calories each.

1 can (8 ounces)
  unsweetened
  pineapple chunks in
  pineapple juice
2 cups diced cooked
  chicken
1 cup chopped celery

¼ cup low-calorie
  mayonnaise
Few drops of liquid
  red-pepper
  seasoning
½ teaspoon salt
Dash of pepper
4 lettuce leaves

1. Drain pineapple, reserving ¼ cup of the juice.
2. Combine pineapple with chicken and celery in a medium-size bowl. Blend in pineapple juice, mayonnaise and red-pepper seasoning. Salt and pepper to taste.
3. Cover; chill several hours. When ready to serve, wash and dry lettuce leaves; arrange on individual salad plates; fill each with ¼ of the chicken salad.

EGG SALAD

Makes 2 servings at 90 calories each.

2 eggs, hard-cooked,
  shelled and chopped
2 tablespoons low-fat
  creamed cottage
  cheese

Dash of lemon juice
Pinch each of dry
  mustard, salt,
  pepper and celery
  salt

1. Combine eggs and cottage cheese in small bowl. Season with all the remaining ingredients, mixing well to blend flavors.
2. Cover; chill until ready to serve.

ROAST BEEF SALAD

Makes 1 serving at 270 calories.

¼ pound sliced rare roast beef	½ grapefruit, sectioned
Shredded lettuce	1½ teaspoons chopped green onions
1 medium-size tomato, cut in wedges	Florida Dressing

1. Cut beef slices into strips. Arrange shredded lettuce on salad plate; top with beef strips.
2. Arrange all the tomato wedges and grapefruit sections around beef. Garnish with onions; drizzle with 2 tablespoons Florida Dressing.

FLORIDA DRESSING

Makes 1⅓ cups at 21 calories per tablespoon.

2 teaspoons cornstarch	1 cup unsweetened grapefruit juice
1 teaspoon sugar	2 tablespoons vegetable oil
¾ teaspoon salt	
½ teaspoon paprika	⅛ teaspoon liquid red-pepper seasoning
½ teaspoon dry mustard	¼ cup catsup

1. Combine dry ingredients in a small saucepan; stir in grapefruit juice. Bring to boiling, stirring constantly, over medium heat. Boil 1 minute. Remove from heat.
2. Add oil, red-pepper seasoning and catsup; mix well. Chill several hours.

HEARTY TUNA-MACARONI SALAD

Makes 14 one-cup servings at 94 calories each.

2 cans (7 ounces each)
  tuna, packed-in-water
8 ounces elbow
  macaroni, cooked
  to tender stage
  (14 to 20 minutes,
  about 2 cups)
3 stuffed olives, sliced
1 large onion, chopped
  (1 cup)
1 medium-size tomato,
  diced
1 cup minced celery
1½ teaspoons salt
½ teaspoon pepper
1 teaspoon celery salt
1 tablespoon olive juice
2 tablespoons low-
  calorie imitation
  mayonnaise

1. Drain and flake tuna. Combine with the cooked, cooled macaroni, olives, onion, tomato and celery in a large salad bowl; add salt, pepper, celery salt and olive juice. Toss to mix well.

2. Fold in the mayonnaise. Cover; chill several hours.

COTTAGE CHEESE "BANANA SPLIT"

Makes 1 large serving at 260 calories.

Cut 1 banana in half lengthwise; top with ⅓ cup of cottage cheese and 3 tablespoons of your favorite yogurt. Garnish with 6 green grapes and 1 teaspoon chopped nuts.

PINEAPPLE-CHEESE SALAD

Makes 8 servings at 91 calories each.

1 package low-calorie
  lemon gelatin
  (2 envelopes)
1 can (20 ounces)
  unsweetened crushed
  pineapple
2 tablespoons lemon
  juice
2 cups (1 pound) low-
  fat cottage cheese
¼ cup skim milk

1. Drain pineapple juice from crushed pineapple into a 1-cup measure and add water to make 1 cup. Pour into small saucepan.

2. Heat liquid to boiling. Remove from heat; add lemon gelatin. Return saucepan to heat and stir until gelatin dissolves.

3. Fold in cottage cheese; add pineapple and milk. Pour into 6-cup ring mold. Chill until firm, about 3 hours.

4. When ready to serve, loosen salad around edge and center; dip mold in and out of hot water. Cover with serving plate; turn upside down; gently lift off mold.

Shimmering Salads

PEACHES WITH HAM MOUSSE

Makes 16 servings at 33 calories each.

1 envelope unflavored gelatin	3 tablespoons low-calorie mayonnaise
1 envelope or teaspoon instant chicken broth	2 egg whites
½ cup water	2 cans (16 ounces each) low-calorie peach slices, drained
1 can (2½ ounces) deviled ham	Lettuce leaves
	Paprika

1. Sprinkle gelatin and broth over water in a small saucepan to soften. Place saucepan over very low heat until gelatin and broth dissolve. Remove from heat; cool.

2. Blend ham and mayonnaise together; gradually add to gelatin mixture. Chill until thick as unbeaten egg white.

3. Beat egg whites until stiff peaks form. Carefully fold into gelatin mixture.

4. Arrange well-drained peach slices in bottom of square pan 8x8x2. Spoon ham mousse mixture over. Chill several hours.

5. When ready to serve, cut into 16 square pieces. Arrange on lettuce leaves; sprinkle with paprika.

GAZPACHO SALAD MOLD

Makes 8 servings at 28 calories each.

2¾ cups tomato juice
2 envelopes low-calorie
  lemon-flavor gelatin
  (2 to a package)
2 tablespoons catsup
½ teaspoon seasoned
  salt

¼ cup chopped celery
¼ cup chopped
  cucumber
2 tablespoons chopped
  green pepper

1. Heat tomato juice to boiling in a small saucepan. Sprinkle gelatin over and stir until gelatin dissolves. Add catsup and seasoned salt. Chill until thick but not set.

2. Fold in celery, cucumber and green pepper. Pour into 4-cup mold. Chill until firm, about 3 hours.

3. When ready to serve, loosen salad around edge; dip mold in and out of hot water. Cover with a serving plate; turn upside down; gently lift off mold. Garnish salad with lettuce leaves, if you wish.

CHICKEN SALAD MOLD

Makes 4 servings at 225 calories each.

1 envelope unflavored
  gelatin
1 cup cold water
1 can condensed cream
  of chicken soup
1 tablespoon lemon
  juice
⅛ teaspoon pepper
2 cups diced cooked
  chicken

½ cup chopped celery
¼ cup chopped green
  pepper
2 tablespoons diced
  pimiento
2 teaspoons grated
  onion
Salad greens

1. Sprinkle gelatin over half of the cold water in medium-size saucepan to soften. Place saucepan over very low heat until gelatin dissolves, 2 to 3 minutes.

2. Remove saucepan from heat; blend in soup. Stir in remaining water, lemon juice and pepper. Chill until mixture mounds slightly when dropped from spoon.

3. Fold in chicken, celery, green pepper, pimiento and onion. Turn into 4-cup mold or 4 individual molds. Chill several hours, or until the gelatin is firm.

4. When ready to serve, loosen salad around edge; dip mold very quickly in and out of hot water. Cover with serving plate; turn upside down; gently lift off mold. Garnish plate with salad greens.

CRANBERRY-ORANGE SALAD

Makes 6 servings at 40 calories each.

1 envelope low-calorie
   cherry-flavor gelatin
   (2 to a package)
1 envelope unflavored
   gelatin
1½ cups boiling water
1⅓ cups cold water

¾ cup fresh cranberries
¼ cup water
Sweetener to equal
   ¼ cup sugar
2 tablespoons sugar
1 medium-size orange

1. Combine cherry-flavor gelatin and unflavored gelatin; sprinkle over boiling water in small saucepan. Remove from heat; stir until dissolved. Add 1⅓ cups cold water; chill until thick but not set.

2. Pour cranberries and ¼ cup water in container of electric blender; blend a few seconds or until cranberries are just coarsely chopped.

3. Combine cranberry mixture and sugar in saucepan. Cover; bring to boiling. Reduce heat; simmer about 5 minutes.

4. Peel the orange; cut into small bite-size pieces; drain off juice.

5. Fold cooked cranberries and juice into gelatin; add oranges. Pour all into 6-cup mold. Chill several hours, or until firm.

6. To unmold: Loosen salad around edge; dip mold very quickly in and out of hot water. Cover with a serving plate and turn upside down; gently lift off mold.

CHEF'S SALAD MOLD

Makes 6 servings at 150 calories each.

2 envelopes unflavored
   gelatin
1 cup cold water
Granulated sugar
   substitute to equal
   ½ cup sugar
1 teaspoon salt
1½ cups ice water
½ cup cider vinegar

2 tablespoons lemon
   juice
½ medium-size green
   pepper, chopped
½ cup chopped celery
2 pimientos, diced
1 cup grated Swiss
   cheese
1 cup finely chopped
   ham

1. Sprinkle gelatin over cold water in small saucepan to soften. Place saucepan over very low heat until gelatin dissolves, 2 to 3 minutes.

2. Remove from heat. Stir in sugar substitute and salt. Add ice water, vinegar and lemon juice.

3. Chill until consistency of an unbeaten egg white.

4. Add remaining ingredients and turn into a 4-cup mold. Chill several hours.

5. To unmold: Loosen salad around edge; dip mold very quickly in and out of hot water. Cover with a serving plate and turn upside down; gently lift off mold.

MOLDED LIME SALAD

Makes 8 servings at 139 calories each.

1 can (8 ounces) crushed pineapple, in juice
¾ cup water
2 envelopes low-calorie lime-flavor gelatin (2 to a package)
1 cup evaporated skimmed milk (from 13-ounce can)
1 cup low-fat creamed cottage cheese
½ cup chopped nuts
½ cup finely chopped celery
½ cup low-calorie imitation mayonnaise
1 tablespoon lemon juice

1. Heat crushed pineapple with juice and water to boiling in small saucepan. Sprinkle gelatin over and stir until gelatin dissolves. Remove from heat; stir in milk. Chill until thick but not set.
2. Fold in the cottage cheese, chopped nuts, celery, mayonnaise and lemon juice.
3. Pour into a 6-cup mold. Chill several hours or until firm.
4. When ready to serve, loosen salad around edge; dip mold very quickly in and out of hot water. Cover with a serving plate; turn upside down; gently lift off mold. Garnish plate with lettuce leaves.

BUFFET CHEESE RING

Makes 10 servings at 88 calories each.

2 envelopes unflavored gelatin

4 cups (from 46-ounce can) mixed vegetable juice

Pinch of instant garlic powder

2 teaspoons sugar

2 tablespoons lemon juice

2 teaspoons prepared horseradish

2 tablespoons low-calorie imitation mayonnaise

4 ounces imitation cream cheese or Neufchâtel cheese

1 container (16 ounces) low-fat cottage cheese

1. Sprinkle gelatin over 1 cup juice in small pan to soften. Add the garlic powder; place saucepan over very low heat until gelatin dissolves. Remove from heat; add remaining 3 cups juice, sugar, lemon juice and horseradish.

2. Combine mayonnaise and cream cheese. Stir in ¾ cup of vegetable-gelatin mixture. (Let remaining vegetable-gelatin mixture stand at room temperature.)

3. Rinse a 5-cup ring mold with cold water. Pour in the cream cheese-gelatin mixture; chill until firm.

4. Pour remaining vegetable mixture over the set gelatin. Chill several hours, or until firm.

5. To unmold: Loosen salad around edge and center with sharp knife; dip mold very quickly in and out of hot water. Cover with a serving plate and turn upside down; gently lift off mold. Garnish with salad greens and fill center of ring with cottage cheese.

VERY BERRY MOLD

Makes 8 servings at 111 calories each.

1 envelope low-calorie
  cherry-raspberry-
  flavor gelatin (2 to
  a package)
¾ cup boiling water
Liquid sugar substitute
  to equal ¼ cup
  sugar

⅔ cup evaporated
  skimmed milk
1 can (16 ounces)
  whole cranberry
  sauce, drained
1 medium-size ripe
  avocado, peeled and
  cubed (1 cup)

1. Sprinkle gelatin over boiling water to soften in small bowl of electric mixer. Stir until dissolved. Chill until thick but not set.

2. Beat thickened gelatin at high speed until foamy. Gradually add milk; continue beating until mixture is fluffy.

3. Stir in cranberry sauce and avocado cubes. Pour into a 6-cup mold. Chill several hours, or until firm.

4. To unmold: Loosen salad around edge and center with sharp knife; dip mold very quickly in and out of hot water. Cover with a serving plate; turn upside down; gently lift off mold.

Slimmer Salad Dressings

MOCK MAYONNAISE

Makes about 1 cup at 15 calories per tablespoon.

1 cup part-skim ricotta
  cheese *OR:* low-fat
  cottage cheese
1 egg, hard-cooked
1 tablespoon lemon
  juice
½ teaspoon dry
  mustard

½ teaspoon salt
½ teaspoon celery salt
½ teaspoon sugar or
  an equivalent
  amount of sugar
  substitute

Combine all the ingredients in container of electric blender. Blend until smooth.

TARTAR SAUCE—Stir 3 tablespoons minced pickle and 1 teaspoon chopped capers into the Mock Mayonnaise. Makes 1¼ cups at 13 calories per tablespoon.

RUSSIAN DRESSING

Makes 1 cup at 19 calories per tablespoon.

⅓ cup instant nonfat
   dry milk
⅓ cup water
2 eggs, beaten
½ teaspoon salt
½ teaspoon paprika

½ teaspoon dry
   mustard
Pinch of pepper
2 tablespoons cider
   vinegar
3 tablespoons chili
   sauce

1. Combine all ingredients except the chili sauce in a medium-size saucepan. Cook, stirring constantly, over very low heat until dressing thickens. Remove from heat; stir in chili sauce.

2. Chill in covered container before using.

LEMON MAYONNAISE

Makes 1½ cups at 12 calories per tablespoon.

2 tablespoons sugar
1 tablespoon
   cornstarch
2 teaspoons dry
   mustard
2 teaspoons salt
1 cup water

2 medium-size eggs,
   lightly beaten
5 tablespoons fresh
   lemon juice
2 tablespoons cider
   vinegar

1. Combine the sugar, cornstarch, mustard and salt

in top of double boiler. Gradually add water, blending until smooth. Stir in remaining ingredients.

2. Place over boiling water; cook, stirring constantly, 7 to 8 minutes, or until thick and smooth.

3. Cover and reduce heat to very low; cook 5 minutes longer, stirring occasionally. Chill before using.

FRENCH DRESSING

Makes 1 cup at 18 calories per tablespoon.

1 tablespoon
  cornstarch
1 cup water
4 tablespoons wine
  vinegar
2 tablespoons vegetable
  or olive oil

1 clove of garlic,
  minced
3/4 teaspoon salt
1/4 teaspoon pepper
3/4 teaspoon paprika

Mix all the ingredients in a small saucepan. Bring to boiling, stirring constantly, over low heat. Cook 5 minutes longer. Cover; chill.

THOUSAND-ISLAND DRESSING

Makes 3/4 cup at 12 calories per tablespoon.

1 egg
2 tablespoons cider
  vinegar
4 tablespoons skim
  milk
1/4 teaspoon paprika
1/2 teaspoon salt
1/4 teaspoon dry
  mustard

1/2 teaspoon chili
  powder
2 tablespoons tomato
  paste
2 tablespoons chopped
  stuffed olives
2 tablespoons chopped
  dill pickle

1. Combine all ingredients except the olives and pickle in container of electric blender. Blend until well mixed.

2. Transfer dressing to small saucepan. Cook, stirring constantly, over very low heat until dressing thickens. Stir in olives and pickle. Chill.

YOGURT DRESSING

Makes 1¼ cups at 7 calories per tablespoon.

1 cup plain yogurt	1 teaspoon salt
3 tablespoons lemon juice	½ teaspoon prepared mustard

Combine all ingredients in a small bowl; stir until thoroughly mixed. Chill before using.

EASY CREAMY ITALIAN SALAD DRESSING

Makes 1⅓ cups at 22 calories per tablespoon.

1 cup part-skim ricotta cheese	1 envelope Italian salad dressing mix
	½ cup skim milk

1. Combine cheese, salad mix and milk in container of electric blender. Blend on low speed, scraping sides frequently with rubber scraper, until thoroughly mixed.

2. Transfer to covered container; chill before using.

EASY BLUE CHEESE SALAD DRESSING

Makes 1⅓ cups at 20 calories per tablespoon.

1 cup small curd dry cottage cheese (from an 8-ounce carton)	**1 envelope Blue Cheese salad dressing mix** **½ cup skim milk**

1. Mix all ingredients in container of an electric blender. Blend on low speed, scraping sides frequently with rubber scraper, until smooth.
2. Transfer dressing to covered container; chill.

VARIATIONS—To 1 cup of cottage cheese and ½ cup skim milk, add one of the following packaged dressing mixes: Bacon, Caesar, Cheese-Garlic or Coleslaw; French, Garlic, Green Goddess, Italian, Onion, Parmesan or Thousand Island. Prepare as for recipe above.

EASY RUSSIAN DRESSING

Makes 1½ cups at 11 calories per tablespoon.

1 cup plain yogurt	**½ cup chili sauce**

Blend well; chill before using.

LEMON-FRENCH DRESSING

Makes 1 cup at 9 calories per tablespoon.

1 teaspoon unflavored
  gelatin
1 tablespoon cold water
¼ cup boiling water
2 tablespoons sugar
½ teaspoon salt
1 teaspoon grated
  lemon peel

½ cup lemon juice
1 teaspoon dry mustard
¼ teaspoon garlic salt
Pinch of pepper
¼ teaspoon Worcester-
  shire sauce

1. Sprinkle gelatin over cold water in small bowl to soften. Add boiling water; stir until gelatin is thoroughly dissolved.
2. Add sugar and salt; stir until dissolved.
3. Combine gelatin mixture with remaining ingredients in container. Shake well; serve at room temperature.

CALIFORNIA CITRUS DRESSING

Makes ¾ cup at 6 calories per tablespoon.

½ cup orange juice
¼ cup lemon juice
1 teaspoon seasoned
  salt
½ teaspoon paprika

½ teaspoon instant
  garlic powder
⅛ teaspoon freshly
  ground pepper

Combine juices, salt, paprika, garlic powder and pepper in 1-cup jar with screw top. Shake until thoroughly mixed.

Chapter 5

A Bonanza of Beef Dishes

Prime ribs . . . or pot roast? Steak or stew? If you're a cost-conscious calorie-counter who feels she can't afford slimming dinners, have we got news for you! The least expensive cuts of beef are usually the leanest—and the least fattening!

Let's start with slow-simmered, fork-tender pot roast. If you're a Creative Low-Calorie Cook, pot roast even with gravy and potatoes, can be less than half the calories—and cost—of steak!

Dollar-wise round, chuck and flank steaks offer unlimited possibilities, too, along with lean ground beef. It may have a higher price-per-pound, but the leanest ground beef is still your best buy. There's less fatty waste—a drawback any way you slice it. And ground beef is so equally at home in hamburgers, meatloaves and meatballs, that you'll never fall into a one-dish beef rut. Continue reading and you're on your way to many exciting, waistline-loving dinners.

Priceless Pot Roasts

Chances are you have limited your recipe repertoire to simple broiling . . . and your beef-buying to steaks only. That's where most would-be skinnies go wrong— the best cuts of beef for broiling are also the most high-calorie. One pound of rib steak (meat only) is 45 percent fat and more than 2,000 calories. Fat-trimmed, lean, round pot roast, on the other hand, is less than 700 calories per pound!

Why Pot Roasts Are Considered Fattening

Because they usually are, if prepared by the usual methods! If you choose a fatty piece of beef (like brisket or cross-rib chuck), brown it in extra fat, cook it so the fat can't escape and serve it with greasy gravy and fat-soaked vegetables, you've got a traditionally fattening pot-roast dish.

If you're a Creative Low-Calorie Cook, however, you can still capture the flavor—including the gravy, sauce, vegetables and even the potatoes—without all those fat calories!

What About the Cholesterol?

Good news for heart-smart beef eaters! The more beef fat you eliminate, the less saturated fat in your diet, and that's just what the doctor ordered! American men have the world's highest heart-disease rate and the highest cholesterol level . . . and a diet rich with saturated animal fats (meat and dairy fats). The American Heart Association's committee on nutrition urges a decrease in fat intake, particularly animal fats. (The Heart Association also recommends a "calorie intake adjusted to achieve proper weight.") In other words, fewer calories!

USDA Grades and Fat Content

Two factors affect the fat content of the beef that you buy: The USDA (U.S. Department of Agriculture) "Grade" and the "cut" (the part of the animal it comes from).

In grading beef, government inspectors consider all tenderness factors, including fatty marbling, and then grade beef into six quality categories. But of these six, only the top three are generally available to consumers. (The bottom three grades are used commercially.)

The qualities that make a piece of beef an expensive, luxurious steak don't necessarily make it a good buy in calories or nutrition.

Which "Cuts" of Beef Are Least Fattening

Cuts from the hind quarter are less fatty than the forequarter. Here's a comparison of the cuts of beef most often used for pot roasts and slow-simmer dishes. (The calorie comparisons given are for U.S. Department of Agriculture "choice" grade, the type of beef most widely available to consumers.)

Calorie-Counter's Comparison Chart

Boneless Beef Uncooked	Fat Content	Calories per Pound
Flank	0%	653
Round	11%	894
Chuck Arm	14%	1,012
Rump	25%	1,374
Roundbone Sirloin	27%	1,420
Doublebone Sirloin	28%	1,510
Blade Steak	29%	1,647
Chuck Rib	30%	1,597
Club Steak	36%	1,723
Porterhouse	37%	1,769
T-Bone	38%	1,800
Hipbone Sirloin	39%	1,869
Short Plate	41%	1,814
Rib (11th and 12th)	45%	2,014

Low-calorie, Two-stage, Make-ahead Method

The pound-wise way to prepare pot roast is to make it a day ahead. Brown and simmer the meat—without vegetables—then refrigerate overnight. Before dinner, remove your pot roast from the refrigerator and lift off all the hardened fat. Now that the fat's gone, add the vegetables and slow simmer until they're tender. Thicken the sauce and you've got it made—without the fat calories.

Here are some pot roast pointers:

How to De-Calorize Your Favorite Pot Roast, Stew or Ragout

• Be sure to trim away *every last bit of fat* before cooking.

• Use a heavy nonstick pot or Dutch oven and *only one tablespoon of oil* to brown the meat. Brown the meat slowly and drain away any remaining fat.

• Or . . . brown the meat under your broiler; it's far less messy! Broiler-browned pot roast won't have a dark brown gravy (which may not be a disadvantage if you desire a light gravy or tomato sauce) but you can "brown" a gravy by adding soy sauce, Worcestershire sauce, beef extract or brown gravy coloring to the meat.

• Don't brown the vegetables with the meat. It isn't necessary . . . and *vegetables are notorious fat sponges!*

• Thicken your meat gravy or sauce with cornstarch rather than flour, to save even more calories. Cornstarch has twice the thickening power of flour, for the same number of calories.

• Don't forget that very lean beef takes more cooking to reach that knife-tender stage . . . anywhere from 25 to 50 percent more cooking time than fatty beef. Don't try to hurry things by "boiling" your pot roast over too-high heat; that will only make it tough. Pot roast should always barely simmer.

• You get more servings from lean beef, another reason why it's a budget-wise buy! One pound of fatty beef may shrink to barely two servings while a lean, boneless pot roast will yield at least three (3-ounce) servings per pound, almost four, if it's really lean!

FLEMISH POT ROAST

Low-calorie, low-carbohydrate beer replaces the more fattening brew in this hearty man-pleasing dish!

Makes 12 three-ounce servings at 204 calories each.

3½ pounds lean, well-trimmed round

2 teaspoons garlic salt

¼ teaspoon pepper

1 tablespoon vegetable oil

1 teaspoon leaf thyme, crumbled

1 bay leaf

1 bottle or can (12 ounces) low-calorie, low-carbohydrate beer

1 teaspoon brown sugar

2 medium-size onions, sliced

2 tablespoons chopped parsley

1. Season the meat with garlic salt and pepper.

2. Heat the oil in a heavy nonstick pan or Dutch oven; brown the meat on all sides. Drain off any remaining fat.

3. Add thyme, bay leaf, beer and the brown sugar. Cover; simmer over very low heat 3 hours, or until meat is tender. Remove from heat; remove bay leaf and refrigerate several hours or overnight.

4. About 30 minutes before serving time, remove the pot roast from refrigerator. Carefully remove hardened fat. Add onions and parsley. Simmer, covered, 20 minutes, or until meat is heated through and onions are tender.

5. Remove meat to serving platter; keep warm. Sim-

mer sauce for a few minutes to thicken it slightly. Serve the sauce with meat.

POT ROAST PROVENCALE

A hearty, French country dish made the modern two-stage way. Shredded carrots and minced onion are added to the wine gravy in the second cooking.

Makes 10 three-ounce servings at 240 calories each.

3 pounds lean, well-
    trimmed round
2 teaspoons garlic salt
1/4 teaspoon pepper
1 tablespoon vegetable
    oil
1/2 cup dry red wine
1/2 cup water

2 cans (8 ounces each)
    tomato sauce
1 bay leaf
1 medium-size onion,
    finely chopped
    (1/2 cup)
1 cup shredded carrot

1. Season the meat with garlic salt and pepper.
2. Heat oil in a heavy nonstick pan or a Dutch oven; brown meat on all sides. Drain off any remaining fat.
3. Add the wine, water, tomato sauce and bay leaf. Cover; simmer over very low heat 2½ to 3 hours, or until meat is tender. Remove from heat; remove bay leaf; refrigerate several hours or overnight.
4. About 30 minutes before serving time, remove the pot roast from refrigerator. Carefully remove all hardened fat. Add onion and carrot. Simmer, covered, 20 minutes, or until meat is heated through.
5. Remove meat to a serving platter; keep warm. Simmer sauce for a few minutes to thicken it slightly.

BURGUNDY POT ROAST

A French classic that's short on calories. Short on work, too! We've pared the preparation time by using canned onion, carrots, and mushrooms and some easy-to-use spices. Don't worry about the wine calories—most of the alcohol (and calories) evaporates in the cooking!

Makes 12 three-ounce servings at 238 calories each.

3½ pounds lean, well-trimmed round
2 teaspoons garlic salt
½ teaspoon pepper
1 tablespoon vegetable oil
1 teaspoon pumpkin-pie spice
1 teaspoon poultry seasoning
½ teaspoon dry orange peel (*optional*)
2 teaspoons parsley flakes

½ cup Burgundy wine (or any red table wine)
1 can (1 pound) whole onions, with liquid
1 can (1 pound) tiny Belgian carrots, with liquid
2 cans (8 ounces each) whole mushrooms, with liquid
½ cup water
1 tablespoon flour
1 tablespoon cornstarch
4 tablespoons cold water

1. Season the meat with garlic salt and pepper.
2. Heat the oil in a heavy nonstick pan or Dutch oven; brown meat on all sides. Drain off any remaining fat.
3. Add pumpkin-pie spice, poultry seasoning, orange peel, parsley flakes, wine, liquid from the vegetables and water. (Refrigerate vegetables until needed.) Cover; simmer over very low heat 3 hours, or until meat is tender. Remove from heat; refrigerate several hours or overnight.
4. About 30 minutes before serving time, remove the pot roast from refrigerator. Carefully remove hardened fat. Heat to boiling; add reserved vegetables. Cover; simmer 20 minutes, or until meat is heated through.
5. Remove meat to a serving platter. Surround with vegetables. Keep warm. Combine flour, cornstarch and cold water; stir into simmering liquid. Cook, stirring

constantly, until sauce thickens and bubbles. Serve sauce with meat and vegetables.

POT ROAST ORIENTALE

Pot roast is strictly Western fare . . . but here it gets a Far East flair with soy, sherry and ginger. Canned mixed Chinese vegetables would make a simple low-calorie side dish. (Four tablespoons of fluffy cooked rice add 50 calories.)

Makes 12 three-ounce servings at 235 calories each.

3½ pounds lean, bone-less, well-trimmed chuck arm roast	1 teaspoon ground ginger
2 teaspoons garlic salt	5 tablespoons soy sauce
¼ teaspoon pepper	1 cup dry sherry
1 tablespoon vegetable oil	½ cup water
	1 medium-size onion, sliced

1. Season the meat with garlic salt and pepper.
2. Heat the oil in a heavy, nonstick pan or Dutch oven; brown meat on all sides. Drain off any remaining fat.
3. Add the ginger, soy sauce, wine and water. Cover; simmer over very low heat 2½ to 3 hours, or until meat is tender. Remove from heat; refrigerate several hours or overnight.
4. About 30 minutes before serving time, remove the pot roast from refrigerator. Carefully remove hardened fat. Add onion. Simmer, covered, 20 minutes, or until meat is heated through and onion is tender.
5. Remove meat to serving platter; keep warm. Simmer sauce to thicken it slightly. Serve sauce with meat.

POT ROAST ITALIANO

A one-step pot roast based on flank steak. The steak is spread with Italian cheese and seasoning before rolling —and so free of fat that the two-stage make-ahead method isn't necessary!

Makes 6 three-ounce servings at 214 calories each.

1½ pounds flank steak
2 tablespoons grated Romano cheese
1 teaspoon leaf oregano, crumbled
1 teaspoon garlic salt
¼ teaspoon pepper
1 tablespoon olive oil

1 can (1 pound) whole tomatoes
1 cup water
1 medium-size onion, chopped (½ cup)
½ teaspoon salt
⅛ teaspoon pepper
¼ teaspoon leaf oregano, crumbled

1. Lay the flank steak flat; score one side (this prevents meat from shrinking out of shape during cooking). Turn steak over; sprinkle unscored side with cheese, 1 teaspoon of the oregano, garlic salt and ¼ teaspoon of the pepper. Roll up from the long side; tie in several places with white cord.

2. Heat the olive oil in a heavy nonstick pan or Dutch oven. Brown rolled steak on all sides. Drain off any remaining fat.

3. Add tomatoes, water, onion, salt and remaining pepper and oregano. Break up tomatoes with a wooden spoon. Cover; simmer over very low heat 1½ to 2 hours, or until meat is tender.

4. Remove meat to serving platter; keep warm. Simmer tomato sauce until slightly thickened. Slice meat; top with sauce.

NEW ENGLAND POT ROAST

A hearty hearthside dinner dish without all those disheartening calories! The two-stage method of preparation eliminates most of the fat.

Makes 12 three-ounce servings at 241 calories each.

3½ pounds lean, boneless, well-trimmed chuck arm roast
2 teaspoons salt
¼ teaspoon pepper
1 tablespoon vegetable oil
2 bay leaves
1 teaspoon poultry seasoning
2½ cups water
2 envelopes or teaspoons instant beef broth

2 stalks celery, thinly sliced
1 pound carrots, scraped and cut into strips
1 pound white turnips, pared and cut into slices
2 cups small white onions, peeled
1 tablespoon flour
1 tablespoon cornstarch
4 tablespoons cold water

1. Season the meat with salt and pepper.
2. Heat the oil in a heavy, nonstick pan or Dutch oven; brown meat on all sides. Drain off any remaining fat.
3. Add bay leaves, poultry seasoning, water and beef broth. Cover; simmer over very low heat 2½ to 3 hours, or until meat is almost tender. Remove from heat; remove bay leaves; refrigerate several hours or overnight.
4. About 30 minutes before serving time, remove the pot roast from refrigerator. Carefully remove hardened fat. Heat to boiling. Add celery, carrots, turnips and onions. Cover; simmer over low heat 25 minutes, or until vegetables are tender.
5. Remove meat to a serving platter; surround with vegetables. Keep warm. Combine flour, cornstarch and cold water; stir into simmering liquid. Cook, stirring

constantly, until sauce thickens and bubbles. Serve sauce with meat and vegetables.

DEVILED POT ROAST

Makes its own zesty "Sauce Diable" as it simmers, helped along by white wine, mustard and tarragon.

Makes 12 three-ounce servings at 221 calories each.

3½ pounds lean, boneless, well-trimmed chuck arm roast
2 teaspoons salt
½ teaspoon pepper
1 tablespoon vegetable oil
¼ cup white vinegar
½ cup dry white wine
1½ cups water
1 tablespoon dry mustard
¼ teaspoon liquid red-pepper seasoning
1 teaspoon parsley flakes
2 teaspoons leaf tarragon, crumbled
1 medium-size onion, chopped (½ cup)
1 tablespoon flour
1 tablespoon cornstarch
4 tablespoons cold water

1. Season the meat with salt and pepper.
2. Heat the oil in a heavy, nonstick pan or Dutch oven; brown the meat on all sides. Drain off any remaining fat.
3. Add vinegar, wine, water, mustard, pepper seasoning, parsley flakes and tarragon. Cover; simmer over very low heat 3 hours, or until meat is tender. Remove from heat; refrigerate several hours or overnight.
4. About 30 minutes before serving time, remove the pot roast from refrigerator. Carefully remove hardened fat. Cover; simmer 20 minutes, or until meat is heated through.
5. Remove meat to serving platter; keep warm. Simmer liquid until reduced to 2 cups. Combine the flour, cornstarch and cold water; stir into simmering liquid.

Cook, stirring constantly, until sauce thickens and bubbles. Serve sauce with meat.

OVERNIGHT SAUERBRATEN

In most sauerbraten recipes, beef is marinated for several days in a pickling mixture, then cooked until it's tender. Here's a hurry-up turn-about in which the beef marinates after cooking. Less wait . . . and fewer calories!

Makes 12 three-ounce servings at 205 calories each.

3½ pounds lean, well-trimmed round	¼ cup catsup
2 teaspoons onion salt	2 bay leaves
½ teaspoon pepper	Pinch of ground cloves
1 tablespoon vegetable oil	1 teaspoon ground ginger
1½ cups water	2 medium-size onions, sliced
5 tablespoons red wine vinegar or cider vinegar	1 tablespoon flour
	1 tablespoon cornstarch
	4 tablespoons cold water

1. Season meat with onion salt and pepper.

2. Heat the oil in a heavy, nonstick pan or Dutch oven; brown the meat on all sides. Drain off any remaining fat.

3. Add water, vinegar, catsup, bay leaves, cloves and ginger. Cover; simmer over very low heat 3 hours, or until meat is tender. Remove from heat; remove bay leaves; refrigerate 24 hours or longer.

4. About 30 minutes before serving time, remove the pot roast from refrigerator. Carefully remove hardened fat. Add onions. Cover; simmer 20 minutes, or until meat is heated through and onions are tender.

5. Remove meat to a serving platter; keep warm. Combine the flour, cornstarch and cold water; stir into

simmering liquid. Cook, stirring constantly, until sauce thickens.

BEEF RAGOUT

Makes 4 servings at 194 calories each.

1 pound lean, well-trimmed round steak, cubed	1 envelope or teaspoon instant beef broth
½ teaspoon garlic salt	Pinch of pepper
2 medium-size onions, finely chopped (1 cup)	¼ teaspoon leaf thyme, crumbled
1 cup water	½ pound mushrooms, sliced
1 tablespoon Worcestershire sauce	1 cup instant nonfat dry milk
	2 tablespoons water

1. Season beef cubes with garlic salt. Brown on all sides in broiler on foil-lined baking sheet.

2. Combine cubes with the onion, water, Worcestershire sauce, beef broth and thyme in large skillet. Cover; simmer over low heat 45 minutes, or until meat is tender.

3. Add mushrooms; cook 10 minutes longer.

4. Stir nonfat dry milk and water together. Gradually add to meat. Heat slowly, stirring occasionally, to thicken. Do not boil.

BOEUF BOURGUIGNONNE

Makes 8 servings at 296 calories each.

1 tablespoon vegetable oil

3 pounds lean, well-trimmed top round, cubed

1 medium-size onion, coarsely chopped (½ cup)

2 cloves of garlic, minced

2 cups Burgundy wine (or any red table wine)

1 teaspoon salt

¼ teaspoon pepper

2 tablespoons parsley

1 bay leaf

1 can (8 ounces) whole mushrooms, with liquid

1 can (1 pound) whole onions, with liquid

1 can (1 pound) small Belgian carrots, with liquid

1. Heat oil in a heavy nonstick pan or a Dutch oven; brown meat on all sides. Add onion and garlic; sauté until tender.

2. Add the wine, salt, pepper, parsley and bay leaf. Cover; simmer over very low heat 2 hours, or until meat is nearly tender.

3. Add the mushrooms, onions and carrots. Cover; cook 10 minutes longer.

4. Uncover and cook until the liquid thickens slightly. Skim off all fat. (For a thick sauce, mix 1 tablespoon flour with 1 tablespoon cornstarch and 4 tablespoons water; add to liquid. Stir until thick.)

EASY RAGOUT (BEEF STEW)

Makes 8 servings at 229 calories each.

2 pounds lean, well-
  trimmed boneless
  round, cubed
1 tablespoon vegetable
  oil
½ cup dry sherry
2 cans (1 pound each)
  carrots, with liquid
1 can (1 pound) whole
  onions, with liquid

1 can (1 pound)
  mushroom stems and
  pieces, with liquid
1 tablespoon parsley
2 small bay leaves
½ teaspoon coarse
  grind pepper
2 teaspoons garlic salt

1. Heat the oil in a heavy nonstick pan or Dutch oven; brown meat on all sides. Drain off any remaining fat.

2. Add sherry, liquid from carrots, onions and mushrooms, parsley, bay leaves, pepper and garlic salt. Cover; simmer over low heat 1¼ hours, or until meat is tender.

3. Add carrots, onions and mushrooms. Cover; cook 10 minutes longer.

4. Remove meat to platter; simmer sauce to thicken.

HUNGARIAN GOULASH

Makes 8 servings at 209 calories each.

1 pound lean, well-
  trimmed boneless
  round, cubed
1 pound lean boneless
  veal shoulder, cubed
1 tablespoon vegetable
  oil
2 medium-size onions,
  chopped (1 cup)

2 teaspoons paprika
2 cups tomato juice
¼ teaspoon coarse
  grind pepper
1 teaspoon salt
⅛ teaspoon instant
  garlic powder

1. Heat the oil in a heavy, nonstick pan or Dutch oven; brown beef and veal on all sides. Add the onions; sauté until soft. Stir in the paprika.

2. Add all remaining ingredients. Cover; simmer 1½ hours, or until meat is tender.

3. Remove meat to a serving platter; keep warm. Simmer sauce to thicken. Skim fat.

Man-Pleasing Steaks

PENNY PINCHER'S STEAK

Makes 6 servings at 250 calories each.

1 boneless chuck arm steak (about 2½ pounds), 1½ inches thick	1 teaspoon meat tenderizer ½ teaspoon garlic powder ¼ teaspoon pepper

1. Trim steak carefully of all border fat; puncture each side with a fork. Wet with cold water and sprinkle liberally with the meat tenderizer. Place on a platter; cover with foil or plastic wrap, and leave at room temperature 3 hours.

2. Season with garlic powder and pepper. Place on a rack in broiler pan. Broil, 2 inches from heat, until cooked to desired doneness.

SKILLET PEPPER STEAK

Makes 8 servings at 202 calories each.

2 pounds lean round
steak, ¾ inch thick,
trimmed of fat
1½ teaspoons salt
½ teaspoon pepper
1 tablespoon vegetable
oil
1 can (1 pound, 12
ounces) tomatoes

2 medium-size onions,
sliced
1 clove of garlic, minced
4 tablespoons water or
dry red wine
2 medium-size green
peppers, cut in strips

1. Cut meat to serving-size pieces. Sprinkle with salt and pepper.

2. Heat oil in a large skillet. Add meat; brown. Drain fat.

3. Add the tomatoes, onions, garlic and water or wine. Cover; simmer 1½ hours, or until meat is just tender.

4. Add green peppers; cook 15 minutes longer. Skim fat; simmer sauce to thicken.

CHUCKWAGON STEAK

Makes 8 servings at 251 calories each.

3 pounds lean boneless
chuck roast, about 2
inches thick
2 teaspoons meat
tenderizer
2 tablespoons dried
onion flakes
2 teaspoons leaf thyme,
crumbled

1 teaspoon leaf
marjoram, crumbled
1 bay leaf, crushed
1 cup wine vinegar
2 tablespoons whole
peppercorns
1 teaspoon salt

1. Trim fat from roast. Sprinkle with tenderizer.

2. Place meat in a shallow dish just large enough to hold it. Combine all remaining ingredients except peppercorns. Marinate 2 to 3 hours.

3. Remove meat from marinade. Crush peppercorns, and press into surface of meat. Grill about 6 inches from hot coals, about 15 minutes each side. Sprinkle with salt. Slice on the diagonal.

CHILLIED BEEFSTEAK

Makes 4 servings at 224 calories each.

1 pound top round
  steak, trimmed of fat
  and cut in 2-inch cubes
1 tablespoon vegetable
  oil
1 large onion, thinly
  sliced
2 tomatoes, peeled and
  chopped

½ teaspoon chili
  powder
½ cup boiling water
2 envelopes or teaspoons
  instant beef broth
½ teaspoon salt
⅛ teaspoon pepper

1. Heat oil in a large nonstick skillet. Add beef; stir until browned. Remove and set aside.

2. Add onion to the skillet; sauté until soft.

3. Add tomatoes, chili powder, water, beef broth, salt and pepper; simmer 5 minutes. Return meat cubes to skillet; simmer 1½ hours, or until meat is tender.

STEAK-IN-BEER

Makes 6 servings at 228 calories each.

1 flank steak (about
  1¾ pounds)
1 tablespoon vegetable
  oil
1 tablespoon all-purpose
  flour

1 tablespoon brown
  sugar or brown sugar
  substitute
1 cup beer
Pinch of sage

1. With a sharp knife, score steak in a diamond pattern on both sides. Trim off all excess fat.

2. Heat oil in a large nonstick skillet. Add meat; brown quickly on both sides. (Meat should be rare.)

3. Reduce heat; sprinkle both sides of steak with flour and sugar. Swish steak around in the skillet, first on one side then on the other, so that the flour and sugar are well moistened by the pan juices.

4. Add beer and sage; continue cooking over moderate heat, turning occasionally, until liquid is reduced to a saucey thickness. Remove steak to a hot platter; cover with any remaining sauce. Garnish with fresh parsley, if you wish.

CREAM-STYLE SWISS STEAK

Makes 6 servings at 211 calories each.

1½ pounds round steak, 1 inch thick
1 teaspoon salt
¼ teaspoon pepper
1 tablespoon vegetable oil
1½ cups boiling water
2 envelopes or teaspoons instant beef broth
1 teaspoon soy sauce
¼ teaspoon ground ginger
2 tablespoons flour
1 tablespoon cornstarch
¾ cup evaporated skimmed milk

1. Season steak with salt and pepper; cut into serving-size pieces.

2. Heat oil in a large skillet. Add steak; brown on all sides. Drain off fat.

3. Add water, beef broth, soy sauce and ginger. Cover; simmer 1½ hours, or until meat is tender. Remove to heated serving platter; keep warm.

4. Combine flour, cornstarch and milk. Stir into meat liquid in skillet. Cook, stirring constantly, over medium heat until thickened. Pour over meat; serve.

SAUTEED LIVER, BACON AND ONIONS

Makes 8 servings at 321 calories each.

½ pound beef bacon	1 teaspoon salt
8 thin slices calf's liver	1 tablespoon bacon fat
(about 1¾ pounds)	1 medium-size onion,
2 tablespoons flour	chopped (½ cup)

1. Place bacon on a rack in broiler pan; broil until crisp. Blot with paper towelling to remove excess fat, but reserve 1 tablespoonful of fat.

2. Coat liver with flour. Heat reserved bacon fat in medium-size skillet. Add liver; sauté. Add onion, and continue cooking until onion is sautéed and just lightly browned. Drain off any excess fat. Serve with bacon.

LIVER WITH WINE AND MUSHROOMS

Makes 6 servings at 185 calories each.

1 tablespoon butter or	6 thin slices calf's liver
margarine	(about 1½ pounds)
1 teaspoon minced	1 cup dry red wine
parsley	1 cup sliced mushrooms
1 tablespoon chopped	(¼ pound)
chives	

1. Melt butter or margarine in large skillet. Add parsley and chives.

2. Add liver and brown.

3. Add wine and mushrooms. Cover; simmer 2 minutes. Remove liver to serving platter; simmer pan juices until they are reduced.

SKILLET BEEF AND MUSHROOMS

Makes 6 servings at 195 calories each.

1½ pounds lean bone-
  less round steak
1 teaspoon salt
¼ teaspoon pepper
1 tablespoon butter or
  margarine
½ pound fresh mush-
  rooms, thinly sliced

1 medium-size onion,
  thinly sliced
1 tablespoon all-purpose
  flour
⅔ cup skim milk
⅓ cup dry white wine

1. Cut beef into thin slices; trim off any excess fat.
Season with salt and pepper.
2. Melt butter or margarine in large skillet. Add
meat, mushrooms and onions. Cook over moderate heat
until meat is browned.
3. Combine flour and milk; add to skillet. Cook,
stirring constantly, until thickened. Add wine; simmer
3 minutes.

FRENCH FLANK STEAK

Makes 6 servings at 200 calories each.

1 tablespoon vegetable
  oil
3 tablespoons minced
  shallots
1 cup cold water
1 envelope or teaspoon
  instant beef broth
2 tablespoons all-
  purpose flour

¼ cup dry red wine
2 teaspoons lemon juice
2 tablespoons dried
  parsley
Pinch of cayenne
1½ pounds flank steak
1 clove of garlic, halved
¼ teaspoon salt
Pinch of pepper

1. Heat 1 teaspoon oil in a large skillet. Add shallots; sauté until tender. Combine cold water, beef broth and flour. Add to skillet; stir until smooth. Add the wine, lemon juice, parsley and cayenne. Continue heating over moderate heat, stirring frequently, until the sauce simmers and thickens, about 5 minutes. Keep warm while preparing steak.

2. Score steak; rub with remaining 2 teaspoons oil and garlic. Broil quickly, 4 to 5 minutes per side. Season with salt and pepper. Cover with sauce.

Pennywise, Poundwise Hamburger

How to Buy Low-Fat Hamburger

Avoid prepackaged ground meat if you're looking to save on calories. The bargain-buy ground meat that saves you pennies may contain 30 percent fat (or more!). Maybe you can't afford that kind of bargain! Meat managers say that there is little flavor difference among ground chuck, sirloin or other beef parts; the only difference is the fat content. And it's the fat content, of course, that determines the calories. When ground meat is naturally lean, as with beef round, meat departments often add additional fat, ostensibly for the consumer who is supposed to believe that extra fat will make a hamburger "juicy." If you don't want extra fat in your ground meat, be a figure-wise shopper and avoid all prepackaged ground meats.

Instead, pick out a lean cut of beef round or chuck, for example—and have it custom ground-to-order, the border fat trimmed away before grinding. It costs more per pound, but not as much as you may think. Your meat money, after all, is buying a much higher proportion of protein . . . and getting only one fifth or one sixth the fat! And the calorie cost of your ground meat will be cut by one half or one third!

The less fat in the meat, the less there is to ooze extra calories into saucy burger creations or casserole dishes as they cook. If you're a Creative Low-Calorie Cook, you can trim down your favorite ground meat classics even more, simply by replacing the fattening ingredients with their slimmer stand-ins.

Calories aren't all we've eliminated from these recipes. Fuss and bother are missing too, thanks to the judicious use of convenience products . . . but only those that won't add to the calorie count!

Comparison Shopper's Guide to Ground Beef

Prepackaged Ground Beef	Fat Content	Calories per Pound
Regular Ground Beef	25 to 30%	1,375 to 1,597
Ground Chuck or Round	17 to 21%	1,160 to 1,265
Ground-to-Order Ground Beef		
Chuck, trimmed of fringe fat	7%	717
Round, trimmed of fringe fat	5%	612

CANTONESE BURGERS IN RED SAUCE

Canned bean sprouts add a subtle flavor and delectable moistness to this quick-and-easy dinner dish with a Far East flair! Roll the meatballs extra tiny and you've got a compliment-catching chafing dish fare for your next cocktail or dinner party.

Makes 6 servings at 231 calories each.

1½ pounds ground lean beef round	¼ cup dry sherry
1 can (1 pound) bean sprouts, drained	¼ cup soy sauce
2 tablespoons instant minced onion	1½ cups water
¼ teaspoon ground ginger	2 tablespoons cornstarch
¼ cup catsup	2 tablespoons finely chopped green peppers

1. Lightly combine ground beef with 1 cup of the bean sprouts, onion and ginger in a large bowl. Shape into 12 patties. Broil just until brown on both sides.

2. Combine catsup, sherry, soy sauce, water and cornstarch in large saucepan. Cook over medium heat, stirring constantly, until sauce thickens and bubbles.

3. Add broiled burgers to sauce, one at a time. Heat sauce to boiling; lower heat. Cover; simmer for 10 minutes. Add green pepper: simmer 10 minutes longer. Skim fat from sauce, if necessary.

4. Heat the remaining bean sprouts; place on a serving platter. Arrange burgers over bean sprouts. Serve with the sauce.

NOTE: A ½-cup serving of instant rice adds 92 calories per serving.

SLIM ITALIAN MEATBALLS

Quick-brown these spicy meatballs under your broiler . . . it's so much simpler than frying in oil. Your kitchen stays cleaner, too. To add an olive-oil flavor without fat, add a minced olive to sauce.

Makes 4 servings at 253 calories each.

1 pound ground lean
   beef round
2 tablespoons instant
   minced onion
½ teaspoon garlic salt
1 package (10 ounces)
   frozen chopped
   spinach, thawed
¼ cup seasoned bread
   crumbs

1 egg
1 tablespoon water
1 can (8 ounces) tomato
   sauce
1½ cups water
1 large stuffed olive,
   minced
1 teaspoon leaf oregano,
   crumbled

1. Lightly combine the ground beef, onion, garlic salt, spinach and bread crumbs in a large bowl. Beat egg with water in a small bowl; blend into beef mixture. Shape into balls, using a tablespoon of beef mixture per ball. Broil, just until brown, turning once.

2. Combine tomato sauce, water, olive and oregano in a large saucepan. Heat until mixture is boiling.

3. Add broiled meatballs to sauce, one at a time. Heat to boiling; lower heat. Cover; simmer 30 minutes. Remove cover during last 10 minutes of cooking to allow sauce to thicken slightly. Skim off fat from sauce, if necessary.

NOTE: A ½-cup serving of tender-cooked spaghetti adds 78 calories per serving.

QUICK GERMAN-STYLE MEATBALLS

Savory little meatballs in the style of "Königsberger Klops," extra easy to make because there's no pre-browning needed; they are simply simmered in a slim stock! Hamburger relish in the sauce is an easy way to add that piquant punch! A quick dinner that's a great appetizer, too!

Makes 6 servings at 226 calories each.

1½ pounds ground lean beef round	1 tablespoon lemon juice
2 eggs, beaten	3 envelopes or teaspoons instant beef broth
2 tablespoons packaged bread crumbs	3 cups boiling water
2 tablespoons instant minced onion	3 tablespoons flour
2 tablespoons parsley flakes	¼ cup cold water
1½ teaspoons salt	1 tablespoon Worcestershire sauce
¼ teaspoon pepper	3 tablespoons hamburger relish

1. Lightly combine the ground beef, eggs, bread crumbs, onion, parsley, salt, pepper and lemon juice in a large bowl. Shape into 2-inch balls.

2. Dissolve the beef broth in boiling water; heat to boiling; add meatballs. Heat again to boiling; lower heat. Cover; simmer 15 minutes.

3. Remove meatballs to serving dish; keep warm. Skim fat from broth, if necessary.

4. Mix flour and cold water to a smooth paste; stir into simmering broth. Add Worcestershire sauce and hamburger relish. Continue stirring over medium heat until sauce thickens and bubbles. Pour over meatballs.

APPLESAUCE MEATBALLS

Everyone knows what applesauce does for cakes. Here it is adding its own special moistness magic to meatballs, plus a mystery tang that's tantalizingly indefinable. Make it a guessing game!

Makes 4 servings at 248 calories each.

2 slices protein bread	1 tablespoon instant
1 pound ground lean	minced onion
beef round	1 teaspoon salt
1 egg	⅛ teaspoon pepper
1 cup unsweetened	5 tablespoons catsup
applesauce	¾ cup water

1. Moisten bread with water; squeeze out well. Crumble bread into large bowl with ground beef, egg, applesauce, onion, salt and pepper. Mix lightly. Shape into walnut-size balls. Broil just until brown, turning once.

2. Combine catsup and water in a large saucepan. Heat to boiling.

3. Add broiled meatballs to sauce. Heat to boiling; lower heat. Cover; simmer 15 minutes. Remove cover; continue simmering until sauce is slightly thickened. Skim fat from sauce, if necessary.

BURGUNDY BEEFBURGERS

Here's budget-wise "Beef Bourguignonne" . . . from chopped meat instead of expensive beef! Calorie-wise, too—when you make it from fat-trimmed, extra-lean ground round. Don't worry about the wine calories, most of them evaporate during the cooking.

Makes 8 servings at 203 calories each.

2 pounds ground lean
  beef round
½ cup cracked ice or
  ice water
1 tablespoon instant
  minced onion
2 teaspoons garlic salt
¼ teaspoon pepper
1 tablespoon vegetable
  oil

1 can (8 ounces) sliced
  mushrooms
¼ cup cold water
2 tablespoons flour
¾ cup Burgundy
2 tablespoons parsley
  flakes
½ teaspoon leaf sage,
  crumbled

1. Lightly combine the ground beef, ice (or ice water), onion, garlic salt and pepper in a large bowl. Shape into 8 oval "steaks."

2. Heat oil in large nonstick skillet; brown the beef-burgers quickly on both sides. Lower heat; continue cooking about 5 minutes longer, or until the beefburgers are medium rare. Remove to serving platter; keep warm.

3. Drain mushrooms, reserving liquid. Combine mushroom liquid with water, flour, wine, parsley flakes and the sage. Cover tightly and shake well. Pour into same skillet. Cook over medium heat, stirring constantly, until it thickens and bubbles. Add mushrooms and cook until mushrooms are hot, about 5 minutes longer. Serve sauce over beefburgers.

Hamburgers Encore! Low-calorie Main Courses from Leftover Broiled Burgers

Having broiled hamburgers tonight? Get a head start on tomorrow's dinner by broiling twice as many as you need. The broiler-browned burgers can serve as a base for any casserole dish that calls for ground beef browned in oil. Your "recycled" leftovers will be much leaner and lower in calories. If you don't want hamburger dishes two nights in a row, simply bag the burgers away in your freezer until needed.

SKINNY SKILLETBURGERS IN SAUERBRATEN SAUCE

A ginger-snappy gravy adds dash to this spur-of-the-minute skillet supper that's short on fat and calories. To cut the calories even more, use diet catsup instead of regular (6 calories a tablespoon instead of 18) and replace the sugar with its equivalent in sugar substitute. Stir it into the sauce after cooking—just before serving—so its sweetening power won't be diminished.

Makes 6 servings at 210 calories each.

1½ pounds ground
   lean beef round
1 egg
2 teaspoons onion salt
Pinch of thyme
1 tablespoon vegetable
   oil
1 cup cold water
1 tablespoon all-purpose
   flour
¼ teaspoon ground
   cloves

¼ teaspoon ground
   ginger
¼ teaspoon coarse
   grind pepper
2 tablespoons diet
   catsup
1 bay leaf
1 tablespoon cider
   vinegar
1½ tablespoons brown
   sugar (or sugar
   substitute)

1. Mix the ground round, egg, onion salt and thyme; shape into 6 oblong burgers. Heat oil in a nonstick skillet. Add the burgers; brown on both sides. Pour off fat, if any, and blot burgers with paper towelling to remove excess fat; reserve burgers.

2. Combine water with flour and add to skillet.

3. Stir in all remaining ingredients. Bring to boiling, stirring. Reduce heat; add burgers. Cover; simmer 20 minutes.

STUFFED PEPPERS PRONTO

Leftover hamburgers, pre-cooked rice and protein-rich bacon-flavored bits speed the preparation of this quick supper dish.

Bake at 350° for 30 minutes.
Makes 4 servings at 230 calories each.

4 large green peppers
4 broiled hamburger patties (from 1 pound ground lean beef round)
¼ cup pre-cooked rice
½ teaspoon salt
⅓ cup water
½ cup frozen chopped onion

2 cans (8 ounces each) tomato sauce
2 tablespoons bacon-flavored vegetable protein product
½ cup water
½ teaspoon leaf basil, crumbled
½ teaspoon garlic salt
⅛ teaspoon pepper

1. Slice the tops from green peppers; remove seeds, leaving shells intact. Cook 3 minutes in boiling water; drain.

2. Mash hamburger patties with fork. Combine with rice, salt, the ⅓ cup water, onion and ½ cup of the tomato sauce. Stuff mixture into pepper shells; sprinkle with protein product. Place peppers in a shallow, 6-cup baking dish.

3. Combine the remaining tomato sauce with the ½ cup water, basil, garlic salt and pepper. Pour over peppers.

4. Bake in a moderate oven (350°) 30 minutes, or until peppers are tender.

SLIM BEEFBURGERS "STROGANOFF"

Makes 8 servings at 182 calories each.

2 pounds ground lean beef round	¼ teaspoon salt
2 tablespoons instant minced onion	⅛ teaspoon pepper
1 teaspoon salt	2 tablespoons catsup
½ cup cracked ice or ice water	1 teaspoon prepared mustard
1 cup water	2 teaspoons parsley flakes
1 tablespoon flour	1 can (8 ounces) mushroom stems and pieces, drained
1 envelope or teaspoon instant beef broth	1 cup buttermilk

1. Combine the ground beef, onion, the 1 teaspoon of salt and cracked ice in a large bowl. Shape into 16 balls and brown under the broiler, turning once.

2. Combine water, flour and beef broth in a large saucepan. Cook over medium heat, stirring constantly, until sauce thickens and bubbles. Add salt, pepper, catsup, mustard and parsley. Reduce heat; drop in meatballs, a few at a time. Heat to boiling; lower heat. Cover; simmer 15 minutes.

3. Uncover; add mushrooms, return to boiling. Stir in buttermilk; reduce heat, cook until warmed through (do not boil), about 3 minutes.

PROTEIN-BOOSTED SWEDISH MEATBALLS

Soya granules (from health food store) add protein power and a smooth texture to these low-calorie meatballs with a party flair. Evaporated skimmed milk serves as a slimmer stand-in for cream in the gravy . . . it has all the dairy-fresh richness, but none of the butterfat

*calories or cholesterol! Here's another hint for choles-
terol watchers (it saves a few calories, too): Simply use
egg whites—egg yolks aren't needed to bind meatball
mixture.*

Makes 8 servings at 203 calories each.

1½ pounds ground
   lean beef round
2 tablespoons dried
   onion flakes
1 egg or 1 egg white
2 teaspoons garlic salt
¼ teaspoon freshly
   ground pepper
Pinch of nutmeg
½ cup water
½ cup soya granules
   (from health food

stores or in the
   health food section of
   your supermarket)
1 can (13 ounces)
   evaporated skimmed
   milk
1½ tablespoons all-
   purpose flour
½ cup water
2 envelopes or teaspoons
   instant beef broth
1 teaspoon dillweed

1. Combine the ground round, onion flakes, egg,
garlic salt, pepper, nutmeg, water and soya granules;
shape into walnut-size meatballs; brown under broiler,
turning once, until cooked through, 10 minutes.

2. While the meatballs brown, combine milk, flour,
water, beef broth and dill in a saucepan. Stir until flour
is dissolved. Cook, stirring constantly, over moderate
heat, to boiling.

3. Drop browned meatballs into sauce, a few at a
time. Reduce heat; cover; cook 10 minutes. Skim off fat,
if any, before serving.

GROUND ROUND STEAK WITH MUSHROOM TOPPING

Makes 4 servings at 162 calories each.

MUSHROOM TOPPING

- 2 tablespoons diet margarine
- 2 teaspoons fine dry bread crumbs
- ¼ teaspoon garlic salt
- ⅛ teaspoon pepper
- 4 tablespoons finely chopped parsley
- ¼ teaspoon grated lemon peel
- 1 teaspoon lemon juice

STEAK

- 1 pound ground lean beef round
- 1 teaspoon garlic salt
- ⅛ teaspoon pepper
- 1 tablespoon lemon juice
- 1 can (2 ounces) sliced mushrooms, drained

1. Combine Mushroom Topping ingredients; set aside. Lightly mix together ground round, salt, pepper and lemon juice; shape into 4 patties.

2. Broil patties 4 minutes, or until lightly browned. Turn and broil 5 minutes longer.

3. Top each patty with sliced mushrooms and 2 teaspoons of topping mixture. Continue broiling 3 minutes, or until bubbly and browned.

HUNGARIAN STUFFED CABBAGE

Makes 8 servings at 327 calories each.

- 1 large head of cabbage
- 1¾ pounds ground lean beef round
- ¾ cup uncooked rice
- 2 medium-size onions, 1 grated, 1 sliced
- 2 eggs
- 1 teaspoon salt
- ¼ teaspoon pepper
- 2 cups tomato juice
- ½ cup catsup
- ⅓ cup brown sugar
- 4 tablespoons lemon juice

1. Fill Dutch oven with water; bring to boiling. Core cabbage; plunge into water and boil for 3 minutes to soften. Remove cabbage and peel off about 12 leaves. Shred rest of cabbage.

2. Combine the ground round, rice, grated onion, eggs, salt and pepper. Place a small mound of the mixture (slightly larger than a walnut) on each leaf. Fold over the sides and roll.

3. Place rolls, seam sides down, in a large skillet or Dutch oven. Add onion slices and shredded cabbage. Combine tomato juice, catsup, sweetener, brown sugar and lemon juice; pour over cabbage rolls.

4. Cover; simmer over low heat for 2 hours. Or bake, covered, in a slow oven (300°) for 2 hours.

5. Before serving taste the sauce. Add more sweetener, if necessary.

PROTEIN-ENRICHED MEATBALLS

Makes 4 servings at 232 calories each.

1 cup high-protein cereal	3 tablespoons instant minced onion
½ cup skim milk	1 egg
3 envelopes or teaspoons instant beef broth	1 pound ground lean beef round
¼ teaspoon powdered sage	

Combine all ingredients and shape into balls. Brown under broiler.

SWEET-AND-SOUR BEEF AND CABBAGE

You might call this "unstuffed cabbage." It has the same flavor, but none of the bother . . . and far fewer calories!

Bake at 400° for 40 minutes.
Makes 4 servings at 223 calories each.

4 broiled hamburger patties (from 1 pound ground lean beef round)	**1 cup tomato sauce**
	½ cup water
1 package (8 ounces) shredded cabbage or coleslaw from supermarket produce department	**1 tablespoon lemon juice**
	1 tablespoon brown sugar or sugar substitute
	½ teaspoon salt
3 tablespoons dried onion flakes	**⅛ teaspoon pepper**

1. Mash the hamburger patties with fork.
2. Rinse the cabbage or coleslaw; drain.
3. Combine all remaining ingredients.
4. Layer cabbage, meat and sauce in a shallow, 8-cup baking dish. Bake in hot oven (400°) 40 minutes, or until cabbage is tender.

EASY MOUSSAKA

The classic Greek beef-and-eggplant casserole is extra lean and easy-to-do when assembled with broiler-browned burgers!

Bake at 350° for 1 hour.
Makes 4 servings at 284 calories each.

4 broiled hamburger patties (from 1 pound ground lean beef round)	**2 teaspoons garlic salt**
	¼ teaspoon nutmeg
2 cans (8 ounces each) tomato sauce	**1 eggplant, pared and cut into cubes (about 1¼ pounds)**
2 tablespoons dried onion flakes	**2 tablespoons grated cheese**

1. Break hamburger patties into chunks.

2. Combine the tomato sauce with onion flakes, garlic salt and nutmeg.

3. Layer meat, eggplant and sauce in a shallow 6-cup baking dish. Sprinkle with cheese; cover dish tightly with foil.

4. Bake in moderate oven (350°) 30 minutes. Remove foil; bake 30 minutes longer, or until eggplant is tender.

Mini-Caloried Meat Loaf

Tips for Calorie-Wise Meat-loaf Makers

• Garlic, mustard, Worcestershire, horseradish, chili, catsup, herbs, spices and seasonings—most of the real flavor-makers are low in calories. Bread crumbs, rice and other starchy stuffers add lots of empty calories.

• The better-choice meat-stretchers include tomatoes and onions; green peppers, mushrooms, celery and such. But why stop there. Grated carrots, canned drained bean sprouts, chopped string beans, cubed eggplant . . . almost any vegetable you like can agreeably fill out a meat loaf with flavor, texture and snuck-in vitamins!

• Meat loaf is best baked on top of a rack in a baking pan—not in a loaf pan or other container that traps fat.

• As with any boneless meat course, meat loaf has a way of looking puny on a too-big dinner plate. A nutritionally adequate serving may leave you psychologically starved, so couple meat loaf with "big" space-hogging vegetables: Big feathery broccoli for example.

• And meat loaf needn't be a loaf at all! Here are some eye-appealing ideas, all so delicious you'll want to give them a try even if you're not watching your weight!

BEEF RING WITH CANDIED CARROTS

Bake at 325° for 1 hour.
Makes 6 servings at 279 calories each.

1½ pounds lean ground beef	1 teaspoon salt
1 egg, beaten	½ teaspoon pepper
3 tablespoons water	Dash of garlic powder
4 tablespoons catsup	1 tablespoon bread crumbs
3 tablespoons grated onion	

1. Combine all the ingredients except bread crumbs. Mix lightly; add enough water to make mixture workable.
2. Pat gently into a 6-cup ring mold, then invert on a rack in a baking pan. Remove ring mold. Or: Shape meat loaf by hand into a big "doughnut."
3. Sprinkle top with crumbs, then bake in moderate oven (325°) for 1 hour. Remove to a platter and fill center with candied carrots.

EASY SUGARLESS "CANDIED" CARROTS—Heat the contents of a 1-pound can of carrots in a saucepan and bring to boiling; drain. Add three tablespoons diet maple syrup, one tablespoon lemon juice, one teaspoon parsley flakes, one teaspoon butter or margarine, salt and pepper. Simmer until most of the liquid evaporates.

SAVORY MEAT LOAF

Bake at 325° for 1 hour.
Makes 6 servings at 258 calories each.

1½ pounds lean ground
    round
1 egg, beaten
1 medium-size onion,
    finely chopped (½
    cup)
1 green pepper, seeded
    and finely chopped
    (½ cup)
2 stalks of celery, finely
    chopped (½ cup)

1 tablespoon chopped
    parsley
½ cup catsup
1 teaspoon dry mustard
1 clove of garlic, minced
1 teaspoon salt
½ teaspoon freshly
    ground pepper
1 green pepper, sliced
    into rings

1. Mix all ingredients except green pepper rings light-ly and shape into a loaf.
2. Place on a rack in a baking pan; top with green pepper rings. Bake in moderate oven (325°) for 1 hour.

MEAT LOAF PIZZA

A meat loaf-turned-piecrust and filled with tomatoes and cheese.

Bake at 425° for 25 minutes.
Makes 6 servings at 280 calories each.

1½ pounds extra-lean
    ground round
1 teaspoon salt
¼ teaspoon pepper
½ teaspoon garlic
    powder

1 cup tomato sauce
3 ounces shredded, part-
    skim mozzarella
    cheese
1 tablespoon leaf
    oregano, crumbled

1. Sprinkle the chopped meat with salt, pepper and

garlic powder. Gently pat into a 10-inch pie plate, including rim.

2. Bake in hot oven (425°) 15 minutes, or until well-browned.

3. Add tomato sauce and sprinkle with the cheese and oregano. Bake 10 minutes longer, or just until hot and bubbly. Drain off any fat. (Chopped peppers, mushroom slices, onions, or whatever else you like on pizza are all good additions. Anything but sausage.)

MINI-SKINNY INDIVIDUAL MEAT LOAVES

Actually flavored-up oven-baked hamburgers! The solo calorie-counter can prepare lots of them and freeze the extras . . . pop one in the oven on a night when the rest of the family is having something horrendously fattening! (This one is eggless.)

Bake at 425° for 20 minutes.
Makes 6 servings at 249 calories each.

1½ pounds ground round	**1 teaspoon leaf basil, crumbled**
1 can (1 pound) tomatoes, drained	**1 teaspoon salt**
1 tablespoon Worcestershire sauce	**½ teaspoon pepper**
1 large onion, chopped (1 cup)	**½ teaspoon garlic powder**
	Sugarless Barbecue Sauce

Shape into six mini-loaves. Place on a rack in a baking pan and bake at 425° for 20 minutes. Serve with Sugarless Barbecue Sauce.

SUGARLESS BARBECUE SAUCE—Combine reserved liquid from canned tomatoes with 3 tablespoons of cider vinegar, 1 tablespoon of the chopped onion, 1 tablespoon Worcestershire sauce, 1 teaspoon of dry mustard, and liquid or granulated no-calories sweetener to equal 2 teaspoons of sugar in a small saucepan. Heat to boiling; lower heat and simmer 15 minutes. Makes 1 cup at 11 calories.

"PRIME RIBS" MEAT LOAF FOR 8

Bake at 425° for 25 minutes.
Makes 8 servings at 220 calories each.

2 pounds extra-lean ground sirloin	**2 teaspoons salt** **½ teaspoon pepper**

1. Always tender and juicy rare, this is "steak" at half the cost—half the calories, too, because steak this lean wouldn't be tender. Sprinkle with salt and pepper and shape into "steak" three inches thick.

2. Bake in hot oven (425°) for about 25 minutes for medium-rare. Check with a meat thermometer to be sure. Serve with fresh broiled mushrooms; garnish with parsley; add your favorite steak sauce. Add a big salad with diet blue cheese dressing and a glass of Burgundy for a low-calorie meal!

ZINGY MEAT LOAF

Bake at 350° for 1 hour.
Makes 6 servings at 220 calories each.

1½ pounds lean ground round	**1 tablespoon minced parsley**
2 eggs, beaten	**2 carrots, grated**
1 medium-size onion, chopped (½ cup)	**1 teaspoon garlic salt**
1 tablespoon prepared horseradish	**1 teaspoon salt**
1 teaspoon dry mustard	**¼ teaspoon coarse grind pepper**
½ cup catsup	**1 medium-size green pepper, chopped**
½ cup minced celery	

1. Mix all ingredients lightly and shape into loaf.
2. Place on a rack in a baking pan; bake in moderate oven (350°) for 1 hour.

CHILI-TOPPED MEAT LOAF

Bake at 350° for 1 hour.
Makes 6 servings at 191 calories each.

1½ pounds lean ground round	1 medium-size onion, grated
1 egg, beaten	1 teaspoon fine dry bread crumbs
4 tablespoons catsup	
1½ teaspoons salt	3 tablespoons water
¼ teaspoon pepper	2 tablespoons chili sauce

1. Mix all ingredients, except the chili sauce, lightly and shape into a loaf.
2. Place on a rack in a baking pan; spread chili sauce over the top. Bake in a moderate oven (350°) for one hour.

HOLIDAY-STUFFED MEAT LOAF

Bake at 325° for 1 hour.
Makes 6 servings at 197 calories each.

1½ pounds lean ground round	¼ teaspoon chili powder
3 tablespoons chopped onion	Pinch of garlic salt
3 tablespoons skim milk	1 teaspoon salt
2 tablespoons Worcestershire sauce	¼ teaspoon pepper
3 tablespoons catsup	"Bacon" Flavored Mushroom Stuffing

Mix all the ingredients lightly and shape into a "bowl," reserving a handful for the cover. Fill "bowl" with stuffing; cover with remaining meat mixture. Garnish with sliced mushrooms or green pepper rings, if you wish. Place on a rack in a baking pan and bake in a moderate oven (325°) for 1 hour.

"BACON" FLAVORED MUSHROOM STUFFING: Sauté ½ cup sliced mushrooms in one teaspoon vegetable oil. Add ¼ cup dry sherry, ¼ cup water, 1 tablespoon bacon-flavor soy protein chips, 2 tablespoons instant rice, a pinch of salt and a pinch of marjoram. Simmer for 1 minute. Cover; let stand for 5 minutes, or until all moisture is absorbed.

SPEEDY MEAT LOAF

Bake at 350° for 1¼ hours.
Makes 8 servings at 223 calories each.

2 pounds lean ground
  round
1⅔ cups evaporated
  skimmed milk

1 package (2 envelopes)
  dried onion soup mix

Mix all ingredients and shape into a loaf in shallow baking pan. Bake in moderate oven (350°) 1¼ hours.

MEAT LOAF III, HERB-FLAVORED

Bake at 350° for 1 hour.
Makes 8 servings at 181 calories each.

2 pounds lean ground
  round
2 eggs, beaten
2 tablespoons chopped
  onions
½ cup skim milk
4 tablespoons parsley

1 clove of garlic, minced
2 teaspoons salt
½ teaspoon oregano
¼ teaspoon leaf basil,
  crumbled
½ teaspoon rosemary

Mix all ingredients lightly but thoroughly and shape into a loaf. Place on a rack in a roasting pan; bake in moderate oven (350°) for 1 hour.

BEEF-VEAL LOAF

Bake at 350° for 1 hour.
Makes 6 servings at 192 calories each.

1 pound lean ground round	1 can (1 pound) tomatoes, drained
½ pound lean ground veal	1 green pepper, chopped
1 tablespoon lemon juice	2 tablespoons parsley
1 medium-size onion, chopped (½ cup)	1 tablespoon oregano
	1 teaspoon fennel seed
	1 teaspoon salt
	¼ teaspoon pepper

1. Mix all ingredients lightly but thoroughly, and shape into a loaf.
2. Place on a rack in a baking pan; bake in moderate oven (350°) 1 hour.

EGGLESS MEAT LOAF

A low cholesterol counter!

Bake at 350° for 1 hour.
Makes 6 servings at 184 calories each.

1½ pounds lean ground round	1 clove of garlic, minced
2 medium-size onions, chopped (1 cup)	1 teaspoon salt
1 can (1 pound) tomatoes, drained	¼ teaspoon coarse grind pepper
	1 teaspoon oregano
	2 tablespoons catsup

1. Mix all ingredients, except the catsup, lightly but thoroughly.
2. Shape into a loaf; place on a rack in a baking pan; spread catsup over the top.
3. Bake in a moderate oven (350°) 1 hour.

PEPPER BEEF LOAFETTES

Each dieter gets his own savory loaf striped with crunchy water chestnuts and green pepper.

Bake at 350° for 30 minutes.
Makes 6 servings at 280 calories each.

1½ pounds lean ground round	1 egg, slightly beaten
½ cup fine dry bread crumbs	¼ cup water
6 tablespoons instant nonfat dry milk	1½ teaspoons salt
	⅛ teaspoon pepper
1 tablespoon chopped onion	1 small green pepper, halved lengthwise
	8 water chestnuts (from a 5-ounce can)

1. Combine the ground beef, bread crumbs, nonfat dry milk, onion, egg, water, salt and pepper in a medium-size bowl.
2. Set half of the green pepper and 3 water chestnuts aside for Step 4; chop remaining and add to meat mixture; mix lightly.
3. Shape into 6 even-size loaves; place in a shallow baking dish.
4. Cut remaining green-pepper half into 24 one-inch-long strips; cut each water chestnut into 4 slices, then halve each slice. Press 4 pepper strips and 4 water-chestnut slices, alternately, into top of each loaf.
5. Bake in a moderate oven (350°) 30 minutes, or until loaves are richly browned.

SPAGHETTI BOWL

Makes 6 servings at 372 calories each.

MEATBALLS

1 pound lean ground
  round
1 small onion, chopped
  (¼ cup)
2 tablespoons chopped
  parsley
1 cup soft whole-wheat
  bread crumbs
  (2 slices)
1 teaspoon salt
⅛ teaspoon pepper
1 tablespoon olive oil

SAUCE AND SPAGHETTI

1 medium-size onion,
  chopped (½ cup)

1 small clove of garlic,
  minced
1 can (about 1 pound)
  tomatoes
1 can (6 ounces) tomato
  paste
¾ cup water
2 teaspoons mixed
  Italian herbs
1½ teaspoons salt
¼ teaspoon pepper
Granulated, liquid or
  tablet no-calorie
  sweetener
1 package (1 pound)
  spaghetti, cooked to
  tender stage (14 to 20
  minutes)
Grated Parmesan cheese

1. Make meat balls: Combine beef, onion, parsley, bread crumbs, salt and pepper in medium-size bowl; mix lightly with fork. Shape into 6 balls.

2. Brown in olive oil in large frying pan; remove from pan with slotted spoon and set aside for Step 4.

3. Make sauce: Sauté onion and garlic until soft in remaining olive oil in a frying pan. Stir in tomatoes, tomato paste, water, Italian herbs, salt, pepper and your favorite no-calorie sweetener, using the equivalent of 1½ teaspoons sugar.

4. Arrange meat balls in the sauce; cover; simmer 1 hour.

5. While the sauce simmers, cook spaghetti.

6. Spoon the spaghetti onto heated serving plates, al-

lowing 1 cup for a dieter; top with ½ cup sauce and a meat ball. Pass cheese separately to sprinkle over.

BEEF-VEGETABLE LOAF

Flecks of carrot add a golden color and a subtle flavor to this herb-seasoned dish.

Bake at 350° for 50 minutes.
Makes 6 servings at 171 calories each.

1 pound lean ground round	1 small onion, chopped (¼ cup)
1 cup (8 ounces) cream-style cottage cheese	1 egg
3 medium-size carrots, scraped and shredded (about 1 cup)	1 teaspoon salt
	½ teaspoon basil
	¼ teaspoon pepper

1. Mix all ingredients lightly in large bowl. Shape into a loaf in middle of an ungreased shallow baking pan.
2. Bake in moderate oven (350°) 50 minutes, or until firm and lightly browned on top. Cut into 12 slices with a sharp knife.

WEIGHT-WISE LASAGNA

It tastes almost as rich as its high-calorie twin, yet hides several cooking tricks to keep the count down.

Bake at 350° for 30 minutes.
Makes 6 servings as 271 calories each.

1 clove of garlic, minced
1 medium-size onion,
    chopped (½ cup)
½ cup diced celery
½ cup water
½ pound lean ground
    round
3 cups Italian tomatoes
    (from a 2-pound can)
¼ cup catsup
¼ cup chopped parsley
1 teaspoon salt
½ teaspoon basil
Granulated, liquid or

tablet no-calorie
    sweetener
1½ cups (12-ounce
    package) pot cheese
1 egg
6 lasagna noodles (from
    a 1-pound package)
Half an 8-ounce package
    mozzarella cheese,
    cut into 6 slices
1 tablespoon grated
    Parmesan cheese
Paprika

1. Combine the garlic, onion, celery and water in a medium-size frying pan. Cook, uncovered, 10 minutes, or until water evaporates and vegetables are tender; push to one side.

2. Shape ground round into a thick patty in same pan; brown 3 minutes on each side; break up into chunks. Stir in onion mixture, then tomatoes, catsup, parsley, salt, basil and your favorite no-calorie sweetener, using the equivalent of 1 teaspoon sugar. Simmer 20 minutes, or until thick.

3. Mix pot cheese and egg in a small bowl.

4. Cook noodles in boiling salted water, following label directions; drain well.

5. Place 2 noodles in bottom of a very lightly greased shallow 6-cup baking dish, 10x6x2; spoon ⅓ of the cheese mixture, then ⅓ of the sauce on top. Repeat with remaining noodles, cheese and sauce mixtures to make 2 more layers of each. Place mozzarella on top; sprinkle with Parmesan and paprika.

6. Bake in moderate oven (350°) 30 minutes.

Chapter 6

Veal for Variety

Spiced with garlic or spiked with wine, sauced with "sour cream" or smothered in onion—no matter how you serve it, veal is a versatile calorie-saver that can lift both dining and dieting out of the doldrums. It's the lowest calorie meat there is. A quarter-pound veal cutlet is only 186 calories, while the equivalent amount of boneless beef-rib steak is a whopping 455! The same-size serving of pork or lamb chops will probably weigh in at 338 to 383 calories.

If you were hazy about where veal fits into the calorie picture, it's no wonder. The best-loved veal dishes seem so rich, it's easy to assume that the meat itself is fattening. Yet veal is such a calorie bargain that even the most spectacular dishes are sometimes slimmer than seemingly more-Spartan fare on the menu. If you're a Creative Low-Calorie Cook, you can work your own special magic to make them slimmer still!

PENNYWISE "CORDON BLEU"

Bake at 425° for 20 to 25 minutes.
Makes 4 servings at 351 calories each.

1 pound (8 slices) veal
    for scaloppine
3 ounces Swiss cheese,
    thinly sliced
3 ounces boiled ham,
    thinly sliced

1 teaspoon dried
    parsley flakes
¼ cup fine dry bread
    crumbs
1 teaspoon vegetable oil

1. Pound veal slices to even thickness with a meat mallet. Sprinkle the cheese and ham with parsley flakes. Divide the cheese and ham between 2 veal slices to make 4 "sandwiches."

2. Combine bread crumbs with oil; spread on wax paper. Coat veal "sandwiches" lightly on both sides; place on a cooky sheet.

3. Bake in hot oven (425°) 20 to 25 minutes, or till veal is done, cheese melted.

WIENER SCHNITZEL

Makes 6 servings at 193 calories each.

¼ cup fine dry bread
    crumbs
1½ pounds veal steak,
    about ¾ inch thick
2 tablespoons butter or
    margarine
1 envelope or teaspoon
    instant beef broth

½ cup boiling water
3 tablespoons lemon
    juice
3 tablespoons chopped
    parsley
½ teaspoon salt
⅛ teaspoon pepper

1. Spread bread crumbs on wax paper; press veal steak into crumbs, coating both sides lightly.

2. Melt butter or margarine in a large nonstick skillet; brown meat on both sides over moderate heat. Dissolve instant beef broth in boiling water; add to skillet with lemon juice, parsley, salt and pepper. Cover; bring to boiling. Simmer 30 minutes, or until meat is tender.

3. Remove steak to serving platter; pour pan juices over.

VEAL PICCATA

Makes 6 servings at 225 calories each.

1½ pounds veal for scaloppine	¼ cup dry white wine
1 tablespoon olive oil	1 tablespoon lemon juice
1 envelope or teaspoon instant chicken broth	1 lemon, cut in slices
½ cup water	Parsley sprigs

1. Heat the olive oil in a large, nonstick skillet. Brown veal quickly, turning once, several pieces at a time; remove to a warm plate.

2. Stir chicken broth, water, wine and lemon juice into skillet, scraping pan to loosen brown bits. Return veal to pan.

3. Cook over high heat 5 minutes, or until veal is tender.

4. Return to serving plate; garnish with lemon slices and parsley sprigs.

VEAL STROGANOFF

Makes 6 servings at 242 calories each.

2 tablespoons flour
1½ teaspoons salt
¼ teaspoon pepper
1½ pounds veal for
scaloppine, cut in
1-inch strips
1 tablespoon butter or
margarine
½ cup sliced onion

½ cup dry white wine
½ teaspoon prepared
mustard
1 tablespoon tomato
paste
1 tablespoon dried
parsley flakes
½ cup buttermilk

1. Put flour, salt and pepper in a plastic bag; add veal pieces. Coat the veal lightly.

2. Melt butter or margarine in a nonstick skillet and brown veal pieces quickly. Add onion, wine, mustard, tomato paste and parsley flakes; stir to blend. Cover; bring to boiling; lower heat. Simmer 10 minutes, or until tender.

3. Stir in buttermilk; cook over low heat a few minutes longer to heat through (do *not* boil). Serve with hot cooked noodles, if you wish.

SWEET-AND-SOUR VEAL

Makes 6 servings at 285 calories each.

1½ pounds veal
shoulder, cut in
cubes
1 can (1 pound,
4 ounces) pineapple
chunks, packed in
juice
1 tablespoon vegetable
oil
1 medium onion, sliced
(½ cup)

1 envelope or teaspoon
instant beef broth
1 cup boiling water
1 cup chopped celery
1 tablespoon cider or
wine vinegar
2 teaspoons cornstarch
3 tablespoons soy sauce
½ teaspoon salt
⅛ teaspoon pepper

1. Drain pineapple and reserve juice. Dissolve beef broth in boiling water. Heat oil in a nonstick skillet and brown the veal on all sides.

2. Add onions, broth and juice; cover and simmer for 45 to 50 minutes, or until veal is nearly tender. Add celery and cook 10 minutes more.

3. Combine cornstarch and vinegar; add to soy sauce; stir all into skillet. Cook until mixture simmers and thickens. Salt and pepper to taste; garnish with parsley. (A ½-cup serving of cooked rice adds 112 calories.)

LOW-CALORIE VEAL LOAF

If you're a meat-loaf lover, count on veal to serve up a savory dish that's calorie-shy and so low in fat that it encores beautifully as tomorrow's take-it-from-home sandwich—much tastier than "cold cuts."

Bake at 325° for 1 hour.
Makes 6 servings at 242 calories each.

1 large onion, chopped (1 cup)	1 tablespoon lemon juice
1 green pepper, chopped	1½ teaspoons salt
2 teaspoons vegetable oil	½ teaspoon coarse grind pepper
1½ pounds ground veal	1 teaspoon paprika
1 egg, beaten	1 clove of garlic, minced
2 tablespoons chopped pimiento	1 tablespoon packaged bread crumbs
	Tomato juice for basting

1. Sauté onion and pepper in oil in nonstick skillet.

2. Combine veal with all remaining ingredients except tomato sauce.

3. Pack into loaf pan, 8½x4½x2½. Bake in slow oven (325°) 1 hour, basting occasionally with tomato juice.

BULGARIAN VEAL SAUSAGE

Lean veal is a friend to sausage lovers on low-fat diets. Simply spice it up to suit your taste, at half the calories of the pork variety.

Makes 24 tiny sausages at 36 calories each.

1 pound veal, finely ground	¼ teaspoon freshly ground pepper
1 small onion, minced (¼ cup)	1 teaspoon paprika
1 teaspoon salt	1 egg, slightly beaten

1. Combine all ingredients; chill for 1 to 2 hours. Shape into 24 balls, using about 1 tablespoon for each, then roll into mini sausages 2 inches long.

2. Cook sausages over coals or under broiler with some smoke cooking sauce added, about 10 minutes.

MOCK ITALIAN SAUSAGE PATTIES

Makes 6 meal-size patties at 233 calories each.

1½ pounds ground veal	2 teaspoons paprika
1 egg, beaten with ¼ cup water	1 tablespoon fennel seeds
1 clove garlic, minced	2 teaspoons oregano
1 small onion, minced	1 tablespoon olive or vegetable oil
1½ teaspoons salt	
¼ teaspoon coarse grind pepper	

1. Combine all ingredients; shape into 6 meal-size patties, mini meatballs or tiny sausage oblongs.

2. Broil or panfry in 1 tablespoon olive or vegetable oil, 5 minutes on each side. Serve plain or top with tomato sauce.

QUICK VEAL IN TUNA SAUCE

Here's a way to recycle *leftover roast veal into a low-calorie version of the classic Italian "Vitello Tonnato," cold sliced veal marinated in tuna sauce.*

Makes 8 three-ounce servings at 263 calories each or 16 appetizer-size servings at 131 calories each.

1½ pounds cold cooked rolled leg of veal roast	1 teaspoon dried parsley flakes
1 bottle (8 ounces) low-calorie Italian dressing	Pinch of ground cloves
	1 teaspoon anchovy paste or dash of Worcestershire sauce
1 can (3¼ ounces) tuna, packed-in-water	½ teaspoon garlic salt
	1 teaspoon capers
	4 or 5 slices of lemon

1. Slice the cold roast in thin, even slices and arrange in a shallow serving dish.
2. Put all remaining ingredients except the capers and lemon slices in blender and beat at high speed. Pour sauce over veal. Marinate in refrigerator for several hours before serving; garnish with capers and lemon slices.

VEAL IN PORT

Makes 4 servings at 244 calories each.

2 veal cutlets, thinly sliced (about 1 pound)	½ pound fresh mushrooms, sliced
½ teaspoon salt	½ green pepper, cut in strips
¼ teaspoon pepper	¼ cup Port wine
1 tablespoon butter or margarine	1 tablespoon flour
	1 cup skim milk

1. Cut veal into serving-size pieces. Brown in butter or margarine in large skillet. Season with salt and pepper. Reduce heat. Cover; cook 10 minutes, or until meat is tender. Transfer to warm platter.

2. Brown mushrooms and green pepper in same skillet.

3. Stir wine into pan juices and cook a few minutes.

4. Mix flour and skim milk. Add gradually to skillet until sauce thickens. Return veal to pan and simmer in sauce until warm.

SOUTH-END VEAL CHOPS

Makes 8 servings at 251 calories each.

8 lean loin veal chops (about 2½ pounds), trimmed of fat	1 can (1 pound) tomatoes
1 tablespoon olive or vegetable oil	½ cup sliced onions
	½ pound sliced mushrooms
1 teaspoon salt	½ cup dry white wine
¼ teaspoon pepper	1 teaspoon leaf basil, crumbled
⅛ teaspoon garlic powder	

1. Heat oil in a large nonstick skillet. Season chops and brown on both sides.

2. Add all remaining ingredients and simmer for 45 minutes, or until chops are tender.

3. Remove chops to serving platter; keep warm. Skim off fat; simmer to thicken sauce. Pour sauce over chops.

HUNGARIAN VEAL CHOPS

Paprika powers this Hungarian-inspired dish that also owes its special dash to the tangy tartness of plain yogurt, so rich and sour-creamy, yet it adds only 30 calories to the recipe.

Makes 6 servings at 239 calories each.

6 loin veal chops, **¾ inch thick**	**1 tablespoon paprika**
½ cup sliced onion	**1½ teaspoons salt**
1 envelope or teaspoon **instant chicken broth**	**¼ teaspoon pepper**
1 cup boiling water	**1 teaspoon caraway** **seeds (optional)**
	¼ cup plain yogurt

1. Heat a large nonstick skillet; rub fat edges of chops over surface to grease. Brown chops well on both sides; add onion and sauté a few minutes longer.

2. Dissolve instant chicken broth in boiling water; pour over the chops. Sprinkle paprika, salt, pepper and the caraway seeds evenly over chops.

3. Cover; bring to boiling; lower heat. Simmer 20 minutes, or until chops are nearly tender.

4. Uncover skillet; simmer chops for about 10 minutes longer, or until most of the liquid is evaporated.

5. Stir in yogurt and heat 1 or 2 minutes longer, but do not boil.

ITALIAN VEAL ROLLS

Bake at 350° for 1 hour.
Makes 6 servings at 267 calories each.

6 slices veal for **scaloppine (1¼** **pounds)**	**4 tablespoons chopped** **parsley**
1 teaspoon salt	**4 tablespoons packaged** **seasoned bread**
⅛ teaspoon pepper	**crumbs**
3 thin slices lean cooked **ham (4 ounces)**	**3 tablespoons tomato** **sauce**
2 hard-cooked eggs, **chopped fine**	**2 tablespoons lemon** **juice**
½ cup minced onion	**1 tablespoon olive oil**

1. Pound the veal thin. Sprinkle with salt and pepper; set aside.

2. Chop the ham and combine with eggs, onion, parsley, bread crumbs and tomato sauce.

3. Spread the ham mixture evenly on veal slices. Fold sides to enclose filling. Roll up; place seam-side down in 6-cup shallow baking dish.

4. Combine lemon juice and oil; brush over rolls. Pour remaining mixture around rolls. Cover, and bake in moderate oven (350°) 1 hour, or until tender. Sprinkle with additional chopped parsley, if you wish.

VEAL AND SPANISH RICE ROAST

Bake at 350° for 2 hours.
Makes 10 three-ounce servings at 237 calories each.

1 veal rump roast,
  3 pounds
1 teaspoon garlic salt
⅛ teaspoon pepper
1½ cups tomato juice
1 package (5½ ounces)
  Spanish rice mix

1 can (4 ounces) sliced
  mushrooms
Mushroom liquid and
  water to make ½ cup
2 teaspoons dried
  parsley flakes
½ teaspoon salt
⅛ teaspoon pepper

1. Trim fat from roast. Season with garlic salt and pepper; place in center of long piece of wide foil.

2. Combine the tomato juice, rice mix, mushrooms, water, parsley, salt and pepper; spoon around roast; seal foil.

3. Place foil packet on rack in shallow roasting pan. Bake in moderate oven (350°) 2 hours, or until meat is tender.

4. Unwrap foil; remove roast to serving platter; surround with vegetables and sauce.

SLIM VEAL PARMIGIANA

Consider the classic Veal Parmigiana, in a rich tomato sauce, topped with melting mozzarella, complete with a side dish of tender-cooked spaghetti. How do you think that would stack up against a broiled steak and naked baked potato? Our Slim Veal Parmigiana is only two-thirds the calories!

The secret is in the simplified crumb coating; a lot less trouble than the dip-dunk-dip procedure of coating the veal in an egg-crumb batter that soaks up a lot of oil and soars the calorie count to 600-plus!

Bake at 350° for 20 minutes.
Makes 6 servings at 298 calories each.

1½ pounds veal for
    scaloppine
¼ cup seasoned bread
    crumbs
1 tablespoon olive oil
2 cans (8 ounces each)
    tomato sauce

2 teaspoons leaf
    oregano, crumbled
1 teaspoon garlic salt
½ teaspoon salt
⅛ teaspoon pepper
3 ounces part-skim
    mozzarella cheese,
    sliced

1. Dip veal in bread crumbs in a pie plate. Tap off any excess.
2. Heat oil in a large nonstick frying pan. Brown veal, turning once, several pieces at a time.
3. Place veal in a shallow baking dish; spoon the tomato sauce over veal; sprinkle with oregano, garlic salt, salt and pepper. Top with mozzarella.
4. Bake in a moderate oven (350°) 20 minutes, or until cheese is melted and bubbly.

Rump of Veal for Scaloppine

Some of the most popular veal dishes are made from the cut known as "scaloppine," which is cut from the leg. True, scaloppine is low in calories, but is also quite high in cost. Calorie watchers can also be penny watchers by buying rump of veal when it is on special and cutting their own thin scaloppine pieces, then pounding thin between two pieces of wax paper.

HAWAIIAN VEAL CHOPS

Makes 8 servings at 294 calories each.

8 lean loin veal chops (about 2½ pounds), trimmed of fat	4 tablespoons soy sauce
1 tablespoon vegetable oil	2 tablespoons cider vinegar
2 envelopes or teaspoons instant chicken broth	1 can (1 pound, 4 ounces) pineapple chunks, packed in juice
1½ cups boiling water	½ pound mushrooms, sliced
½ cup sliced onions	½ teaspoon salt
1 cup sliced celery	⅛ teaspoon pepper
2 tablespoons cornstarch	

1. Heat oil in a large nonstick skillet and brown chops on both sides. Remove chops and blot with paper towel to remove excess fat. Dissolve the broth in the boiling water.

2. Add the broth, onions and pineapple juice to skillet. Return chops to skillet. Cover; simmer 30 minutes, or until chops are nearly tender.

3. Add celery and simmer 10 minutes longer.

4. Combine cornstarch with soy sauce and vinegar; mix well and stir into skillet.

5. Stir in the pineapple and mushrooms; simmer, uncovered, until liquid thickens to sauce consistency. Add salt and pepper.

NOTE: ¼ cup fluffy cooked rice will add 56 calories.

Low-Calorie Veal for Wallet-Watchers

No doubt about it, veal wears a higher price tag than beef, but the cost difference is not nearly so great as it seems, when you consider that veal's lower fat content means less shrinkage.

Boneless veal cutlet, one of the costliest cuts, averages 90 percent meat and only 10 percent fat, while boneless beef-rib steak may contain as much as 45 percent fat (and even more in well-marbled prime ribs). With a higher meat-to-fat ratio, veal offers more protein per pound than beef, too.

But there are bargain cuts in veal that you can turn into pocketbook-conscious fare, using the same slow-simmer techniques that work magic on the less tender cuts of beef.

Here's what to look for in your store: *Cubes of Veal,* generally cut from the shoulder. This is veal "chuck," but only 785 calories per pound, compared with 1,166 per pound for beef chuck. Use it as a stand-in for beef in any stew or ragout your family favors and you'll automatically reduce the calorie count almost by half!

Keep it in mind, too, for any dish where garlic, wine, herbs, green pepper, mushrooms or tomatoes play a prominent role.

VEAL GOULASH

Makes 8 servings at 281 calories each.

2 pounds veal shoulder, cut into 1-inch cubes
1 tablespoon vegetable oil
2 medium-size red onions, sliced
1 can (16 ounces) whole peeled Italian tomatoes in purée

1½ teaspoons salt
2 teaspoons paprika
¼ teaspoon pepper
¼ teaspoon caraway seeds
2 cups hot cooked noodles

1. Brown meat in oil in a large nonstick skillet; add remaining ingredients, except noodles.
2. Heat to boiling; cover; lower heat. Simmer for 1¼ hours, or until meat is tender.
3. Prepare noodles according to package directions; drain. Serve with veal and vegetables.

VEAL IN WINE WITH MUSHROOMS

Makes 6 servings at 260 calories each.

2 pounds veal shoulder, cut into 1-inch cubes
1 tablespoon vegetable oil
½ cup sliced onion
1 clove of garlic, minced
1 pound fresh mushrooms

¾ cup dry sherry
1½ teaspoons seasoned salt
¼ teaspoon lemon pepper
2 teaspoons dried parsley flakes
1 small bay leaf

1. Brown meat in oil in a large nonstick skillet. Add onion, garlic and chopped mushroom stems (reserve

caps). Stir until onion is tender; pour in sherry. Cover; bring to boiling; lower heat.

2. Simmer 45 minutes, or until veal is almost tender. Add sliced mushroom caps. Cover; simmer 15 minutes longer. Remove bay leaf; serve immediately.

ITALIAN VEAL AND PEPPER STEW

"Veal and Peppers" is a dish that's normally made with the costlier cuts of veal, sautéed quickly in oil. Here's a more cost-conscious version that's also a calorie-saver.

Makes 8 servings at 228 calories each.

2 pounds veal shoulder, cut in cubes
1 tablespoon olive oil
2 medium-size onions, quartered
1½ teaspoons salt
½ teaspoon pepper
2 teaspoons dried oregano

1 clove of garlic, minced
½ cup white chianti (or any dry white wine)
1 can (1 pound) Italian tomatoes
3 green peppers, halved, seeded and cut in strips

1. Heat oil in a heavy skillet or Dutch oven; brown veal.

2. Add all remaining ingredients except peppers. Cover; simmer over low heat for 30 minutes. Uncover; simmer 45 minutes, or until meat is tender.

3. Uncover; simmer a few minutes more to thicken stew.

LOW-CALORIE SALTIMBOCCA
(VEAL AND HAM ROLL-UPS)

Makes 6 servings at 282 calories each.

1¼ pounds lean veal
round, cut into
12 even slices
½ pound cooked ham,
thinly sliced

½ teaspoon leaf sage,
crumbled
1 tablespoon olive oil
½ cup dry white wine

1. Pound veal slices lightly with meat mallet or edge of heavy plate. Cover each veal slice with a piece of ham; sprinkle with sage. Roll up; secure with wooden picks.

2. Heat oil in a nonstick skillet; brown veal rolls well on all sides. Pour in wine; bring to boiling. Lower heat; simmer until wine is evaporated.

Chapter 7

Diet Happy Pork

Ask any dieter the one meat to avoid . . . and chances are the answer will be "Pork!" Which really isn't fair to the modern porker. Today's little piggie goes to market with a much slimmer figure. The important "vital statistics" on today's pork is 36-57-22 . . . 36 percent fewer calories, 57 percent less fat and 22 percent more protein!

As a result, many cuts of pork are actually slimmer than steak. Of course pork isn't as trim as fish or chicken, but there's no reason to rule out pork if you're a Creative Low-Calorie Cook. But first you must be a figure-wise shopper, knowledgeable about the calorie counts of pork and pork products. The calories can range to less than 700 per pound for fat-trimmed pork shoulder to over 3,000 calories for bacon! Compare the cuts of pork and products in the chart. The counts given are calories-per-pound, meat only, without bones. And follow the Pork Pointers to get the most meat for the least calories.

Pork Pointers

• Always, ALWAYS trim away all fat before cooking. Or ask the butcher to do it.
• Quality pork is smooth and firm. Pork is naturally

tender, so fatty marbling is not an asset. Look for the leanest pork you can find.

• For succulent, easy-to-carve roasts, have the pork boned and rolled. And tell the butcher to trim away all fat while he's at it!

• Fresh ham (uncured leg-of-pork) makes a marvelously-tender rolled boneless pork roast once it's been trimmed of its thick layer of outside fat. Take note that the inner meat of fresh ham has fewer calories than the pork loin.

• For slow-simmer dishes, choose boned, fat-trimmed pork shoulder. For minimum fat and maximum flavor, use the "make-ahead method." Prepare the pork; cook it and then refrigerate the cooked pork dishes overnight. Lift off the hardened fat before reheating.

• Instead of sugary glazes, couple baked ham and other cured pork products with juice-packed pineapple. Try spreading crushed low-calorie pineapple on a heat-and-serve cooked ham slice or on a canned ready-to-eat ham such as we've done in the recipe for Quick Glazed Ham on page 126.

• Canned ham is a calorie bargain . . . only 875 calories per pound and virtually no waste!

• And of course, all pork products must be thoroughly cooked before eating (internal temperature of 170°).

Calorie Guide

	Calories	
	1 lb. Fat and Lean	1 lb. Lean only
Boneless Fresh Pork		
Fresh Ham	1397	726
Loin of Pork	1352	857

Boston Butt	1302	816
Picnic		
(shoulder)	1315	680
Spareribs	1637	*

Boneless Cured Pork

Ham (country)	1765	*
Ham		
(commercial)	1279	762
Boston Butt	1320	907
Picnic	1293	758

Boneless Pork Product

Canned ham	875	*
Bacon	3016	*
Canadian		
Bacon	960	*
Frankfurters	1402	*
Sausage	2259	*

* not available

PORK STEAK WITH APPLEKRAUT

Makes 6 servings at 218 calories each.

1 thick pork steak
  trimmed of fat (about
  1½ pounds)
1 tablespoon water
1 can (1 pound, 11
  ounces) sauerkraut,
  drained and rinsed

2 medium-size onions,
  chopped (1 cup)
1 large apple, pared,
  cored and sliced
2 teaspoons caraway
  seeds
½ teaspoon salt
⅛ teaspoon pepper

1. Put water and pork steak in large nonstick skillet. Cook over moderate heat until the water evaporates

and steak browns in its own fat (brown both sides). Drain off excess fat. Remove meat from pan.

2. Combine all remaining ingredients and stir into skillet. Add meat. Cover; cook over low heat for 1 hour.

PORK CUTLETS IN WINE

Makes 6 servings at 223 calories each.

8 pork cutlets, ⅛ inch thick (about 1½ pounds)
½ teaspoon salt
⅛ teaspoon pepper
2 cloves of garlic, minced
½ cup dry white wine
8 thin slices ready-to-eat ham (¼ pound)

1. Trim fat from the cutlets; pound thin with meat mallet or edge of plate. Season with salt and pepper.

2. Place cutlets and garlic in nonstick skillet. Sauté 5 minutes on each side. Drain off excess fat. Stir in wine. Cover; simmer 10 minutes. Top each cutlet with a slice of ham. Cover; simmer 5 minutes longer.

BROILED HAM STEAK

Makes 4 servings at 195 calories each.

1 slice ready-to-eat ham
2 tablespoons low-
calorie maple syrup

Trim all fat from ham steak. Place on rack in broiler pan. Brush with syrup. Broil 5 minutes on each side.

SLIVERED ORIENTAL PORK

Makes 6 servings at 185 calories each.

1½ pounds pork steak
  (cut from shoulder
  or leg)
2 tablespoons soy sauce
2 tablespoons dry white
  wine
1 medium-size green
  pepper, shredded

1 green onion, sliced
½ teaspoon ground
  ginger
1 teaspoon sugar
2 teaspoons cornstarch
2 tablespoons cold water

1. Trim off fat from meat; slice into thin 1-inch-long strips. Combine with sauce and wine in a large bowl.
2. Heat a large nonstick skillet or Oriental wok. Add pork-wine mixture; cook and stir until pork is cooked through. Add green pepper and onion; stir-fry 2 minutes.
3. Add ginger and sugar. Combine the cornstarch and water, add to skillet; stir until evenly glazed.

MARINATED PORK STEAK

Makes 6 servings at 230 calories each.

1 pork steak, trimmed
  of fat (about
  1¾ pounds)
1 medium-size onion,
  sliced
¼ cup lemon juice

¼ cup water
2 tablespoons brown
  sugar substitute
1 teaspoon garlic salt
Pinch of pepper
2 tablespoons soy sauce

1. Slash the edges of steak. Combine steak and onions in large shallow dish.
2. Mix juice, water, brown sugar substitute, garlic

salt, pepper and soy sauce; pour over steak and onions. Let stand at room temperature at least 2 hours.

3. Drain and reserve marinade and onions. Broil steak 10 to 12 minutes on each side, or until well-done. Remove to serving platter.

4. Pour marinade-onion mixture into saucepan; heat over low heat; pour over steak.

CALIFORNIA PORKCHOPS

Makes 8 servings at 255 calories each.

8 lean center-cut pork chops, ½ inch thick	3 tablespoons orange juice
Salt	1 teaspoon lemon juice or cider vinegar
2 tablespoons honey	1 medium-size orange, peeled and sliced into half cartwheels
½ teaspoon grated orange peel	

1. Trim off all fat from lean center portion of the chops; score edges to prevent curling. Season with salt.

2. Place chops in cold nonstick skillet; sauté over low heat until nicely browned.

3. Combine honey, orange peel, orange juice and lemon juice. Pour mixture over meat. Cover; simmer gently over very low heat 30 to 40 minutes, or until tender. Remove chops to warm serving platter. Simmer pan drippings until syrupy. Add the orange slices; heat until just warm; pour over meat.

QUICK GLAZED HAM

Bake at 350° for 1 hour.
Makes 10 servings at 272 calories each.

1 can (3 pounds) ready-to-eat ham	½ cup water
⅔ cup calories-reduced pineapple preserves	½ envelope onion soup mix
	Pinch of ground cloves

1. Place ham in a shallow baking pan.
2. Combine the preserves, water, soup mix and cloves; pour over ham. Bake, uncovered, in a moderate oven (350°) until meat thermometer registers 130°, about 1 hour. Baste often with glaze.

CANTONESE PORK STEAKS

Makes 6 servings at 195 calories each.

2 fresh ham slices (about 1½ pounds), trimmed of all fat	½ cup dry sherry
	6 tablespoons soy sauce
	2 tablespoons catsup
½ teaspoon instant garlic powder	2 teaspoons cornstarch

1. Sprinkle the garlic powder over pork steaks. Place in plastic bag; pour in sherry and soy sauce; place bag in bowl (to catch any leakage). Draw the sides of the bag up; twist sides together so marinade completely covers the meat. Marinate, in the refrigerator, 2 to 4 hours or longer.
2. Drain and reserve marinade. Broil steaks over hot coals or in your broiler, turning once, until browned and cooked through, about 12 minutes per side.
3. Meanwhile, prepare the sauce: Combine the re-

served marinade in a medium-size saucepan with
enough water to make 1 cup. Stir in catsup and cornstarch. Cook, stirring constantly, over moderate heat
until mixture thickens. Reduce heat; simmer 1 minute.
Pour over steaks on a heated platter. Cut into serving-
size portions.

FRESH HAM ROAST, ROLLED

*A fresh ham is leg-of-pork, uncured and unprocessed.
Like all fresh pork dishes, it must be thoroughly cooked
before serving. Pick out a lean fresh ham and tell the
butcher you want it boned, rolled and tied for roasting.
Tell him that you want all the fat removed.*

Each 3-ounce serving is 186 calories.

1. Marinate roast for several hours in equal parts
water and white wine. (For an Oriental accent, add
soy sauce.)
2. Season the roast well. Place on a rack in a roasting pan. Add ½ cup of the marinade. Cover loosely
with a tent of aluminum foil.
3. Bake in a slow oven (325°) about 25 minutes per
pound, or until a meat thermometer reads 170. Roast,
uncovered, for the last 20 minutes to brown the meat.

PERFECT PORK LOIN

*Pick out a lean loin roast of pork. Tell the butcher that
you want it trimmed of fat, boned and tied. What you'll
get back is an easy-carving rolled roast, with all the
fat and bones on the side. Discard the fat; use the
bones to flavor spaghetti sauce!*

Each 3-ounce serving is 215 calories.

1. Season the roast with salt and pepper. Place it on a rack in a roasting pan.

2. Roast, uncovered, in a slow oven (325°) about 40 minutes per pound or until a meat thermometer reads 170.

PORK CHOPS ITALIANO

Bake at 350° for 1½ hours.
Makes 6 servings at 287 calories each.

6 lean center-cut pork chops trimmed of all fat (about 2¼ pounds)
1½ teaspoons salt
⅛ teaspoon pepper
1 clove of garlic, minced
1 pound mushrooms, sliced
2 medium-size green peppers, halved, seeded and chopped
1 medium-size onion, sliced
1 can (1 pound) tomatoes
1 teaspoon leaf oregano, crumbled

1. Season the chops with salt and pepper. Broil until brown on both sides.

2. Remove to a medium-size roasting pan. Combine all remaining ingredients; pour over chops. Cover with foil; bake in moderate oven (350°) 1½ hours, or until tender.

SPANISH SAUSAGE PATTIES

Makes 16 patties at 87 calories each.

1 pound lean ground pork	2 teaspoons leaf oregano, crumbled
1 pound lean ground veal	½ teaspoon ground cumin
Pinch of cayenne	3 tablespoons wine vinegar
1 tablespoon garlic salt	
1 teaspoon pepper	

1. Combine all ingredients and toss lightly to mix. Shape into 16 patties. Wrap tightly in aluminum foil and store in freezer.

2. When ready to use, place frozen patties on a rack in broiler pan. Broil until patties are thoroughly cooked, about 10 minutes per side.

(CAUTION: Uncooked pork can't be taste-tested for seasoning!)

FRANKS IN BARBECUE SAUCE

Makes 6 servings at 261 calories each.

8 frankfurters (about 1 pound), cut in ¼-inch slices	½ teaspoon chili powder
4 tablespoons chopped onion	¼ teaspoon dry mustard
½ teaspoon salt	1 can (8 ounces) tomato sauce
Pinch of pepper	

1. Brown the frankfurters and onions slowly in a large nonstick skillet. Drain off excess fat.

2. Add the salt, pepper, chili powder, dry mustard and tomato sauce to the skillet. Mix well. Simmer 10 minutes to blend flavors.

PINEAPPLE PORK STEAK

Bake at 350° for 1 hour.
Makes 4 servings at 253 calories each.

1¼ pounds pork steak,
    trimmed of fat
1 teaspoon salt
⅛ teaspoon pepper

1 can (8 ounces)
    pineapple slices,
    packed in juice
4 tablespoons pineapple
    juice (from the can)

1. Brown steak in nonstick skillet. Season with salt and pepper. Arrange in baking dish. Top with pineapple slices and juice.

2. Cover with foil. Bake in moderate oven (350°) 1 hour, or until steak is tender.

LOW-CALORIE SPARERIBS

Bake at 400° for 30 minutes.
Makes 10 servings at 398 calories each.

4 pounds top spareribs
1 cup water
1½ teaspoons garlic salt
¼ teaspoon pepper
½ cup cold water

½ cup calories-reduced
    peach, apricot or
    pineapple jam
4 tablespoons soy sauce

1. Place spareribs in large saucepan with water. Cover; simmer over moderate heat 45 minutes, or until nearly tender.

2. Remove ribs to a baking dish. Season with garlic salt and pepper. Combine cold water, jam and soy sauce; pour over ribs.

3. Bake in a hot oven (400°) 30 minutes, or until crisp and brown.

BEEFY DOGS

Makes 5 servings at 134 calories each.

5 frankfurters	**1 envelope or teaspoon**
1½ cups boiling water	**instant beef broth**

Drop frankfurters and beef broth into boiling water. Remove from heat; cover, let stand 7 minutes.

To "De-Fat" Franks and Sausages

Heat a potful of water to boiling and drop in the franks or sausages. Remove from heat; allow to stand for 7 to 10 minutes. Much of the fat will melt into the water. Remove the franks from the water; place on rack in broiler pan. Broil until brown; serve.

APPLE-GLAZED PORK ROAST

Roast at 375° for 1½ hours.
Makes 6 servings at 309 calories each.

1 two-pound loin of	**1 small apple, pared,**
pork (6 chops)	**quartered, cored and**
½ teaspoon salt	**sliced**
⅛ teaspoon pepper	**1 tablespoon bottled**
½ cup apple juice	**steak sauce**

1. Trim all fat from roast; rub roast with salt and pepper; place on a rack in a roasting pan. If using a meat thermometer, insert bulb into center of roast without touching bone.
2. Pour the apple juice over roast; cover pan with foil, fastening it tightly around edges.
3. Roast in moderate oven (375°) for 1 hour; re-

move foil. Lay apple slices on top of roast; brush with steak sauce.

4. Continue roasting, brushing again with remaining sauce, 30 minutes, or until richly glazed and thermometer registers 170°. Remove to a heated serving platter; carve into chops.

SPANISH PORK

Makes 6 servings at 310 calories each.

1½ pounds lean boneless pork shoulder	¾ cup water
	½ cup chopped celery
	¼ cup chopped green pepper
1 large onion, chopped (1 cup)	1 teaspoon salt
1½ teaspoons chili powder	⅛ teaspoon pepper
	Granulated or liquid no-calorie sweetener
1 can (about 1 pound) tomatoes	3 cups cooked hot rice

1. Trim all fat from pork, then cut pork into ½-inch cubes. Brown in a large frying pan; push to one side.

2. Stir in the onion and chili powder; sauté until onion is soft, then stir into meat with the tomatoes, water, celery, green pepper, salt and pepper; cover. Simmer 50 minutes, or until meat is tender.

3. Just before serving, stir in your favorite no-calorie sweetener, using the equivalent of 2 teaspoons sugar. Serve over rice.

PORK RAGOUT

Hankering for stew but feel it's too high in calories? Try this version with lean pork and vegetables.

Makes 4 servings at 341 calories each.

1 pound lean pork leg,
  cubed
1 large onion, peeled
  and sliced thin
2 cups shredded lettuce
1 teaspoon salt
Dash of pepper
½ teaspoon rosemary
1 envelope instant
  chicken broth *OR:*

1 chicken-bouillon
  cube
1 cup hot water
8 small new potatoes
2 medium-size yellow
  squashes
½ pound green beans
2 tablespoons
  cornstarch
2 tablespoons cold water

1. Trim all fat from the pork. Combine pork, onion, lettuce, salt, pepper and rosemary in a kettle or Dutch oven.

2. Dissolve instant chicken broth or bouillon cube in hot water in a 1-cup measure; pour over pork; cover. Simmer 2 hours, or until pork is tender.

3. About 45 minutes before meat is done, scrub potatoes well; cut off a band of skin around the middle of each. Wash, trim, and then slice squashes thin. Wash, tip and cut green beans diagonally into ½-inch-long pieces.

4. Place potatoes on top of meat mixture; cook 30 minutes, or until tender. Cook squashes and green beans in slightly salted boiling water in separate medium-size saucepans 15 minutes, or until crisply tender; drain; keep hot.

5. Smooth the cornstarch and cold water to a paste in a cup; stir into the hot meat mixture; cook, stirring constantly, until broth thickens and boils 3 minutes.

6. Spoon meat mixture, dividing evenly, and 2 potatoes into each of 4 heated serving dishes; spoon squash and the green beans in separate piles at edge.

ORIENTAL PORK AND VEGETABLES

Makes 6 servings at 248 calories each.

1½ pounds lean
    boneless pork
    shoulder
4 tablespoons soy sauce
1 can (6 ounces)
    unsweetened
    pineapple juice
2 teaspoons salt
1 cup water

½ pound green beans,
    tipped and cut in
    1-inch-long pieces
2 large yellow squashes,
    trimmed, quartered
    lengthwise, and cut in
    2-inch-long sticks
2 tablespoons
    cornstarch
2 tablespoons cold water

1. Trim all the fat from pork, then cut the pork into thin strips; place in a shallow dish. Drizzle soy sauce over; let stand about 15 minutes to season.

2. Sauté strips, stirring several times, in a large frying pan 5 minutes; stir in pineapple juice, salt, and water; cover. Simmer 1 hour.

3. Place green beans and squash sticks around meat; cook 15 minutes longer, or until meat and vegetables are tender.

4. Smooth cornstarch and cold water to a paste in a cup; stir into meat mixture; cook, stirring constantly, until mixture thickens and boils 3 minutes. Spoon onto heated serving plates.

Chapter 8

Lean, Lovely Lamb

Luscious lovely lamb can liven any dieter's dinner . . .
if you're a calorie-wise shopper and careful cook! Most
calorie counters are confused about lamb. Some main-
tain that broiled lamb chops are slimming, while others
swear that all lamb is fattening.

Both opinions are dead wrong! Fatty lamb chops,
particularly those cut from the rib, are higher in calories
than many beef or pork dishes, even when broiled. On
the other hand, most lamb wears its fatty overcoat outside the meat, making it easy to "decalorize." A deter-
mined cook can trim away a hefty portion of lamb's
excess fat calories, leaving only the lean.

If you have to count calories, leg of lamb will be
your favorite dish . . . it's the leanest of all! Have your
butcher cut several steak-size slices from a leg roast
for low-calorie lamb chops. Every bit as flavorful as
loin chops. Have the rest of the leg trimmed of fat and
cut in cubes for stew or ground for patties.

ROAST LEG OF LAMB

Roast at 325° for 2½ hours (30 minutes per pound).
Makes 14 three-ounce servings at 302 calories each.

1 leg of lamb (about 5 pounds)	1 teaspoon garlic salt
	¼ teaspoon pepper

1. Carefully trim fat from the roast, leaving only a thin covering. Rub garlic salt and pepper into surface. Place roast on a rack in shallow roasting pan.

2. Roast in slow oven (325°) 30 minutes per pound (or 5 minutes longer per pound if well done lamb is desired).

WEST COAST SHISH KABOB

Makes 4 servings at 204 calories each.

MARINADE

⅓ cup water
1 teaspoon salt
¼ teaspoon thyme
¼ teaspoon crushed rosemary
⅛ teaspoon pepper
½ teaspoon grated lemon peel
3 tablespoons lemon juice
2 teaspoons Worcestershire sauce
1 small clove of garlic, pressed

SHISH KABOB

1 pound lean lamb (from leg), cut into 1-inch cubes
1 medium-size green pepper, cut into 8 wedges
4 small firm tomatoes, cut into 8 wedges
4 small onions, peeled and cut into 8 wedges
1 tablespoon vegetable oil

1. Combine all ingredients for marinade; add lamb. Marinate at least 2 hours.

2. Drain meat; reserve marinade. Thread cubes on 4 skewers, alternating with vegetables. Brush each lamb cube with a little oil.

3. Arrange on rack of broiler pan. Broil, 3 inches from the heat, for 10 minutes. Turn the skewers; brush meat with remaining oil. Broil about 10 minutes longer.

SKEWERED LAMB AND PINEAPPLE

Makes 4 servings at 253 calories each.

2 teaspoons vegetable oil	(from leg), cut in cubes
4 tablespoons cider vinegar	1 can (1 pound, 4 ounces) unsweetened pineapple chunks
¼ teaspoon rosemary	Meat tenderizer
¼ teaspoon basil	1 teaspoon salt
¼ teaspoon marjoram	⅛ teaspoon pepper
1 pound lean lamb	

1. Combine oil, vinegar, rosemary, basil and marjoram in a large bowl; add meat and marinate at least 3 hours.

2. Drain meat. Thread cubes on 4 skewers, alternating with pineapple chunks. Sprinkle with tenderizer, salt and pepper.

3. Arrange on rack of broiler pan. Broil, 2 inches from the heat, turning periodically, about 10 minutes per side.

SWEET-AND-SOUR LAMB STEAKS

Makes 6 servings at 316 calories each.

3 lamb steaks, ¾ inch thick (about 2 pounds)	3 tablespoons honey
2 tablespoons Worcestershire sauce	4 tablespoons cider vinegar
	4 tablespoons water
	Garlic salt

1. Trim excess fat from lamb steaks and cut in half to make 6 portions. Combine all remaining ingredients. Pour over steaks. Stack coated steaks on a platter and refrigerate 1 hour.

2. Broil, 3 to 4 inches from heat, 10 minutes per side. Salt and pepper to taste.

LAMBURGERS

Makes 6 patties at 150 calories each.

1½ pounds lean leg of lamb, ground	1 teaspoon allspice
	Pinch of curry
1 teaspoon onion salt	½ teaspoon crushed
½ teaspoon marjoram	mint leaves
½ cup parsley, chopped	

1. For the leanest burgers, select the lamb yourself and have it chopped to order. Combine lamb with all remaining ingredients; shape into 6 patties.

2. Broil, 2 inches from heat, 4 to 5 minutes per side.

NOTE: Each patty may be topped with 1 slice of unsweetened pineapple at an additional 27 calories each.

MARJORAM-BROILED LAMB STEAK

Makes 2 three-ounce servings at 211 calories each.

1 lamb leg steak, about ¾ inch thick (8 ounces)	⅛ teaspoon pepper
	1 tablespoon leaf marjoram, crumbled
½ teaspoon garlic salt	

1. Carefully trim all fringe fat from steak with a sharp knife. Slash edges to prevent curling during broiling.

2. Sprinkle steak with garlic salt and pepper. Press marjoram onto both sides. Place on rack in broiler pan.

3. Broil, 3 inches from heat, 8 minutes to the side, or to desired degree of doneness.

CURRIED LAMB ENCORE

Makes 4 servings at 287 calories each.

1 pound cooked lamb, cut in cubes	½ teaspoon ground ginger
3 tablespoons dried onion flakes	1⅔ cups canned tomatoes in purée (from 1-pound, 12-ounce can)
1 teaspoon garlic salt	
1 teaspoon curry powder	

Combine all ingredients in a large saucepan; stir well. Cover; bring to boiling; lower heat. Simmer 10 minutes. (A ½-cup serving of instant rice adds 89 calories per serving.)

LAMB AND RICE EN CASSEROLE

A great way to use leftover roast leg of lamb.

Bake at 350° for 1 hour.
Makes 6 servings at 210 calories each.

2 cups diced cooked lean lamb (1 pound)	1 medium-size onion, chopped (½ cup)
2 envelopes or teaspoons instant beef broth	1 teaspoon salt
	¼ teaspoon pepper
2 cups boiling water	½ cup uncooked rice
1 cup canned tomatoes (from 1-pound can)	2 tablespoons Worcestershire sauce

1. Combine all ingredients in an 8-cup baking dish. Bake, covered, in a moderate oven (350°) 40 minutes.
2. Uncover; bake 20 minutes longer, or until most of the liquid is evaporated. Garnish with chopped parsley, if you wish.

SKILLET MOUSSAKA

Makes 6 servings at 205 calories each.

1½ pounds ground lamb (trimmed of fat and ground to order)	3 tablespoons chopped parsley
1 eggplant (1 pound), pared and cut into small cubes	1½ teaspoons salt
	1½ teaspoons leaf oregano, crumbled
1 medium-size onion, chopped (½ cup)	1 cup canned tomatoes
	2 tablespoons grated Romano cheese

1. Heat a large skillet; brown ground lamb well, draining off fat as it accumulates.

2. Add the eggplant, onion, parsley, salt and oregano; cook 3 minutes, stirring several times. Add tomatoes, breaking up with a spoon. Mix well. Bring to boiling. Lower heat; cover; simmer 30 minutes, or until eggplant is very tender. Uncover; sprinkle with cheese and a little more of the chopped parsley, if you wish.

IRANIAN PARTY MEATBALLS IN YOGURT SAUCE

Makes 12 party servings at 159 calories each. (Three meatballs per serving.)

2 pounds ground lamb (trimmed of fat and ground to order)	1 cup chopped parsley
	1 teaspoon apple pie spice
1½ teaspoons garlic salt	2 slices protein bread
2 eggs	2 containers (8 ounces each) plain yogurt
4 tablespoons tomato paste (from a 6-ounce can)	

1. Combine lamb, garlic salt, eggs, tomato paste, parsley and apple pie spice in a large bowl. Dip bread in water; squeeze out excess. Add to meat mixture; mix well. Use a teaspoon to shape into small meatballs. Place on rack in broiler pan.

2. Broil, 3 inches from heat for 10 minutes, turning frequently to brown evenly.

3. Heat yogurt in a large skillet or chafing dish over low heat; do not allow to boil. Stir in meatballs. Garnish with some additional chopped parsley, if you wish.

SHASHLIK

Makes 6 servings at 186 calories each.

¼ cup lemon juice
1 tablespoon olive oil
¼ cup water
1 teaspoon salt
¼ teaspoon pepper
1½ pounds boneless
    leg of lamb, cut
    in cubes

2 medium-size onions,
    cut into 6 wedges each
½ pound small
    mushroom caps
2 lemons, sliced
2 tomatoes, cut in
    wedges
4 green onions, cut in
    2-inch pieces

1. Combine lemon juice, oil, water, salt and pepper in a glass or ceramic bowl; stir in the lamb cubes. Cover; marinate in the refrigerator 6 hours, or overnight.

2. Drain the meat; thread on skewers alternately with onion wedges and mushrooms. Place on rack in broiler.

3. Broil, 3 inches from heat for 15 minutes, turning frequently.

4. Slide meat and vegetables off the skewers onto a serving platter. Garnish with lemon slices, tomato wedges and green onions.

Shopper's Guide to Lamb

For Roasting: Choose a whole leg of lamb and have it carefully trimmed of fat. Or, ask the butcher to remove the bone and prepare a "rolled roast."

For Broiling or Pan-Frying: "Leg steaks" or "leg chops" are your most calorie-wise buy. These are oval-shaped, lean lamb steaks with a small bone in the middle.

For Skewering or Barbecuing: Tender, boneless cubes of lamb cut from the leg. These will be more tender than cubes from the shoulder.

For Stews and Ragouts: For leanness and tenderness, choose cubes of meat cut from the leg. For economy, choose a shoulder roast trimmed of all fat.

For Ground Lamb Dishes: Choose a leg or shoulder roast and have it trimmed of fat, then ground to order.

Chapter 9

Trim Chicken Tempters

Chicken is such a beautiful bargain in calories and cost, you can afford to dress it up with flourishes you might not otherwise consider. You can enjoy chicken often, too, because it's so spectacularly versatile—glamorous one day and "just folks" the next. Plain or fancy, nearly everyone can eat it. In fact, chicken's easy digestibility and low cholesterol level make it just what the doctor ordered on so many special diets.

If you want to be a real diet heroine, you can strip off the skin, a particularly good idea in recipes where the meat simmers or bakes in a sauce or liquid. Without the skin, there's no chicken fat to ooze extra calories into the sauce, yet the chicken can't dry out the way it does when you broil or bake it bare. And every tablespoon of chicken fat you eliminate from your plate is 126 calories you might spend on something else—dessert, for example!

LEMON-BAKED CHICKEN

Bake at 400° for 55 minutes.
Makes 4 servings at 196 calories each.

1 broiler-fryer (about 2 pounds), quartered	½ teaspoon grated lemon peel
1 teaspoon garlic salt	⅓ cup lemon juice
2 teaspoons paprika	½ cup water
½ teaspoon leaf oregano, crumbled	

1. Wash chicken; pat dry. Arrange in a 12-cup baking dish, skin side down. Sprinkle with the garlic salt and paprika.

2. Combine remaining ingredients and pour over chicken. Bake, uncovered, in hot oven (400°) 30 minutes.

3. Uncover; turn the chicken. Cover and continue baking, basting once or twice with pan drippings, 25 minutes, or until chicken is tender. Garnish with parsley, if you wish.

NOTE: One 4-ounce serving is 1 thigh and drumstick or half a chicken breast.

CHICKEN WITH ORANGES

Bake at 375° for 1 hour.
Makes 6 servings at 222 calories each.

2 broiler-fryers (about
 1½ pounds each),
 cut up
1 small onion, sliced
4 tablespoons chopped
 green pepper
1 cup sliced mushrooms
 (fresh or canned)
1 cup orange juice
3 tablespoons dry
 sherry

½ cup water
1½ teaspoons salt
¼ teaspoon pepper
1 teaspoon grated
 orange rind
1 tablespoon all-purpose
 flour
2 teaspoons dried
 parsley flakes
Orange slices

1. Wash chicken; pat dry. Place, skin side up, in a shallow 12-cup baking dish. Add the onion, pepper and mushrooms.
2. Combine all remaining ingredients except the orange slices in a shallow saucepan. Cook over moderate heat, stirring frequently, until mixture thickens and bubbles. Pour over chicken.
3. Bake in moderate oven (375°), basting occasionally, 1 hour, or until chicken is tender. Skim fat from pan juices. Garnish with orange slices, if you wish.

CHICKEN MEXICANA

Makes 6 servings at 191 calories each.

3 large chicken breasts,
   split (about 12 ounces
   each)
1 clove of garlic, split
1 teaspoon oregano
Pinch of cayenne
Pinch of ground
   nutmeg
1 teaspoon salt

1 envelope or teaspoon
   instant chicken broth
1 cup water
2 cans (8 ounces each)
   tomato sauce
1 cup sliced onions
1 medium-size green
   pepper, halved,
   seeded and chopped

1. Wash chicken; pat dry. Arrange, skin side down, in a cold nonstick skillet. Rub with garlic; sprinkle with the oregano, cayenne, nutmeg and salt.

2. Heat slowly to melt fat from skin. Continue cooking until chicken is browned.

3. Add all remaining ingredients. Cover; simmer 30 minutes, or until tender.

QUICK "COUNTRY" CHICKEN

Makes 4 servings at 243 calories each.

1 broiler-fryer (about 2
   pounds), cut up
1 tablespoon all-purpose
   flour
2 teaspoons garlic salt
¼ teaspoon coarse-
   grind pepper
Pinch of instant garlic
   powder
Small bay leaf
1 tablespoon dried
   parsley flakes

1 can (about 8 ounces)
   sliced carrots, with
   liquid
1 can (8 ounces) sliced
   mushrooms, with
   liquid
1 can (8 ounces) small
   boiled onions, with
   liquid
½ cup dry sherry

1. Wash chicken; pat dry. Arrange the chicken pieces, skin side down, in a flameproof casserole or large skillet. Heat slowly to melt fat from skin; continue cooking over moderate heat until the chicken is browned. Drain all fat from pan.

2. Return chicken to skillet. Sprinkle with flour, salt, pepper and garlic powder; add bay leaf, parsley flakes and onion liquid. Add liquid from the carrots and mushrooms; reserve the vegetables. Add the wine.

3. Cover; simmer over low heat for 45 minutes, or until chicken is nearly tender. Add carrots, mushrooms and onions; simmer, uncovered, a few minutes longer until the sauce is thickened.

CHICKEN BREASTS WITH CHERRIES

Bake at 375° for 50 minutes.
Makes 8 servings at 188 calories each.

4 large chicken breasts, split	unsweetened pitted red tart cherries
1 teaspoon salt	2 tablespoons sugar
1/8 teaspoon pepper	Pinch of salt
1 tablespoon cornstarch	Few drops red food coloring
1 can (1 pound)	

1. Wash the chicken; pat dry.

2. Place chicken pieces, skin side up, on a rack in a shallow baking pan. Season with salt and pepper. Bake in a moderate oven (375°) 50 minutes, or until tender.

3. Combine cornstarch and cherries in a nonstick saucepan. Add the sugar and salt; stir to dissolve cornstarch. Heat over moderate heat, stirring constantly, until the juice thickens and clears. Add food coloring. Serve with baked chicken.

SMOTHERED CHICKEN

Bake at 350° for 45 minutes.
Makes 6 servings at 267 calories each.

1 broiler-fryer (about 3 pounds), cut up	1½ cups boiling water
1 teaspoon salt	½ teaspoon poultry seasoning
½ teaspoon paprika	1 cup evaporated skimmed milk
1 envelope (2 ounces) chicken-vegetable soup mix	2 tablespoons cornstarch

1. Wash chicken; pat dry. Arrange on rack in broiler pan. Sprinkle with salt and paprika. Broil until brown. Turn; brown other side.

2. Place browned chicken in a 2-quart casserole, skin side up. Stir in soup mix, water and poultry seasoning.

3. Cover; bake in moderate oven (350°) 45 minutes, or until tender.

4. Remove chicken to serving platter; keep warm. Combine milk and cornstarch; stir into ingredients in casserole dish. Cook over low heat, stirring constantly, until sauce is thickened. Pour sauce over chicken; serve immediately.

SPICED CHICKEN

Bake at 350° for 1 hour.
Makes 6 servings at 262 calories each.

1½ cups orange
    sections (4 or 5
    oranges), drained
1 cup orange juice from
    sections
1 tablespoon brown
    sugar or granulated
    brown sugar substitute
2 tablespoons cider
    vinegar

1 teaspoon mace or
    nutmeg
1 teaspoon leaf basil,
    crumbled
1 clove of garlic, minced
1 broiler-fryer (about 3
    pounds), cut up
1 teaspoon salt
¼ teaspoon pepper

1. Combine orange juice with brown sugar, vinegar, mace, basil and garlic in a medium-size saucepan. Simmer over low heat 10 minutes.

2. Wash chicken pieces; pat dry with paper toweling.

3. Place chicken, skin side up, on rack of broiler pan. Sprinkle with salt and pepper. Broil until brown.

4. Remove chicken to a shallow baking dish. Pour orange juice mixture over chicken and bake, uncovered, in a moderate oven (350°) for 55 minutes, or until chicken is tender. Baste occasionally.

5. Add orange sections to baking dish. Bake 5 minutes longer.

HARVEST CHICKEN

Bake at 350° for 40 minutes.
Makes 6 servings at 254 calories each.

2 broiler-fryers (about
  1½ pounds each),
  cut up
1 large onion, coarsely
  chopped (1 cup)
3 medium-size tomatoes,
  peeled and diced
1½ teaspoons salt
¼ teaspoon pepper
1 envelope or teaspoon
  instant chicken broth
1 cup boiling water

1 clove of garlic, minced
¾ teaspoon liquid red-
  pepper seasoning
½ teaspoon thyme
1 package (10 ounces)
  frozen mixed
  vegetables
1 small zucchini, thinly
  sliced (1 cup)
2 teaspoons cornstarch
1 tablespoon water

1. Wash chicken; pat dry. Place, skin side up, on rack of broiler pan. Broil to brown.

2. Remove to large skillet or Dutch oven. Add onion, tomatoes, salt, pepper, chicken broth, water, garlic, red-pepper seasoning and thyme. Bring to boiling. Reduce heat; simmer 30 minutes.

3. Add mixed vegetables and squash. Simmer 15 minutes. Remove chicken to platter.

4. Skim fat from sauce. Combine cornstarch and water; stir into sauce; heat to thicken.

CHICKEN A LA KING

Makes 8 servings at 242 calories each.

1 tablespoon diet margarine	2 teaspoons salt
1 large onion, peeled and chopped (about 1 cup)	⅛ teaspoon pepper
	⅛ teaspoon thyme
	1 cup water
4 cups cooked cubed chicken	⅓ cup all-purpose flour
	½ cup instant nonfat dry milk
1 envelope or teaspoon instant chicken broth	8 slices diet white bread, toasted
1 cup boiling water	

1. Heat margarine in skillet. Add onions; sauté over very low heat 15 minutes. Add chicken, broth, boiling water, salt, pepper and thyme.

2. Combine water, flour and milk in a bowl; beat until smooth; add to pan. Cook over low heat, stirring occasionally, until mixture thickens and bubbles. Cook 2 minutes longer. Serve over toast.

VARIATIONS—Any one of the following can be added to the recipe for Chicken A La King, for extra flavor and very few calories: 4 sprigs of parsley, chopped; 2 tablespoons dry sherry; 3 stalks of celery, sliced; ½ pound mushrooms, sliced; 4 tablespoons diced green pepper; 4 tablespoons sliced pimiento. Serve the chicken and sauce over toast.

QUICK CHICKEN FLORENTINE

Makes 4 servings at 288 calories each.

1 package (10 ounces) frozen spinach	1 cup skim milk
1 can (15 ounces) boned chicken	½ teaspoon salt
	⅛ teaspoon pepper
1½ tablespoons all-purpose flour	4 tablespoons extra-sharp grated Cheddar cheese

1. Cook spinach according to package directions. Drain and place in a shallow 8-cup baking dish.
2. Drain and flake chicken; layer on top of spinach.
3. Combine flour, milk, salt and pepper in a medium-size saucepan. Heat to simmering, stirring constantly. Pour sauce over chicken; top with grated cheese.
4. Heat under broiler until cheese is brown and bubbly.

SOUTH-OF-THE-BORDER CHICKEN

Makes 6 servings at 250 calories each.

1½ teaspoons salt	2 medium-size onions, chopped (1 cup)
½ teaspoon pepper	
1 teaspoon paprika	1 medium-size green pepper, chopped
½ teaspoon oregano	
1 teaspoon instant garlic powder	2 envelopes or teaspoons instant chicken broth
2 broiler-fryers (about 1½ pounds each), cut up	1 cup water
	1 can (1 pound) tomatoes
1 tablespoon vegetable oil	1 can (8 ounces) sliced mushrooms, drained

1. Combine salt, pepper, paprika, oregano and garlic powder; rub into chicken.

2. Heat oil in a heavy skillet. Add onions and green pepper; sauté for 10 minutes. Push aside and add chicken pieces; cook until skin is well browned.

3. Add remaining ingredients. Cover; simmer over moderate heat 45 minutes, or until chicken is tender and sauce is reduced. Skim off fat before serving.

CORN CRISPED OVEN-FRIED CHICKEN

Bake at 375° for 1 hour.
Makes 6 servings at 251 calories each.

2 broiler-fryers (about 1½ pounds each), cut up	1½ teaspoons onion salt
½ cup skim milk	¼ teaspoon pepper
1 cup packaged corn flake crumbs	1 teaspoon paprika

1. Wash chicken pieces; pat dry. Pour milk into a shallow dish. Combine the corn flake crumbs, onion salt, pepper and paprika in a plastic or paper bag.

2. Dip chicken pieces in the milk; shake pieces, a few at a time, in crumb mixture to coat well.

3. Arrange chicken, skin side up, in a single layer on a nonstick baking pan. Bake in moderate oven (375°) 1 hour, or until tender.

COQ AU VIN ROUGE
(CHICKEN IN RED WINE)

Makes 6 servings at 213 calories each.

2 broiler-fryers (about 1½ pounds each), cut up	½ cup tomato juice
	1 bay leaf
	Pinch of thyme
1 can (8 ounces) small boiled onions	Pinch of sage
	1½ teaspoons salt
½ cup dry red wine	¼ teaspoon pepper
½ cup water	

1. Wash chicken pieces; pat dry. Trim off excess fat. Arrange on rack in broiler pan; broil until skin is crackly. Remove from heat.

2. Place chicken, skin side up, in a heavy pan or Dutch oven. Combine all remaining ingredients and pour over chicken. Cover; simmer over low heat 45 minutes, or until chicken is just tender.

3. Uncover; continue cooking until pan juices thicken to sauce consistency. Skim off fat.

CHICKEN SHERRY

Makes 6 servings at 210 calories each.

2 broiler-fryers (about 1½ pounds each), cut up	1 tablespoon chopped parsley
2 medium-size onions, chopped (1 cup)	½ teaspoon leaf rosemary, crumbled
1 clove of garlic, minced	1½ teaspoons salt
½ cup dry sherry	¼ teaspoon pepper
½ bay leaf	½ pound fresh mushrooms, whole or sliced

1. Wash chicken pieces; pat dry. Trim off the excess skin. Place, skin side down, in a large nonstick skillet. Cook over low heat until well-browned on all sides. Drain off excess fat.

2. Add onions and garlic to pan; sauté until soft.

3. Add sherry, bay leaf, parsley, salt and pepper. Cover; simmer over low heat 35 minutes, or until chicken is just tender.

4. Add mushrooms. Cover; simmer 10 minutes longer. Uncover; cook until the pan juices thicken to sauce consistency. Skim off fat.

CAN-OPENER SHERRIED CHICKEN WITH CARROTS: Substitute 1 can (8 ounces) boiled onions, drained and 1 can (8 ounces) sliced mushrooms, drained for fresh ingredients in Chicken Sherry. Also, add 1 can (1 pound) sliced carrots, drained to the recipe. Prepare as above, adding canned ingredients during the last 15 minutes of cooking time. Makes 6 servings at 233 calories each.

CHICKEN HAWAIIAN

Bake at 350° for 45 minutes.
Makes 6 servings at 255 calories each.

2 broiler-fryers (about 1½ pounds each), cut up	½ green pepper, chopped (½ cup)
1½ teaspoons salt	½ cup water
1 can (1 pound, 4 ounces) pineapple chunks, packed-in-juice	1 tablespoon soy sauce
	2 envelopes or teaspoons instant chicken broth
1 cup sliced mushrooms	½ teaspoon ground ginger

1. Wash chicken pieces; pat dry. Arrange, skin side up, in single layer on rack of broiler pan. Sprinkle with

salt; broil until brown. Turn, brown other side. Remove to shallow 12-cup baking dish.

2. Combine pineapple with pineapple juice, mushrooms, green pepper, water, soy sauce, chicken broth and ginger; pour over chicken.

3. Bake, uncovered, in moderate oven (350°) 45 minutes, or until the chicken is tender.

CHICKEN MARENGO CAN-CAN

Makes 6 servings at 252 calories each.

2 broiler-fryers (about 1½ pounds each), cut up	1 can (1 pound) small boiled onions, with liquid
1 can (10¾ ounces) condensed tomato soup	Pinch of instant garlic powder
½ pound mushrooms	Pinch of thyme
	1 teaspoon salt

1. Wash chicken pieces; pat dry. Place, skin side down, in a cold nonstick skillet. Brown slowly over moderate heat. (Chicken will brown in its own fat.) Turn; brown other side; drain fat.

2. Add the soup, mushrooms, onion liquid, garlic powder, thyme and salt.

3. Cover; simmer over low heat for 45 minutes, or until the chicken is tender. Add onions. Uncover; continue cooking until sauce thickens, about 10 minutes.

OVEN-FRIED CHICKEN ROMANO

Bake at 375° for 1 hour.
Makes 6 servings at 274 calories each.

1 cup crushed herb-
 seasoned stuffing
4 tablespoons grated
 Romano cheese

4 tablespoons snipped
 parsley
2 broiler-fryers (about
 1½ pounds each),
 cut up

1. Combine stuffing, cheese and parsley in shallow bowl.

2. Moisten chicken pieces with water and roll in stuffing mixture to coat.

3. Arrange, skin side up, in a single layer on a non-stick baking pan. Sprinkle with remaining crumbs. Bake in moderate oven (375°) for 1 hour, or until tender.

ROAST CHICKEN WITH WILD RICE STUFFING

Bake at 375° for 1½ hours.
Makes 10 servings at 281 calories each.

1 can (8 ounces)
 mushroom stems
 and pieces
1 package (6 ounces)
 long grain and wild
 rice mix
1 tablespoon instant
 minced onion
1 can chicken broth
 plus mushroom liquid
 and water to make
 2½ cups

2 whole broiler-fryers
 (about 2½ pounds
 each)
SAUCE
2 tablespoons thinly
 slivered orange peel
¼ cup orange juice
½ cup diet maple syrup
¼ teaspoon ground
 ginger

1. Drain mushrooms, reserving liquid. Combine rice mix and onion in medium-size saucepan; stir in the chicken broth, reserved mushroom liquid and water. Cook according to rice package directions. Stir in mushrooms.

2. Wash chickens; pat dry. Lightly stuff with rice mixture; secure with poultry skewers.

3. Place chickens, breast side up, on rack in large shallow baking pan; tuck wings under or tie across back.

4. Roast in moderate oven (375°) for 1¼ hours, or until just tender. Drain excess fat.

5. Combine the orange peel, juice and maple syrup in small bowl. Brush glaze over chickens; roast 15 minutes longer. Remove the cord and skewers; carve.

CHICKEN TARRAGON

Makes 8 servings at 204 calories each.

2 broiler-fryers (about 2 pounds each), cut up
1 can (8 ounces) small boiled onions, with liquid
½ cup dry white wine
1 tablespoon chopped parsley
1 clove of garlic, minced
1 teaspoon tarragon
1 teaspoon salt
⅛ teaspoon pepper
½ cup water
1 tablespoon lemon juice
1 lemon, thinly sliced

1. Wash chicken pieces; pat dry. Trim away excess fat. Place on rack in broiler pan; broil until skin is brown.

2. Place the browned chicken pieces, skin side up, in a skillet; add onion liquid, wine, parsley, garlic, tarragon, salt, pepper and water. Cover; simmer 55 minutes, or until chicken is tender.

3. Uncover; add lemon juice and onions. Cook a few minutes longer until sauce thickens. Garnish with lemon.

FRUIT STUFFING FOR POULTRY

Makes 8 servings at 65 calories each.

4 slices protein bread,
    cut in cubes
1 large apple, pared,
    cored and diced
    (1½ cups)
1 medium-size onion,
    chopped (½ cup)

½ cup seedless raisins,
    chopped
¾ teaspoon salt
¼ teaspoon crumbled
    leaf sage
¼ teaspoon crushed
    rosemary
½ teaspoon pepper

Toss all ingredients together in bowl. Makes 4 cups of dressing, or enough for 2-2½ pound chicken.

ARROZ CON POLLO
(SPANISH CHICKEN WITH RICE)

Makes 8 servings at 260 calories each.

2 broiler-fryers (about
    1½ pounds each),
    cut up
2 medium-size onions,
    chopped (1 cup)
2 cloves of garlic,
    minced
1 cup tomato juice
1 cup water
3 tomatoes, peeled and
    chopped

1 bay leaf
½ teaspoon ground
    saffron
1½ teaspoons salt
¼ teaspoon pepper
1 cup uncooked rice
1 medium-size green
    pepper, diced
1 pimiento, sliced
4 tablespoons dry
    sherry

1. Trim away excess fat from chicken pieces. Wash; pat dry. Arrange, skin side down, in a cold nonstick skillet. Brown slowly over low heat.

2. Add the onions and garlic. Sauté; pour off any fat.

3. Add tomato juice, water, tomatoes, bay leaf, saffron, salt, pepper. Cover; simmer over low heat 20 minutes.

4. Add rice, green pepper, pimiento and wine. Cover; cook 30 minutes longer, or until chicken is tender.

CHICKEN CACCIATORE

Makes 6 servings at 219 calories each.

2 broiler-fryers (about 1½ pounds each), cut up	2 teaspoons oregano
	1 teaspoon salt
	¼ teaspoon pepper
1 can (1 pound) tomatoes	½ cup dry white wine
	1½ tablespoons grated Romano cheese
1 medium-size green pepper, halved, seeded and sliced	

1. Wash chicken pieces; pat dry. Trim off excess fat. Place chicken on rack of broiler pan; brown until skin is crisp and brown. Remove to large skillet or baking dish. Place skin side up in skillet.

2. Add all the remaining ingredients except the cheese. Cover; simmer over low heat 45 minutes, or until chicken is tender. (Or, cover and bake in moderate oven [350°] the same amount of time.)

3. Uncover; skim off fat, continue cooking until sauce thickens. Sprinkle lightly with cheese before serving.

NOTE: Tender-cooked spaghetti adds 77 calories per ½-cup serving.

CRANBERRY-GLAZED CHICKENS

Bake at 400° for 1½ hours.
Makes 12 servings at 247 calories each.

2 large broiler-fryers
  (about 3 pounds
  each), cut up
2 teaspoons salt
Pinch of pepper
1 can (1 pound) jellied
  cranberry sauce

4 tablespoons lemon
  juice
Dash of liquid red-
  pepper seasoning
½ teaspoon curry
  powder

1. Wash chicken; pat dry. Arrange chicken in large nonstick baking pan. Sprinkle with salt and pepper. Bake in hot oven (400°) 1 hour, or until brown.

2. Combine cranberry sauce, lemon juice, red-pepper seasoning and curry powder in a medium-size saucepan. Cook over low heat, stirring occasionally to break up the cranberry sauce, until ingredients are well blended, about 10 minutes.

3. Spread part of cranberry mixture over chicken. Continue baking, basting frequently, 30 minutes longer, or until chicken is tender. Serve with any remaining cranberry sauce.

BAKED CHICKEN WITH ARTICHOKES

Bake at 350° for 1 hour.
Makes 6 servings at 198 calories each.

1 broiler-fryer (about
  2½ pounds), cut up
1 teaspoon salt
Pinch of pepper
1 large tomato, chopped
1 medium-size onion,
  chopped (½ cup)
1 clove of garlic, minced

3 medium-size carrots,
  pared and cut into
  2-inch pieces
¼ teaspoon thyme
1 small bay leaf
1 can (14 ounces)
  artichokes, drained

1. Wash chicken pieces; pat dry. Place on rack in broiler pan; broil on both sides, until brown. Remove to a shallow 8-cup baking dish.

2. Add all remaining ingredients, except the artichokes. Cover; bake in a moderate oven (350°) 50 minutes, basting several times with the pan juices and a little water, if necessary.

3. Add artichokes; bake 10 minutes longer. Sprinkle with chopped parsley, if you wish.

CHICKEN NIVERNAISE

This is a calorie cop-out on the classic French Provincial dish, "Duck Nivernaise," a rich and hearty main course that's more than 1,000 calories a serving. The blend of flavors works equally well with low-calorie chicken.

Bake at 350° for 1 hour.
Makes 6 servings at 252 calories each.

1 broiler-fryer (about
 2½ pounds), cut up
¾ cup sliced onion
4 carrots, pared and cut
 into 1-inch lengths
¼ teaspoon thyme
¼ bay leaf
1 teaspoon salt
⅛ teaspoon pepper
2 teaspoons dried
 parsley flakes
¾ cup dry white wine

2 envelopes or
 teaspoons instant
 chicken broth
2 cups boiling water
3 white turnips, peeled
 and quartered
1 package (10 ounces)
 frozen peas
1 tablespoon flour
1 tablespoon cornstarch
¼ cup cold water

1. Wash chicken; pat dry. Arrange on rack in broiler pan; broil until well-browned.

2. Place chicken in a deep 8-cup casserole; add onion, carrots, thyme, bay leaf, salt, pepper, parsley, wine, chicken broth and water. Cover; bake in a moderate oven (350°) 30 minutes, or until nearly tender.

3. Strain fat. Add turnips and peas to casserole.

Cover; continue baking 30 minutes, or until turnips are tender.

4. Drain liquid into a medium-size saucepan. Combine flour, cornstarch and the cold water; stir into sauce. Heat to simmering over low heat; pour over chicken.

SHREDDED ORIENTAL CHICKEN

Makes 6 servings at 142 calories each.

2 chicken breasts
  (about 12 ounces
  each), skinned
  and boned
2 teaspoons cornstarch
2 teaspoons soy sauce
1½ teaspoons salt
1 tablespoon dry white
  wine or water
1 egg white
1 tablespoon vegetable
  oil

1 carrot, pared and
  shredded
1 medium-size green
  pepper, halved,
  seeded and shredded
1 green onion, sliced
½ teaspoon ginger
1 teaspoon sugar
SAUCE
2 teaspoons cornstarch
2 tablespoons dry white
  wine or cold water
2 tablespoons soy sauce

1. Cut chicken breasts into paper-thin strips (slightly frozen chicken is easier to cut). Combine strips in a medium-size bowl with cornstarch, soy sauce and salt. Add wine and egg white; mix well.

2. Heat oil in a large nonstick skillet or Oriental wok; add chicken. Cook and stir until chicken turns white, about 5 minutes. Add carrot, green pepper and green onion; stir-fry for 2 minutes. Add ginger and sugar.

3. Dissolve cornstarch, wine or water and soy sauce in small bowl. Add to skillet; stir until evenly glazed.

CHICKEN LIVERS JARDINIERE

Makes 8 servings at 198 calories each.

2 tablespoons diet
  margarine
1 onion, chopped
  (½ cup)
2 pounds chicken livers
1 can (4 ounces)
  mushroom stems and
  pieces, with liquid

1 can (8½ ounces)
  water chestnuts,
  drained and sliced
3 stalks of celery, cut
  into ½-inch pieces
1 package (9 ounces)
  frozen cut green beans
2 teaspoons salt
Pinch of pepper

1. Melt margarine in a 12-inch skillet over medium heat. Add onion; sauté until soft. Add the chicken livers; cook, turning frequently, 1 or 2 minutes, or until livers are pale pink in color.

2. Add mushrooms, mushroom liquid, water chestnuts, celery and the green beans. Cook over moderate heat until beans are completely defrosted. Add salt and pepper. Cover; simmer 20 minutes, stirring occasionally. Add a little water if necessary to prevent sticking.

CHILLED "PICKLED" CHICKEN

Makes 6 servings at 173 calories each.

1 broiler-fryer (2¼ to 3
  pounds), cut into
  serving-size pieces
1 clove of garlic,
  minced

⅛ teaspoon pepper
½ cup cider vinegar
½ cup soy sauce

1. Wash chicken; pat dry. Arrange in a large skillet; add garlic, pepper, vinegar and soy sauce. Cover; marinate for 20 minutes.

2. Place skillet over medium heat; bring to boiling. Lower heat and simmer 45 minutes, or until chicken is tender.

3. Chill thoroughly. Remove all hardened fat; serve.

CHICKEN PATTIES

Makes 4 patties at 138 calories each.

1 cup minced cooked chicken	Worcestershire sauce
½ cup instant nonfat dry milk	½ teaspoon instant minced onion
1 tablespoon water	2 drops liquid red-pepper seasoning
1 teaspoon lemon juice	Paprika
1 teaspoon	

1. Combine all ingredients except paprika in medium-size bowl; blend well. Shape into 4 equal-size patties.

2. Place on foil-lined baking sheet. Sprinkle each patty with paprika.

3. Broil until browned on one side. Turn; sprinkle with paprika and brown other side.

CHICKEN IN ASPIC

Makes 4 servings at 196 calories each.

1 envelope unflavored gelatin	2 cups diced cooked chicken
½ cup cold water	½ cup chopped celery
1 can condensed chicken broth	¼ cup chopped green pepper
¼ teaspoon salt	2 tablespoons diced pimiento
2 tablespoons lemon juice	

1. Sprinkle gelatin over cold water in saucepan to soften. Place over low heat, stirring constantly, until gelatin dissolves, 2 to 3 minutes.

2. Remove from heat; stir in the bouillon, salt and lemon juice. Chill until mixture is the consistency of unbeaten egg white.

3. Fold in the chicken, celery, green pepper and pimiento.

4. Turn into a 4-cup mold or four individual salad molds. Chill until set, about 3 hours.

5. When ready to serve, loosen salad around edge with a sharp knife; dip mold in and out of hot water. Cover with serving plate; turn upside down; gently lift off mold.

CHICKEN CORDON BLEU

Bake at 350° for 35 minutes.
Makes 6 servings at 236 calories each.

3 chicken breasts (about 12 ounces each), split	Instant garlic powder *(optional)*
4 ounces lean cooked ham, sliced thin	1 teaspoon salt
4 ounces Swiss cheese, sliced thin	$\frac{1}{4}$ teaspoon pepper
Fresh minced parsley	5 tablespoons fine dry bread crumbs
	2 teaspoons vegetable oil

1. Skin and bone the chicken breasts. Flatten slightly with edge of plate.

2. Place a ham and cheese slice on each chicken piece; sprinkle with the minced parsley, garlic powder, salt and pepper.

3. Roll up chicken to enclose ham and cheese; secure with wooden picks or skewers and string, if necessary.

4. Blend bread crumbs with oil and pour onto a flat

plate. Press each chicken roll into the mixture to coat lightly.

5. Place chicken rolls on a nonstick baking sheet; bake in moderate oven (350°) 35 minutes, or until chicken is tender.

CHICKEN CHOW MEIN

Makes 6 servings at 247 calories each.

1 tablespoon diet margarine	1 cup drained bean sprouts
2 medium-size onions, sliced	1 cup water chestnuts, drained and sliced
¼ cup dry sherry	1 can (5 ounces) bamboo shoots, drained and sliced
2 cups sliced celery	
¾ pound fresh mushrooms, sliced	3 cups diced cooked chicken
1 can chicken broth plus water to make 1½ cups	4 tablespoons soy sauce
	2 tablespoons cornstarch

1. Melt the margarine in a large skillet. Add onion; sauté 10 minutes. Add sherry; simmer until it is almost all evaporated.

2. Add the celery, mushrooms, broth and water. Simmer over low heat 5 minutes.

3. Stir in bean sprouts, water chestnuts, the bamboo shoots and diced cooked chicken.

4. Combine soy sauce and cornstarch in small cup or bowl; mix until paste is smooth. Stir into ingredients in skillet. Continue cooking over low heat, stirring frequently until mixture is thickened.

5. Garnish with one of the following: 4 tablespoons fried chow mein noodles (55 calories); 1 de-shredded wheat biscuit (65 calories); ½ cup dry crisp rice cereal (53 calories).

CHICKEN MANDARIN

Bake at 350° for 1 hour.
Makes 6 servings at 221 calories each.

1 broiler-fryer (about 3 pounds), quartered	1 tablespoon seedless raisins
1½ teaspoons salt	1 tablespoon chutney
⅛ teaspoon pepper	1 tablespoon slivered almonds
1 can (8 ounces) low-calorie Mandarin-orange segments, with liquid	½ teaspoon cinnamon
½ cup water	½ teaspoon curry powder
	¼ teaspoon thyme

1. Wash chicken pieces; pat dry. Arrange in single layer, skin side up, in a shallow 12-cup baking dish. Broil until brown.
2. Combine remaining ingredients and pour over chicken.
3. Bake in a moderate oven (350°) 1 hour, or until chicken is tender. Baste frequently and add more water if chicken seems dry.

CHICKEN TERIYAKI

Makes 6 servings at 159 calories each.

First marinate 6 split chicken breasts (6 ounces each) with a sauce made from ½ cup lemon juice, ¼ cup water, 3 tablespoons soy sauce, ¼ teaspoon ground ginger and 1 teaspoon garlic salt. Barbecue about 30 minutes or until tender, on the hibachi or under your broiler, basting frequently with marinade.

OVEN-BAKED "SOUTHERN FRIED" CHICKEN

Crisp and crunchy perfect chicken every time, thanks to an inexpensive easy-to-do "convenience mix" you make yourself and keep in the pantry to use as needed.

Bake at 375° for 45 minutes.
Makes 6 servings at 244 calories each.

½ cup "Skinny Shake"
2 broiler-fryers (about

2½ pounds each),
cut up

1. Measure out ½ cup of "Skinny Shake" mix and put it in a heavy paper bag. Moisten the pieces of chicken with water and shake them in the bag, a few pieces at a time.

2. Arrange, skin side up, in a single layer on a non-stick baking pan and bake in a moderate oven (375°) about 45 minutes, adding absolutely no other fats or oils.

NOTE: Don't be alarmed if the chicken seems dry for the first 20 minutes; then the "Skinny Shake" starts to work, and at the end of the baking period, it will be crisp and perfect.

BASIC "SKINNY SHAKE": It makes enough to coat about 20 cut-up chickens or 30 servings of fish fillets.

Empty one 16-ounce container (about 4 cupfuls, dry measure) of bread crumbs into a deep bowl and stir in ½ cupful of vegetable oil with a fork or pastry blender until evenly distributed. Add 1 tablespoon salt, 1 tablespoon paprika, 1 tablespoon celery salt and 1 teaspoon pepper. This is a good seasoning for chicken, fish or chops. Or season it to suit yourself: Onion or garlic powder, sesame or poppy seeds, dried herbs, lemon pepper ... use your imagination!

BONELESS CHICKEN CACCIATORE

Plump chunks of chicken and bright green strips of pepper in a spicy tomato sauce spiked with wine. How could this be diet fare?

Makes 6 servings at 248 calories each.

2 broiler-fryers (about
    1½ pounds each)
2 cups water
2 cans (8 ounces each)
    tomato sauce
1 tablespoon leaf
    oregano, crumbled
½ cup dry white wine

1 medium-size onion,
    chopped (½ cup)
1 large green pepper,
    halved, seeded and
    sliced
1 clove of garlic, minced
½ teaspoon salt
¼ teaspoon pepper

1. Simmer chicken in water in a large covered saucepan for 30 minutes. Remove. Cool until easy to handle. Pour stock into a 4-cup measure. Refrigerate.

2. Remove meat from chicken. Discard skin and bones. Skim any fat from chicken stock.

3. Put chicken, 2 cups of the stock and remaining ingredients in a saucepan; cover. Simmer 20 minutes. Uncover. Allow to simmer, stirring occasionally, until sauce has thickened, about 10 minutes.

NICE FLOURISHES: A teaspoon of grated Romano cheese (8 calories), ½ cup cooked, well-rinsed spaghetti (78 calories), 1 glass, 3½ ounces, red or white chianti (85 calories). A tossed green salad of: 1 cup mixed greens and 1 tablespoon diet Italian dressing (27 calories). Half a cup of Italian green beans with a teaspoon of diet margarine (17 calories).

AFTER DINNER: A demitasse of cappucino: Instant espresso (or strong dark coffee) with ¼ teaspoon cinnamon and sugar substitute topped with one tablespoon of pressurized whipped cream (10 calories). It all adds up to only 473 calories!

LOW-CALORIE CHICKEN ORIENTALE

A sweet-and-sour chicken dish that's off the "forbidden list," thanks to today's easy-to-use sugar substitutes.

Bake at 325° for 55 minutes.
Makes 6 servings at 248 calories each.

2 broiler-fryers (about
   1½ pounds each),
   cut up
1 can (1 pound)
   unsweetened
   pineapple chunks in
   pineapple juice
3 tablespoons wine
   vinegar

1 tablespoon soy sauce
½ teaspoon dry
   mustard
1 teaspoon salt
¼ teaspoon pepper
2 green peppers, seeded
   and cut in strips
1 tablespoon cornstarch
2 tablespoons water

1. Place the chicken pieces, skin side up, in a shallow baking dish and surround with pineapple chunks. Mix juice with vinegar, soy sauce, mustard, salt and pepper and pour over chicken.

2. Bake, uncovered, in moderate oven (325°) for 40 minutes, basting occasionally.

3. Add pepper strips. Combine cornstarch with water in a cup. Stir into liquid in baking dish and bake an additional 15 minutes, or until thickened and bubbly.

Chicken Calorie Guide

Chicken	Calories	Amount
Broiled	248	½ broiler
Fried	201	½ breast
Fried	101	1 drumstick
Roast	200	½ breast
Roast	101	1 drumstick
Roast	147	1 thigh

Chapter 10

Fish and Seafood

There's simply nothing else so calorie-wise as fish! Many of the most popular types of seafood average around 400 calories per pound (sans skin and bones or shell) while the equivalent in boneless beef, lamb, ham or pork is around 1,600 calories per pound—four times as fattening. And, ounce for ounce, no other main course is lower in fat and higher in protein than heart-smart, cholesterol-shy fish! Americans seem to eat far more fish in restaurants than at home, a sure tip-off that we enjoy seafood, but that most of us feel unsure about buying and preparing it.

Unfortunately, most restaurant fish dishes are fattening. Fast-food eateries usually serve their seafood in a bready overcoat of fat-soaked starch, while the fancier feeding places favor rich sauces. But you can duplicate America's eat-out seafood favorites without all those extra calories, as you'll see in this chapter.

A "Fishing Guide" for Supermarket Shoppers

Cookbooks tell you that fresh fish should be shiny-eyed, firm of flesh and free of any "fishy" smell. But what help is that when most seafood is packed away inside inscrutable boxes or bagged in plastic? Here's a how-to guide for hauling in a calorie-wise catch from the depths of your supermarket frozen-food cabinet:

• In the frozen-food case, look for telltale signs of accidental defrosting and refreezing. Dented or misshapen boxes, frozen cartons with a pushed-in appearance and excess frost are tip-offs to careless frozen-food handling. Bagged seafood such as shrimp or scallops should always be loose-packed, not clumped together in an icy mass.

• At the seafood counter, be sure you know the difference between fresh fish and frozen fish that's been defrosted. (Nonlocal or out-of-season seafood specialties are likely to be defrosted.) Don't buy defrosted fish unless you plan to use it immediately. Ask the counterman for the still-frozen fish instead.

• Thaw frozen fish overnight in your refrigerator or for one or two hours in cold (never hot) water. Always defrost fish for use in any recipe unless directions say otherwise. Never refreeze defrosted raw fish.

• Calorie-wise, pure, plain fish is a better choice than prepared "heat-and-serve" convenience products.

• Don't overlook canned seafood products for meal-in-a-minute ease—canned shrimp, crabmeat, lobster and salmon are all low-calorie menu boosters. But do choose items packed in water rather than oil: A seven-ounce can of water-packed tuna is 254 calories; oil-packed 394!

FLOUNDER FILLETS FLORENTINE

Here's a Continental specialty that seems squanderously rich. Next time try it with perch and extra-sharp Cheddar—a whole different dish, but the calorie count is in the same range!

Bake at 350° for 15 minutes.
Makes 6 servings at 137 calories each.

2 packages (10 ounces
  each) frozen leaf
  spinach
1½ pounds frozen
  flounder fillets,
  thawed
½ cup water

2 tablespoons lemon
  juice
1 teaspoon salt
½ teaspoon pepper
¼ cup skim milk
1½ tablespoons flour
¼ cup grated Parmesan
  cheese

1. Cook spinach following label directions; drain well.

2. Carefully separate flounder fillets; fold neatly in small bundles. Arrange in shallow 6-cup baking dish. Pour over the water and lemon juice; sprinkle with salt and pepper. Cover dish tightly with foil.

3. Bake in a moderate oven (350°) 15 minutes, or until fish flakes easily with a fork.

4. Remove from oven. Drain cooking liquid into measuring cup. (There should be ¾ cup.) Heat liquid to boiling in a saucepan. Combine milk and flour; mix well. Stir into bubbling liquid. Cook over moderate heat, stirring constantly, until the sauce thickens and bubbles.

5. Spread drained spinach around fish fillets; pour sauce over. Top with grated cheese.

6. Bake in hot oven (425°) 5 minutes, or until the sauce bubbles.

TUNA MARENGO

It's a hot-day quickie with canned tuna and garden-fresh tomatoes.

Makes 4 servings at 216 calories each.

1 tablespoon vegetable oil
1 medium-size onion, chopped (½ cup)
1 clove of garlic, minced
2 cans (7 ounces each) water-packed tuna, drained
½ teaspoon salt
Pinch of pepper

¼ teaspoon leaf marjoram, crumbled
½ cup dry white wine
1 can (4 ounces) mushroom stems and pieces, drained
2 tomatoes, peeled and seeded
1 tablespoon parsley flakes

1. Heat oil in a large nonstick skillet. Sauté onion and garlic until tender.

2. Break the tuna into large chunks; add to skillet with salt, pepper, marjoram, wine, mushrooms, tomatoes and parsley. Cover; bring to boiling; lower heat. Simmer 5 minutes; stir twice.

SOUTH SEAS SKEWERED SCALLOPS

Another slim seafood specialty for the backyard chef, this one with a Polynesian punch!

Makes 4 servings at 207 calories each.

1 pound frozen sea
  scallops
1 can (8 ounces)
  pineapple chunks,
  juice drained
1 can (4 ounces) whole
  mushrooms, drained

1 large green pepper,
  halved, seeded and cut
  into 1-inch squares
2 tablespoons vegetable
  oil
¼ cup lemon juice
¼ cup soy sauce

1. Combine scallops with the pineapple chunks, mushrooms and green pepper squares in deep bowl. Add oil, lemon juice and soy sauce. Let stand 1 hour, stirring occasionally, until scallops are thawed.

2. Thread scallops on long skewers alternately with pineapple, mushrooms and pepper. Brush with marinade.

3. Broil 10 minutes, turning once, or until scallops are done (opaque and firm). Brush scallops and fruit with remaining marinade. Remove skewers; serve.

SLIM HALIBUT TERIYAKI

Seafood over the coals on your hibachi or backyard grill. What a fun, entertaining idea!

Makes 6 servings at 176 calories each.

1½ pounds frozen
    halibut fillets
½ cup dry white wine
2 tablespoons vegetable
    oil
3 tablespoons soy sauce
½ teaspoon dry
    mustard

½ teaspoon ground
    ginger
¼ teaspoon garlic
    powder
2 teaspoons parsley
    flakes

1. Place frozen fillets in a plastic bag. Combine wine, oil, soy sauce, mustard, ginger, garlic powder and parsley flakes; pour into bag with fillets. Close the bag tightly; place in a shallow dish. Allow fish to thaw in the marinade about 2 hours at room temperature. Turn bag several times.

2. Drain the fillets, reserving marinade.

3. Broil 5 minutes; brush with marinade. Broil 1 minute longer; turn. Brush with marinade; broil 5 minutes, or until fish is brown and flakes easily with a fork.

HALIBUT FILLETS IN "SOUR CREAM"

At only 125 calories a cupful, low-calorie yogurt offers a splendid stand-in for calorie-crammed sour cream (close to 500 calories a cupful!). Try this with salmon, too . . . or any favorite fish steak.

Bake at 350° for 25 minutes.
Makes 4 servings at 172 calories each.

1 pound frozen halibut
   fillets
½ cup dry white wine
1 envelope or teaspoon
   instant chicken broth
½ cup boiling water
½ teaspoon dillweed

¼ teaspoon salt
⅛ teaspoon pepper
2 teaspoons parsley
   flakes
1 container (1 cup)
   plain yogurt

1. Place frozen fillets in a shallow 6-cup baking dish. Pour wine over. Dissolve instant chicken broth in boiling water; pour over fish. Sprinkle with dillweed, salt, pepper and parsley flakes. Let thaw at room temperature.

2. Bake in moderate oven (350°) 25 minutes, or until fish flakes easily with a fork. Baste several times with liquid. Drain liquid from baking dish; measure ⅔ cup into a saucepan. Bubble over high heat until reduced to ⅓ cup. Stir in yogurt; heat just until sauce is hot (do not boil). Place fish on serving platter; pour sauce over.

CRABMEAT FLOUNDER ROLLS

Delicate rolls of flounder filled with a savory onion-mushroom-crabmeat filling, sauced with wine and Swiss cheese! Elegant dinner-party fare that seems extravagantly rich for its scant calorie count.

Bake at 400° for 30 minutes.
Makes 8 servings at 189 calories each.

2 pounds frozen
 flounder fillets,
 thawed
1 can (4 ounces)
 mushroom stems and
 pieces, drained
3 tablespoons minced
 onion
1 can (7½ ounces)
 crabmeat, drained
 and picked over
¼ cup fine dry bread
 crumbs

1 tablespoon parsley
 flakes
1 teaspoon salt
⅛ teaspoon pepper
3 tablespoons flour
1½ cups skim milk
¼ cup dry white wine
2 ounces process Swiss
 cheese, shredded
 (½ cup)
Paprika

1. Separate flounder fillets; trim into 8 pieces.
2. Chop mushrooms finely; combine with onion, crabmeat, bread crumbs, parsley, ½ teaspoon of the salt and pepper. Spread over fillets; roll up. Place rolls, seamside down, in a shallow 8-cup baking dish. Tuck any remaining filling around the rolls.
3. Combine flour, milk, wine and remaining ½ teaspoon salt in saucepan. Cook over moderate heat, stirring constantly, until sauce thickens and bubbles. Add cheese; stir until melted. Pour over fish rolls. Sprinkle lightly with paprika.
4. Bake in hot oven (400°) 30 minutes, or until fish flakes easily with a fork.

OVEN-FRIED FISH FILLETS

Here's a decalorized version of everyone's favorite fish dish, "fried" in the oven, so there's no range-top mess to clean up!

Bake at 450° for 12 minutes.
Makes 8 servings at 146 calories each.

2 pounds frozen
   flounder, sole or
   perch fillets, thawed
½ cup fine dry bread
   crumbs
1 teaspoon salt

⅛ teaspoon pepper
1 tablespoon parsley
   flakes
1 teaspoon paprika
2 tablespoons vegetable
   oil

1. Separate fillets carefully.
2. Combine bread crumbs, salt, pepper, parsley flakes and paprika in a bowl; add oil. Blend with a fork until thoroughly combined. Spread on wax paper.
3. Press the fish fillets into crumb mixture to coat both sides. Place on a nonstick baking sheet.
4. Bake in a very hot oven (450°) 12 minutes, or until fish flakes easily with a fork.

GREENLAND TURBOT AMANDINE

This turbot is the "hamburger" of fish—plentiful, reasonable and somewhat fatty. It's sometimes miscalled the Greenland halibut and often confused with the rare English turbot. The Greenland turbot is neither, but here's a recipe that turns this commoner into royalty. Poaching the fillets helps remove some fish fat—and calories!

Makes 6 servings at 209 calories each.

1½ pounds frozen
   Greenland turbot
   fillets
Water
1 tablespoon mixed
   pickling spices
2 teaspoons salt
1 cup skim milk
½ cup water

2 tablespoons flour
⅛ teaspoon white
   pepper
1 egg yolk, beaten
2 tablespoons lemon
   juice
1 tablespoon toasted
   sliced almonds

1. Place frozen fish in a large skillet; pour in water just to cover fish. Add the pickling spices and 1½ teaspoons of the salt; cover. Bring to boiling; lower heat and simmer 10 minutes, or until fish flakes easily with a fork. Remove to warm serving platter.

2. Combine milk, water, flour, remaining ½ teaspoon salt and pepper in a saucepan. Cook over moderate heat, stirring constantly, just until sauce thickens and bubbles. Pour some of sauce into beaten egg yolk; mix well. Return to rest of sauce in pan; cook 1 minute longer, stirring constantly. Add lemon juice. Pour over fish; sprinkle with almonds.

CLAMBAKE IN A PIE PAN

Here's a slimmed-down self-tending, no-fuss dinner to serve at your vacation retreat. It looks after itself while you join your guests for a predinner swim. Afterwards, throw out the dishes!

Bake at 350° for 40 minutes.
Makes 4 servings at 228 calories each.

4 frozen rock lobster
   tails (4 ounces each)
4 small chicken
   drumsticks
2 ears of corn in the
   husks
1 can (8 ounces) whole
   onions, drained

1 can (24 fluid ounces)
   steamed clams in
   shells
4 teaspoons parsley
   flakes
2 lemons, cut in wedges

1. Combine one lobster tail, chicken drumstick and a ½ ear of corn in each of 4 aluminum-foil pie pans. Divide onions and clams among the pans; pour about ½ cup of the clam liquid over each. Sprinkle with parsley flakes, 1 teaspoon per serving.

2. Cover pans tightly with foil.

3. Bake in moderate oven (350°) 40 minutes. Remove foil covering; place pie pans in decorative plate holders. Garnish with lemon wedges.

FILLET OF SOLE "BONNE FEMME"

"Bonne femme" means a "good wife," or cooked the way a good wife makes it—a well-deserved bit of praise considering the low calorie and cholesterol count!

Bake at 450° for 10 minutes.
Makes 4 servings at 144 calories each.

1 pound frozen fillets of sole, thawed	Pinch of white pepper
1 can (4 ounces) sliced mushrooms	1 tablespoon fresh chopped parsley
2 tablespoons instant chopped onion	½ teaspoon leaf tarragon, crumbled
½ cup dry white wine	½ cup skim milk
½ teaspoon salt	1 tablespoon flour
	Paprika

1. Carefully separate sole fillets. Pour mushrooms with liquid into a shallow 6-cup baking dish; sprinkle with onion. Fold fillets neatly into small bundles; place on mushrooms. Pour wine over; sprinkle with salt, pepper, parsley and tarragon.

2. Bake in very hot oven (450°) 10 minutes.

3. Drain liquid from baking dish; measure ⅔ cup into saucepan. Bubble over high heat until reduced to ⅓ cup. Combine milk and flour; stir into bubbling liquid.

Cook over medium heat, stirring constantly, until sauce thickens and bubbles. Pour over fish; sprinkle lightly with paprika.

4. Place baking dish under broiler for about 3 minutes, or until sauce is bubbly.

CANTONESE SHRIMP AND CRUNCHY VEGETABLES

It's a super-slender, 10-minute one-dish dinner.

Makes 6 servings at 161 calories each.

1 tablespoon vegetable oil	½ teaspoon ground ginger
1½ pounds peeled and deveined frozen raw shrimp, thawed	1 package (9 ounces) frozen French-style green beans
¼ cup thinly sliced green onions	1 package (10 ounces) frozen chopped broccoli
1 clove of garlic, minced	1 can (4 ounces) sliced mushrooms, drained
1 envelope or teaspoon instant chicken broth	1 tablespoon cornstarch
1 cup boiling water	1 tablespoon soy sauce

1. Heat oil in large nonstick skillet. Add shrimp, onions and garlic; stir-fry 3 minutes. Add instant chicken broth and water; stir to dissolve.

2. Add ginger, green beans, broccoli and mushrooms. Cover. Bring to boiling; lower heat; simmer 6 minutes, or until vegetables are crisp but tender. Break up the frozen vegetables with a fork for even cooking.

3. Combine cornstarch with soy sauce; stir into shrimp mixture. Cook, stirring constantly, until sauce thickens.

CHEESE-TOPPED SOLE

Makes 8 servings at 113 calories each.

2 pounds fresh or
frozen fillets
of sole
1 tablespoon diet
margarine
¼ cup grated sharp
Cheddar cheese
1 tablespoon fresh
chopped parsley

2 teaspoons grated
onion
¼ teaspoon salt
Dash of liquid red-
pepper seasoning
1 egg white, stiffly
beaten

1. Thaw fillets, if frozen. Place in a single layer on nonstick baking pan. Spread each fillet with margarine. Broil 7 minutes, or until fish flakes easily with a fork.

2. While fish broils, combine cheese, parsley, onion, salt and red-pepper seasoning. Fold into egg white and spread on fillets. Broil 3 minutes longer, or until lightly browned.

ORIENTAL CODFISH

Makes 6 servings at 146 calories each.

2 pounds fresh or
frozen cod fillets
1 tablespoon vegetable
oil
5 tablespoons soy sauce

1 tablespoon lemon
juice
½ teaspoon ground
ginger
1 teaspoon garlic salt

1. Thaw fillets, if frozen, and cut into 2-inch cubes.

2. Combine oil, soy sauce, lemon juice, ginger and garlic salt in large skillet over medium heat. Add fish.

3. Cover and cook over low heat about 7 minutes, or until fish flakes easily with a fork.

SAUCY SOLE

Makes 8 servings at 120 calories each.

2 pounds frozen fillets of sole, thawed	1 tablespoon vegetable oil
5 tablespoons bottled steak sauce	1 tablespoon cider vinegar
¼ cup catsup	1 teaspoon salt
	Pinch of curry powder

1. Separate sole fillets. Combine remaining ingredients; spread half mixture on fish.
2. Broil, 3 inches from heat, for 5 minutes.
3. Turn fish carefully; brush with remaining sauce. Broil 5 minutes longer, or until fish flakes easily with a fork.

FLOUNDER CREOLE

Makes 4 servings at 149 calories each.

1 tablespoon butter or margarine	2 tablespoons lemon juice
¼ cup chopped onion	¼ teaspoon tarragon
¼ cup chopped green pepper	1 bay leaf
¼ pound mushrooms, sliced	¼ teaspoon liquid red-pepper seasoning
1 can (1 pound) tomatoes, drained	½ teaspoon salt
	1 pound fresh or frozen flounder fillets, thawed

1. Melt butter or margarine in a large skillet. Add onion and green pepper; sauté until tender.

2. Add mushrooms; cook 3 minutes. Add the tomatoes, lemon juice, tarragon, bay leaf, red-pepper seasoning and salt. Cover; simmer 15 minutes.

3. Add flounder fillets. Cover; simmer 5 to 10 minutes, or until fish flakes easily.

FLORIDA HALIBUT

Makes 8 servings at 212 calories each.

2 tablespoons melted butter	1 can (about 1 pound) unsweetened grapefruit sections, with liquid
⅛ teaspoon paprika	
½ teaspoon salt	
¼ teaspoon ground marjoram	4 halibut steaks (3 pounds), about 1½ inches thick

1. Combine butter, paprika, salt, marjoram and 2 tablespoons of juice from canned grapefruit. Place halibut on foil on broiler pan; brush with grapefruit-butter sauce. Broil 2 inches from heat, 7 minutes, or until lightly browned.

2. Turn fish, brush with more grapefruit-butter sauce. Broil 2 minutes longer, basting several times with sauce.

3. Place grapefruit sections on and around fish; brush again with sauce. Broil 2 minutes longer, or until the fish flakes easily with a fork. Cut steaks in serving-size portions. Garnish with additional grapefruit sections and parsley, if desired.

BARBECUED HALIBUT STEAKS

Makes 4 servings at 126 calories each.

1 pound fresh or frozen
  halibut steaks (about
  ¾ inch thick)
1 can (6 ounces)
  tomato juice
1 teaspoon instant
  minced onion
¼ teaspoon salt

¼ teaspoon sugar
⅛ teaspoon oregano
¼ teaspoon freshly
  grated lemon peel
2 teaspoons lemon juice
1 teaspoon
  Worcestershire sauce

1. Thaw the steaks, if frozen, and cut into four serving-size pieces.
2. Combine remaining ingredients in small saucepan. Bring to boiling. Reduce the heat; cook, uncovered, for 5 minutes or until thick and reduced to ⅓ cup. Stir frequently.
3. Place fish 4 inches above medium coals; grill about 7 minutes. Turn; brush with sauce. Grill 7 minutes longer, or until fish flakes easily with a fork, brushing with more sauce as needed. Serve with any remaining sauce on the side.

CALIFORNIA HALIBUT

Bake at 400° for 20 minutes.
Makes 4 servings at 160 calories each.

1 pound fresh or frozen
  halibut fillets (¾
  inch thick)
½ teaspoon salt
⅛ teaspoon pepper
⅛ teaspoon paprika
12 large stuffed olives

1 small lemon, peeled,
  sectioned and chopped
1 medium-size tomato,
  cut into 4 slices
⅓ cup snipped fresh
  parsley
8 teaspoons imitation
  sour cream

1. Thaw fish, if frozen. Cut into four serving-size pieces and place in shallow baking dish. Sprinkle with salt, pepper and paprika.

2. Slice olives; combine with chopped lemon. Spoon half of olive-lemon mixture over fillets; top each with tomato slice, parsley and remaining lemon mixture.

3. Cover; bake in hot oven (400°) 10 minutes. Uncover; bake 20 minutes longer. To serve, garnish with imitation sour cream.

CRAB NEWBURG

Makes 6 servings at 166 calories each.

3 egg yolks, beaten	1 tablespoon chopped
1 cup evaporated	pimiento
skimmed milk	Pinch of ground
2 cans (7 ounces each)	nutmeg
crab meat, drained,	2 tablespoons dry
flaked and rinsed	sherry
2 tablespoons chopped	6 slices melba-thin
parsley	white bread, toasted

1. Mix egg yolks and milk in top of a double boiler. Add crabmeat and all remaining ingredients except the toast; cook, stirring occasionally, until mixture thickens and is heated through.

2. Trim crusts from toast; cut into triangles. Cover toast points with crabmeat and sauce.

SHRIMP CHOW MEIN

Makes 4 servings at 231 calories each.

1 medium-size onion, finely chopped (½ cup)

½ cup green pepper strips

½ cup sliced celery

1 can (4 ounces) mushroom stems and pieces, drained

½ cup instant nonfat dry milk

½ cup water

¼ cup soy sauce

1 tablespoon Worcestershire sauce

1 pound peeled and deveined frozen raw shrimp, thawed

1 can (1 pound) bean sprouts, drained

1 can (5 ounces) water chestnuts, drained and sliced

1 tablespoon chopped pimiento

1. Combine the onion, green pepper and celery in large saucepan in water to cover. Cook until tender; drain; add mushrooms.

2. Mix milk with water, soy sauce and Worcestershire sauce; add to saucepan.

3. Add shrimp, bean sprouts, water chestnuts and the pimiento. Stir to mix well; heat until shrimp are pink (do not boil).

SERVING SUGGESTIONS—Serve Chow Mein over 1 cup steamed celery, cut into 1-inch pieces. Adds only 17 calories per cup of celery.

QUICK LOBSTER NEWBURG

Makes 4 servings at 166 calories each.

1 tablespoon butter
  or margarine
1 tablespoon all-purpose
  flour
¼ teaspoon salt
¼ teaspoon white
  pepper
1 cup skim milk
2 cups cooked lobster
¼ cup dry sherry

1. Melt butter or margarine in medium-size saucepan.
2. Add flour, salt and pepper; stir to form smooth paste. Remove from heat.
3. Gradually stir in milk. Return to heat. Cook, stirring constantly, over medium heat until thickened.
4. Add the lobster; heat until steaming; stir in sherry. Serve over toasted protein bread. Garnish with chopped parsley.

SHRIMP-STUFFED PEPPERS

Makes 4 servings at 158 calories each.

1 medium-size onion,
  chopped (½ cup)
½ cup chopped celery
1 can (1 pound)
  tomatoes, with
  liquid
1 tablespoon
  Worcestershire sauce
1 teaspoon salt
½ teaspoon chili
  powder
¼ teaspoon instant
  garlic powder
1 package (1 pound)
  frozen peeled shrimp,
  thawed
½ cup chopped green
  pepper
4 medium-size green
  peppers, cored

1. Combine onion and celery in a medium-size saucepan with water to cover. Cook until tender, about 5 minutes; drain well.

2. Add the tomatoes, tomato juice, Worcestershire sauce, salt, chili powder and garlic powder.

3. Mix nonfat dry milk with baking soda, and stir into tomato mixture. Add shrimp and chopped green pepper.

4. Cover; cook 5 minutes, or until shrimp turns pink.

5. Spoon into pepper shells. Arrange shells in a 1½-quart baking dish. Pour any remaining liquid around peppers. Cover; bake in moderate oven (350°) 30 minutes, or until peppers are withery.

SEABURGERS

Makes 4 patties at 306 calories each.

1 pound leftover cooked fish (flounder, sole or halibut)	1 tablespoon fresh chopped parsley
1 teaspoon salt	1 clove of garlic, minced
2 eggs, beaten	Pinch of pepper
2 tablespoons grated Romano cheese	1 tablespoon vegetable oil
	4 tablespoons fine dry bread crumbs

1. Remove any skin and bones from fish; flake with a fork. Combine with salt, eggs, cheese, parsley, garlic and the pepper; shape into 4 "burgers." Brush lightly with oil and roll in bread crumbs.

2. Broil about 7 minutes on each side, or until well-browned. Serve with lemon wedges, if you wish.

SLIM JAMBALAYA

Bake at 350° for 1 hour and 10 minutes.
Makes 8 servings at 192 calories each.

2 pounds frozen bone-
less perch fillets,
thawed
1 cup sliced onions
½ cup chopped green
pepper
4 tablespoons chopped
fresh parsley
1 clove of garlic, minced
1 envelope or teaspoon
instant chicken broth
½ cup hot water
1 can (1 pound)
tomatoes
1 can (8 ounces)
tomato sauce
¾ cup uncooked rice
2 tablespoons bacon-
flavored soy protein
product
1 teaspoon salt
¼ teaspoon thyme
Pinch of ground cloves
Dash of liquid red-
pepper seasoning

1. Cut the fillets into 1-inch pieces. Combine with all remaining ingredients in a shallow 3-quart casserole.
2. Cover; bake in moderate oven (350°) 1 hour and 10 minutes, or until fish flakes easily with a fork.

TUNA CHEESE DIP

Makes 1 cup at 46 calories per tablespoon.

1 package (8 ounces)
Neufchâtel cheese
1 can (3½ ounces) tuna
packed-in-water
1 teaspoon grated onion
2 envelopes or teaspoons
instant chicken broth
2 tablespoons skim milk

1. Soften cheese to room temperature. Drain and flake tuna. Combine cheese and tuna with onion and chicken broth in a medium-size bowl. Mix until blended. Stir in milk.
2. Cover bowl and chill at least 1 hour. Mix again before serving with fresh celery, cucumber or cherry tomatoes.

SEAFOOD DIP

Makes 1 cup at 11 calories per tablespoon.

1 cup low-fat cream-style cottage cheese	1 tablespoon finely chopped parsley
2 envelopes or teaspoons instant chicken broth	1 teaspoon finely cut chives
4 tablespoons water	½ teaspoon dillweed

1. Combine cottage cheese, chicken broth and water in container of electric blender. Blend on high speed until mixture is smooth.

2. Stir in remaining ingredients. Cover; chill at least 1 hour. Pour into dipping bowl and serve with chilled shrimp or lobster.

CRABWICH

Makes 1 serving at 262 calories.

Combine one 4-ounce can crabmeat, drained, with 1 teaspoon soy sauce, 1 teaspoon dried onion flakes and ½ teaspoon dried parsley flakes. Spread on 1 toasted thin slice sandwich bread; top with 1 ounce process American cheese food. Broil until topping is bubbly.

SEVICHE
(MEXICAN MARINATED FISH)

Makes 8 servings at 55 calories each.

1 pound fresh or frozen (thawed) flounder fillets
½ teaspoon salt
¼ teaspoon pepper
1 bay leaf
1 clove of garlic, pressed
6 tablespoons lime juice
1 tablespoon cider vinegar
1 medium-size onion, sliced
4 tablespoons coarsely chopped green pepper
2 tablespoons chopped pimiento
1 lime (or lemon), sliced
4 tablespoons chopped parsley

1. Cut raw flounder into bite-size pieces. Place in shallow (nonmetallic) serving bowl.

2. Combine salt, pepper, bay leaf, garlic and lime juice; brush over fish pieces. Pour remaining mixture around fish. Cover; chill well.

2. Add vinegar, onion, green pepper and pimiento to the chilled sauce. Mix thoroughly but carefully. Decorate fish with lime slices and parsley.

Chapter 11

Zesty Italian Dishes

Tetrazzini with fresh mushrooms. Lasagna layered with tangy cheese. Eggplant topped with melting mozzarella. Spaghetti and spicy meatballs. If you have to count your calories, chances are you count yourself out when it comes to Italian food.

But you don't have to if you're a Creative Low-Calorie Cook. Even Italian cuisine will yield up its extraneous calories to the kitchen wizardry of a weight-wise cook! Far from being off-limits, Italian cooking has a lot going for it. It's easy to serve and is great for the cook with a mixed bag of fatties and skinnies to feed. The main course can be low in fat and calories, augmented with extra cheeses and pasta to flesh out the calorie counts for the trimmer members. But there's no reason why the dieter can't enjoy a fair share of pasta, too, if you follow the de-calorizing suggestions and recipes in this chapter.

How to "De-calorize" Pasta Dishes

Spaghetti's bad reputation among calorie-counters is totally unmerited; there are many foods far more fattening. Depending on how you cook it, pasta can be as low as 155 calories per cupful—a bargain for so much appetite appeasement. The important thing is to measure accurately, and keep spaghetti away from all greasy sauces, rich gravies and other calorific companions.

Linguine, vermicelli, macaroni, fusilli, rigatoni, whatever the size or shape, all spaghetti products are pretty much the same in calories, varying little from one type to another, or brand to brand. However, you *can* cut the calorie count of any pasta product simply by cooking it longer.

Pasta purists prefer their spaghetti cooked "al dente" —firm "to the teeth"—but the calorie-wise cook knows that tender spaghetti costs less in calories, as the following shows:

Pasta Calories Per Cupful

Cooked only until firm (8 to 10 minutes):
  192 calories.
Cooked until tender (14 to 20 minutes):
  155 calories.
After cooking, be sure to rinse the spaghetti
  well.

Spaghetti Sauces

It you'd like to avoid needless calories, leave those convenient canned and jarred "spaghetti sauce" products to the skinnies; make your own. Most canned sauces contain starches, syrups and other fillers (all calorie-adders), plus varying amounts of vegetable oil. Depending on the ingredients, some are as high as 400 calories a cupful.

For quick can-opener convenience, *plain* tomato sauce (as opposed to "spaghetti sauce") is your best bet. One of the best-known brands is only 70 calories per cupful.

Be a fine-print reader, and rule out products that contain added vegetable oil.

Dos & Don'ts for Creative Low-Calorie Italian Cooks

• *Don't* buy bargain hamburger for your meatballs or meat sauce; it's packed with fat, and the fat remains in the sauce and finally winds up on your hips! One pound of ordinary hamburger that's 30 percent fat is 1,600 calories; one pound of extra lean round with all the fat trimmed before grinding is only 612 calories.

• *Do* use chicken, fish and veal whenever you can—they're only half the calories, on the average, of beef, lamb, ham or pork!

• *Don't* add bread crumbs to meatballs—save your starch calories for the spaghetti.

• *Do* pre-brown meats under the broiler instead of frying them in oil—it's slimmer, simpler and will save your kitchen from spatter!

• *Do* make your gravy early in the day and refrigerate. At dinner time, you can simply lift off the chilled hard fat before reheating—very cholesterol-wise!

• *Don't* add any extra oil to sauces—oil is 125 calories a tablespoon and simply not worth the cost! If you want to add an "olive oil" flavor, add the olive instead of the oil—simply add one or two minced olives to the sauce.

• *Don't* be afraid to cook with wine—it's a grand Italian tradition! Most of the calories evaporate in the cooking, along with the alcohol!

SLIM CHICKEN TETRAZZINI

Here's a wonderful way to recycle leftover white meat chicken or turkey—all that's missing is the heavy cream and extra calories. The flavor remains!

Bake at 350° for 30 minutes.
Makes 6 servings at 227 calories each.

1 tablespoon olive oil
½ pound fresh mushrooms, sliced
2 tablespoons nonfat dry milk
1½ tablespoons cornstarch
2 envelopes or teaspoons instant chicken broth
1 teaspoon salt
¼ teaspoon pepper
½ teaspoon onion powder

Pinch of nutmeg
2 cups cold water
3 cups cooked breast of chicken or turkey, cut into 2-inch pieces
6 ounces broad egg noodles, cooked to tender stage (14 to 20 minutes, about 3 cups)
2 tablespoons grated Romano cheese
Paprika

1. Heat olive oil in a skillet; sauté mushrooms until tender.
2. Combine dry milk, cornstarch, chicken broth, salt, pepper, onion powder and nutmeg with cold water in a large saucepan. Cook over medium heat until mixture bubbles and thickens.
3. Arrange noodles in a 2-quart shallow baking dish. Spread mushrooms in a layer over the noodles; top with a layer of chicken. Pour sauce over all; sprinkle with grated cheese and paprika.
4. Bake in moderate oven (350°) 30 minutes, or until bubbly.

LOW-CALORIE LASAGNA

Here's a meatless main course that gets a protein boost from extra quantities of low-fat skim milk cottage cheese (between 155 and 180 calories per cup) instead of the far-more-fattening ricotta cheese (400 calories a cupful). Look for uncreamed or pot-style cottage cheese marked "99 percent fat free."

Bake at 350° for 45 minutes.
Makes 6 servings at 224 calories each.

8 ounces lasagna noodles
2 cups (1 pound) low-fat cottage cheese
1 egg
3 tablespoons grated Romano cheese
1 teaspoon salt
¼ teaspoon pepper
1 teaspoon leaf oregano, crumbled
1 tablespoon parsley flakes
1½ cups canned tomato sauce (from 2 cans, 8 ounces each)
1 tablespoon Italian seasoned bread crumbs

1. Cook noodles in boiling, salted water 18 to 20 minutes, or to the tender stage (this is longer than the directions on the package). Drain; rinse well.
2. Combine the cottage cheese with egg, Romano cheese, salt, pepper, oregano and parsley in a bowl.
3. Arrange the noodles, cheese mixture and tomato sauce in layers in a 2-quart shallow baking dish. Sprinkle bread crumbs evenly over the top.
4. Bake in moderate oven (350°) 45 minutes, or until cheese is set.

LOW-CALORIE EGGPLANT PARMIGIANA

Beware of the innocuous spongelike eggplant; it can soak up prodigious amounts of oil when it's fried! In this recipe, the calorie-wise cook first soaks the eggplant in water, minimizing the amount of oil it can absorb in the browning. For a nice variation, use Romano cheese instead of Parmesan.

Bake at 350° for 30 minutes.
Makes 6 servings at 126 calories each.

1 large eggplant, cut in ¼-inch slices	1 teaspoon leaf oregano, crumbled
1 tablespoon olive oil	1 can (8 ounces) tomato sauce
3 tablespoons grated Parmesan cheese	
½ teaspoon salt	3 ounces part-skim mozzarella cheese, thinly sliced
¼ teaspoon pepper	
Pinch of garlic powder	¼ cup Italian seasoned bread crumbs

1. Bring large kettle of water to boiling; remove from heat. Drop in eggplant slices; let stand 5 minutes. Drain slices; blot dry with paper toweling.

2. Heat oil in nonstick skillet; brown eggplant slices on all sides.

3. Combine the Parmesan cheese, salt, pepper, garlic powder and oregano with tomato sauce. Spread a little tomato sauce mixture over bottom of a 9-inch square shallow baking dish. Arrange eggplant in layers with mozzarella cheese. Pour remaining sauce mixture over all; top with bread crumbs.

4. Bake in moderate oven (350°) 30 minutes, or until bubbly.

SLIM SPAGHETTI AND MEATBALLS

Here's a recipe that does everything right: The beef is extra lean and trimmed of fat. Browning it under the broiler, instead of in a skillet, subtracts rather than adds calories. The spaghetti is tender-cooked and well rinsed to reduce calories. The sauce is made early and chilled so fat can be removed before reheating.

Makes 6 servings at 285 calories each.

MEATBALLS

1¼ pounds lean ground round
¼ cup chopped parsley
2 tablespoons minced onion
1 teaspoon leaf oregano, crumbled
1 teaspoon salt

SAUCE

1 can (1 pound, 13 ounces) Italian plum tomatoes
1 can (6 ounces) tomato paste
1 cup water
1 medium-size onion, chopped (½ cup)
1 clove of garlic, minced
1 teaspoon leaf oregano, crumbled
½ teaspoon salt
⅛ teaspoon pepper
Pinch of cayenne
8 ounces spaghetti, cooked to tender stage (14 to 20 minutes, about 4½ cups)

1. Combine the ground round, parsley, 2 tablespoons onion, 1 teaspoon oregano and 1 teaspoon salt. Shape into 18 meatballs.

2. Broil meatballs 3 inches from heat, about 5 minutes for each side, turning once.

3. Combine tomatoes, tomato paste, water, onion, 1 teaspoon oregano, ½ teaspoon salt, ⅛ teaspoon pepper and cayenne in a large saucepan. Bring to boiling; add meatballs; lower heat; cover; simmer, stirring occasionally, 1 hour, to blend all ingredients.

4. Remove from heat Uncover; refrigerate until serving time. Remove surface fat; reheat.

5. Serve mixture on the hot spaghetti.

LOW-CALORIE OSSO BUCCO (BRAISED VEAL KNUCKLES)

A slow-simmer dish that's thrifty and flavorful—and easy to decalorize if you make it ahead and chill it in your refrigerator until dinnertime.

Makes 6 servings at 348 calories each.

6 veal knuckles
2 teaspoons salt
¼ teaspoon pepper
¼ teaspoon leaf
  oregano or basil,
  crumbled
1 medium-size onion,
  chopped (½ cup)
2 cloves of garlic,
  minced
½ cup finely chopped
  celery

½ cup dry white wine
1 can (1 pound) Italian
  plum tomatoes
1 envelope or teaspoon
  instant beef broth
1 cup boiling water
1 tablespoon grated
  lemon rind
1 tablespoon chopped
  parsley

1. Place veal knuckles in a heavy kettle or Dutch oven. Sprinkle with salt, pepper, and oregano or basil. Add onion, garlic, celery, wine and tomatoes. Dissolve beef broth in boiling water; add to kettle. Sprinkle with lemon rind and parsley. Bring to boiling. Lower heat; cover; simmer 1½ hours, or until tender.

2. Remove from heat. Uncover; refrigerate until serving time. Remove surface fat; reheat.

LOW-CALORIE TUNA MARINARA

Be sure the tuna is water-packed. A 7-ounce can has only 231 calories. Oil-packed tuna has many more— 581 calories for the same amount.

Makes 4 servings at 318 calories each.

2 cans (7 ounces each) water-packed tuna, drained
2 cans (8 ounces each) tomato sauce
2 tablespoons instant minced onion
½ cup water
1 envelope or teaspoon instant chicken broth

1 teaspoon leaf oregano, crumbled
Pinch of garlic powder
Pinch of cayenne
8 ounces spaghetti, cooked to tender stage (14 to 20 minutes, about 4½ cups)
4 teaspoons grated Romano cheese

1. Drain and flake tuna; combine with the tomato sauce, onion, water, chicken broth, oregano, garlic powder and cayenne in large saucepan.
2. Bring to boiling; lower the heat; simmer 15 minutes.
3. Remove saucepan from heat; add cooked spaghetti. Mix thoroughly. Top each serving with 1 teaspoon of cheese.
SHRIMP MARINARA: Substitute 1 pound of cooked, cleaned shrimp for the tuna. Makes 4 servings at 309 calories each.

SPAGHETTI WITH CLAM AND MUSHROOM SAUCE

Here's a slimmed-down version of that calorific classic, White Clam Sauce. Standard recipes often call for as much as a cup of butter, and can add up to 600 calories a serving. If you can't locate butter-flavored salt in your supermarket, look for bottled butter flavoring in the extracts section. One bottle can save you thousands of calories!

Makes 4 servings at 299 calories each.

1 tablespoon butter or margarine
2 cloves of garlic, minced
¼ pound fresh mushrooms, sliced
1 cup chopped parsley
2 cans (10½ ounces each) minced clams, with liquid
1 tablespoon cornstarch

1 teaspoon imitation butter-flavored salt
¼ teaspoon pepper
1 teaspoon leaf oregano, crumbled
8 ounces spaghetti or macaroni, cooked to tender stage (14 to 20 minutes, about 4½ cups)

1. Melt butter in a skillet; add garlic and brown slowly. Stir in mushrooms and parsley; cook 5 minutes, stirring frequently.
2. Drain clams, reserving liquid. Dissolve cornstarch in reserved liquid. Stir clams and cornstarch mixture into mushrooms in skillet. Add salt, pepper and oregano; simmer for 5 minutes. Pour sauce over cooked pasta, ¾ cup per serving.

ITALIAN CHEESE OMELET WITH TOMATO SAUCE

Makes 3 servings at 208 calories each.

1 can (8 ounces) tomato sauce	1 tablespoon extra sharp grated Romano cheese
1 teaspoon vegetable oil	
4 eggs, lightly beaten	½ teaspoon salt
1 cup low-fat cottage cheese	⅛ teaspoon pepper
	1 teaspoon leaf oregano, crumbled

1. Put tomato sauce in a small saucepan; simmer over low heat while preparing the omelet.
2. Rub nonstick skillet with oil; heat over medium heat; pour in eggs. Cook, lifting edges to allow the uncooked portion to flow underneath.
3. Spread cottage cheese over surface of eggs and sprinkle with the Romano cheese, salt, pepper and oregano.
4. Continue cooking over low heat for a few minutes, until cheese is heated through.
5. Fold and turn out onto a heated serving platter. Pour tomato sauce over omelet. Serve immediately.

LOW-CALORIE "ZUPPA DI PESCE" (ITALIAN FISH STEW)

This is Italy's version of the French Bouillabaisse. We've added American convenience by using frozen fish, shrimp and whole canned clams. Any boneless, skinless fish fillets can be used. Simply vary the cooking time according to package directions. Frozen scallops can also be used instead of fish.

Makes 8 servings at 140 calories each.

1 tablespoon olive oil	1 package (1 pound)
2 cloves of garlic, chopped	frozen halibut steaks, partially thawed, cut
½ cup dry white wine	in 2-inch strips
1 can tomatoes (2 cups)	1 package (12 ounces)
½ cup water	frozen, cooked,
½ teaspoon salt	cleaned shrimp
¼ teaspoon pepper	1 can (24 ounces)
2 tablespoons chopped parsley	clams in shells, with liquid
Pinch of cayenne	

1. Heat oil in a large skillet over medium heat; add garlic and sauté until soft. Add wine, tomatoes, water and seasonings. Cover. Bring to boiling; lower heat; simmer 10 minutes.

2. Add fish to sauce. Cover; simmer until cooked but still firm (about 7 minutes).

3. Add shrimp, clams and the clam broth; simmer until heated through.

SAUSAGE-FLAVORED BEEF ROLLETTES

Italian sausage, at a whopping 2,272 calories per pound, is off limits for most calorie counters, but here's a way to add the flavor without the fat—smoke-flavored soy protein chips, at only 29 calories a tablespoon.

Makes 6 servings at 252 calories each.

1½ pounds lean round, cut into 12 even slices (minute steaks or beef braciola)	3 tablespoons smoke-flavored vegetable protein chips
	1½ teaspoons salt
	Pinch of pepper
1 package (6 ounces) part-skim mozzarella cheese, thinly sliced	1 teaspoon leaf oregano, crumbled

1. Trim all fat from steaks. Pound thin with meat mallet or edge of a heavy plate.

2. Slice cheese into 12 thin slices. Place 1 cheese slice on each piece of beef. Sprinkle with protein chips, salt, pepper and oregano. Roll up and secure each roll with wooden picks.

3. Place rolls on a rack of broiler pan. Broil about 2 inches from heat, about 8 minutes on each side.

FLORENTINE BEEFSTEAK

Lean, low-calorie steak with an Italian accent, marinated briefly in dry red wine. Be sure to use round steak, well-trimmed of all extra fat; it's only 612 calories per pound.

Makes 6 servings at 174 calories each.

1½ pounds lean round steak, 1½ inches thick
¼ cup dry red wine
¼ cup water
1 tablespoon olive oil

1 teaspoon garlic salt
½ teaspoon pepper
½ teaspoon leaf rosemary, crumbled
Lemon slices

1. Trim steak of all fat; place in a shallow dish.

2. Combine wine, water, oil, garlic, salt, pepper and rosemary; pour over steak. Marinate steak 30 minutes; turn and marinate for 30 minutes longer. Drain.

3. Broil about 2 inches from heat, 4 to 5 minutes on each side. Serve rare, thinly sliced on the diagonal. Garnish with lemon slices.

MACARONI, CHEESE AND MUSHROOMS

Makes 6 servings at 171 calories each.
Bake at 350° for 25 minutes.

2 cups (8 ounces uncooked) elbow macaroni, cooked to tender stage (14 to 20 minutes)
2 cans (4 ounces each) mushroom stems and pieces, drained
¼ cup minced pimiento
1 cup shredded extra-sharp Cheddar cheese
1 cup skim milk
1 medium-size onion, sliced (½ cup)
2 teaspoons dry mustard
1 teaspoon salt
1 teaspoon Worcestershire sauce
⅛ teaspoon pepper

1. Combine macaroni, mushrooms and the pimiento in a greased 6-cup baking dish.

2. Stir cheese, milk, onion, mustard, salt, Worcestershire sauce and pepper in medium-size saucepan over low heat until cheese is completely melted.

3. Stir sauce into macaroni mixture. Bake in moderate oven (350°) 25 minutes, or until bubbly hot.

PROTEIN LASAGNA

This low-calorie special is made with eggs instead of pasta.

Bake at 325° for 45 minutes.
Makes 4 servings at 276 calories each.

5 eggs
¼ cup water
Pinch of salt
1 tablespoon olive oil
2 cups low-fat cottage cheese
3 tablespoons grated Parmesan cheese

1 teaspoon oregano
2 tablespoons chopped parsley
½ teaspoon salt
2 cans (8 ounces each) tomato sauce
1 tablespoon fine dry bread crumbs

1. Beat 4 of the eggs, water and salt together until light and fluffy. Heat oil in a nonstick skillet over low heat; add egg mixture. Cook until eggs are set. Remove from heat; cut cooked egg mixture into ½-inch strips. (Don't fret if you're not too neat; the sauce covers mistakes.)

2. Combine remaining egg, cottage cheese, Parmesan, oregano, parsley and salt.

3. Layer egg strips in greased 2-quart casserole. Top with cheese mixture and tomato sauce. Repeat layers until all ingredients are used. Top with crumbs and bake in slow oven (325°) 45 minutes, or until bubbly hot.

Chapter 12

Quick 'N' Easy Oriental Fare

If you'd like to "get away from it all"—especially that dreary diet—why not take a trip to China or Japan, via your kitchen. What better way to disguise low-calorie fare than to dress it up with a Far Eastern flair! Going Oriental one or two nights a week has a lot of advantages for the low-calorie cook with a family to feed. The main course can be slim-but-satisfying for you, (and other family members in need of a little girth control), yet it's easy enough to add some fluffy rice or Chinese noodles for the skinnies who need the caloric extras.

Despite its fanfare appearance, Oriental cuisine is the most budgetwise in the world, in both cost and effort! Most dishes take only 15 minutes or less to prepare. But of all the advantages, none is greater than that "who's on a diet?" feeling you have when you sit down to a seemingly sumptuous dish that's under 300 calories!

EGG DROP SOUP

A soup course is likely to appear anywhere in a true Oriental meal, not necessarily at the beginning. But a calorie-shy "de-appetizer" like Egg Drop Soup is a good start for a calorie-counter's dinner. This recipe is half the calories of frozen Egg Drop Soup.

Makes 4 servings at 32 calories each.

3 cups water (for broth)	1 tablespoon cornstarch
	3 tablespoons water
2 envelopes or teaspoons instant chicken broth	1 egg lightly beaten with 1 teaspoon water

1. Heat water and chicken broth to boiling in a large saucepan.

2. Combine cornstarch with the 3 tablespoons water in a cup. Add to the broth mixture. Cook, stirring, until soup thickens and clears.

3. Add the beaten egg gradually, stirring all the time.

LOW-CALORIE FRIED RICE

Oriental fare is so slimming that great bowls of steaming white rice are added at every meal to provide needed calories. Fried rice is especially fattening (about 218 calories per half-cup serving). Here's a protein-boosted, slimmed-down version you can enjoy.

Makes 4 servings at 82 calories each.

½ cup packaged precooked rice	½ cup canned bean sprouts or Chinese vegetables, drained
¾ cup boiling water	
1 egg	¼ cup canned small shrimp, drained
2 egg whites	
1 medium-size onion, minced	2 tablespoons soy sauce

1. Place rice in a small bowl; add boiling water; let stand 15 minutes, or until almost all water is absorbed.

2. Beat egg and egg whites lightly in a second small bowl.

3. Heat a nonstick skillet over medium heat; add eggs; stir to scramble.

4. Add prepared rice, onion, bean sprouts, shrimp

and soy sauce. Stir-fry about 2 minutes more, or until hot.

Beef Dishes

Orientals are skimpy meateaters by Western standards; fish, poultry and soybeans are more their meat. Lamb and veal were unheard of in classic Chinese cuisine. Most of the Chinese beef dishes we're familiar with are the inventions of Chinese-American restaurants.

But good beef, specially raised for leanness and tenderness, is a Japanese delicacy. The dish *Sukiyaki* can be an elaborate company dinner, with slender slices of the finest beef tenderloin and crisp vegetables prepared at the table. Of course it takes a steely-nerved host or hostess to carry off the stir-fry-and-serve procedure in public!

Here's a family-style version that's more convenient because it's prepared in the kitchen—and it's slimmer and less expensive because you use flank steak, with only 653 calories per pound.

FAMILY-STYLE SUKIYAKI

Makes 6 servings at 237 calories each.

1½ pounds flank steak
1 large onion, sliced
1 cup sliced mushrooms
½ cup soy sauce
½ cup dry sherry
1 cup canned Chinese
  vegetables or bean
  sprouts, drained

½ plastic package (8
  ounces) mixed fresh
  salad vegetables
  (shredded cabbage,
  lettuce, celery,
  carrots, etc., from
  supermarket produce
  department)

1. Slice the meat diagonally against the grain into ⅛-inch strips; slice strips in half. (Partially frozen meat is easiest to slice.)

2. Heat a large nonstick skillet. Brown the meat very quickly over high heat, stirring all the time. Push meat to one side, and leave in skillet while cooking vegetables.

3. Add the onion and mushrooms; stir-fry 3 minutes.

4. Add soy sauce, sherry and vegetables; cook, stirring frequently, for an additional four to five minutes. (Don't overcook; vegetables should be crisp.)

NOTE: This is a good dish to prepare with leftover rare roast beef. (Use about ¾ pound. Makes 6 servings.)

LOW-CALORIE CHINESE PEPPER STEAK

Here's a dish that's strictly an American invention.

Makes 4 servings at 237 calories each.

1 pound flank steak	Pinch of pepper
½ cup sliced onion	Pinch of garlic powder
3 green peppers, cut in squares	(optional)
¼ cup soy sauce	3 ripe tomatoes, cut in bite-size pieces
¼ cup dry sherry	1 teaspoon cornstarch mixed with 2 tablespoons cold water
⅓ cup water	
½ teaspoon sugar	
½ teaspoon ground ginger	

1. Slice the meat diagonally against the grain into ⅛-inch strips. Heat a large nonstick skillet and brown the steak quickly over high heat. Push aside.

2. Add the onion and green pepper and stir-fry for 1 minute.

3. Add the soy sauce, sherry and water; stir in the seasonings. Cook for 3 to 4 minutes.

4. Uncover and add tomatoes and cornstarch mixture. Stir and continue cooking another minute or two.

NOTE: This is another good dish for about ½ pound leftover rare roast beef.

What About Those Chinese Pork Dishes?

Oriental cooking is so marvelously versatile that you can substitute boneless white-meat poultry for pork in many recipes and still come up with a dish that's authentic. For dishes that call for a small amount of pork, the least calorie-damaging cut you can buy is fresh ham steak, trimmed of all border fat. Pork spareribs, on the other hand, are so fattening that you're best off to forget it altogether—or come up with your own slimmed-down Westernized version, substituting veal "spareribs" (veal plate or a breast of veal, trimmed of fat and cut into ribs). Far leaner and much meatier, three pounds of veal breast will serve eight generously for only 249 calories for each serving. The same amount of pork spareribs serves up only six skimpy portions at a whopping 550 calories each! Keep breast of veal in mind for all your sparerib recipes.

VEAL SPARERIBS, ORIENTAL STYLE

Bake at 325° for 2 hours.
Makes 8 servings at 265 calories each.

3 pounds breast of veal	Garlic salt
¾ cup pineapple juice	2 tablespoons soy sauce
¼ cup wine vinegar	Dieter's Sweet-and-Sour
Pepper	Sauce

1. Cut veal ribs into serving-size pieces, trimming all visible fat. Place in baking pan.

2. Combine pineapple juice and vinegar; pour over ribs. Sprinkle with pepper and garlic salt. Cover the pan tightly with foil.

3. Bake in slow oven (325°) 1 hour. Uncover; baste with pan liquid; sprinkle with soy sauce. Bake 1 hour longer, turning and basting ribs with pan liquid several times, or until ribs are brown and tender. Discard liquid remaining in pan. Serve with Dieter's Sweet-and-Sour Sauce.

DIETER'S SWEET-AND-SOUR SAUCE

Makes 1 cup at 5 calories per tablespoon.*

1 teaspoon brown sugar	**1 teaspoon wine vinegar**
3 to 4 tablespoons	**1 teaspoon catsup**
boiling water	**1 teaspoon soy sauce**
½ cup sugar-free	
apricot preserves	

Dissolve brown sugar in boiling water; stir in preserves, vinegar, catsup, soy sauce.
Compared with 30 calories per tablespoon for commercial sweet-and-sour sauce or "Chinese duck sauce."

LOBSTER CANTONESE

Here's a simplified version for the squeamish that's not only more convenient than the original, but lower in calories because it uses leftover ground roast pork—most of the fat has been cooked away!

Makes 4 servings at 212 calories each.

1 tablespoon cornstarch	1 clove of garlic,
1½ cups water	crushed
1 envelope or teaspoon	½ teaspoon salt
instant chicken broth	Pinch of sugar
1 pound cooked lobster	Dash of pepper
¼ pound cooked pork,	1 green onion, chopped
finely chopped	1 teaspoon soy sauce
	1 egg, slightly beaten

1. Combine cornstarch and 3 tablespoons of the water in a cup. Heat remaining water with chicken broth to boiling in a large skillet.

2. Stir in the cornstarch mixture, lobster, pork, garlic, salt, sugar, pepper, green onion and soy sauce.

3. Heat, stirring constantly, until mixture bubbles and is thickened.

4. Stir in egg slowly, blending well.

SHRIMP IN LOBSTER SAUCE: This classic-but-lobsterless dish gets its name from the fact that the shrimp is prepared in the same sauce as Lobster Cantonese! Substitute one pound of cooked, cleaned shrimp (237 calories per serving) for the lobster.

BAY SCALLOPS IN LOBSTER SAUCE can be prepared with one pound of steamed scallops (204 calories per serving) substituted for the cooked lobster.

JAPANESE-STYLE VEGETABLES

Makes 8 servings at 30 calories each.

1 can (3 or 4 ounces)	1 package (9 ounces)
mushroom stems and	frozen French-style
pieces	green beans
1 teaspoon cornstarch	1 medium-size onion,
2 envelopes or teaspoons	sliced into rings
instant chicken broth	1 tablespoon soy sauce
1 package (10 ounces)	
frozen broccoli spears	

1. Drain the mushrooms; add enough water to make one half cup of liquid. Pour into a medium-size saucepan; stir in cornstarch and chicken broth.

2. Add the broccoli, green beans, onion and soy sauce. Cook slowly over low heat, breaking up frozen vegetables for even thawing. Cover; cook 4 minutes—vegetables should still be crisp.

MOO GOO GAI PAN (CHINESE CHICKEN AND MUSHROOMS)

Makes 4 servings at 204 calories each.

1 pound boned chicken breasts (fillets)
1 can (8 ounces) mushrooms, including liquid
1 cup mixed Chinese vegetables, including liquid
1 teaspoon vegetable oil
1 pound Chinese or Savoy cabbage
1 package (9 ounces) Italian green beans, thawed
½ teaspoon salt
Pinch of pepper
¼ teaspoon ground ginger
½ teaspoon sugar
1 envelope or teaspoon instant chicken broth
1 teaspoon cornstarch
3 tablespoons water

1. Remove skin from chicken breasts. Cut chicken into ¼-inch-thick slices, crosswise.

2. Drain the mushrooms and Chinese vegetables, reserving ½ cup of the combined liquids.

3. Heat oil in a large skillet. Add chicken; quickly stir-fry until the color turns from pink to white. Stir in mushrooms, Chinese vegetables, liquid from the vegetables, Chinese cabbage, green beans, salt, pepper, ginger, sugar and chicken broth. Cover; cook 2 minutes.

4. Combine cornstarch and water in a small cup; add to skillet. Cook and stir one or two minutes until mixture thickens.

TORI TERIYAKI
(JAPANESE BARBECUED CHICKEN)

This delightful main course is served with tangy Oriental Mustard.

Makes 4 servings at 173 calories each.

1 pound boneless chicken breasts (fillets)	½ cup water
	1 teaspoon cornstarch
¼ cup dry sherry	1 envelope or teaspoon instant chicken broth
¼ cup soy sauce	Dry parsley flakes
1 tablespoon sugar	Oriental Mustard

1. Remove skin from chicken breasts. Place chicken in a small shallow dish.

2. Combine the sherry, soy sauce and sugar in a small cup; pour over chicken. Marinate for 30 minutes or more, turning once.

3. Remove chicken from the marinade; pour marinade into small saucepan.

4. Broil chicken, 4 inches from heat, for 10 minutes on each side, brushing occasionally with the marinade.

5. Add water, cornstarch and chicken broth to marinade in saucepan. Cook over medium heat, stirring constantly, until sauce ˈhickens and comes to boiling. Bubble 1 minute. Remove from heat; serve with Oriental Mustard.

ORIENTAL MUSTARD: Combine 2 tablespoons dry mustard with ¼ cup boiling water in a small bowl; stir until smooth. Let stand 15 minutes to develop the "fire."

SWEET-AND-SOUR "MOCK DUCK"

Bake at 375° for 50 minutes.
Makes 6 servings at 159 calories each.

1 cup Dieter's Sweet-and-Sour Sauce (recipe page 215)	**1 teaspoon cornstarch** **2 pounds broiler-fryer chicken thighs**

 1. Mix Dieter's Sweet-and-Sour Sauce and cornstarch in small bowl.
 2. Remove skin from chicken; arrange chicken in a shallow baking dish; spoon part of sauce over.
 3. Bake in moderate oven (375°), basting occasionally, for 50 minutes, or until the chicken is tender.
 NOTE: Domestic duckling and commercial sweet-sour duck sauce is about 424 calories per serving.

CHICKEN EGG FOO YUNG

Here's an unconventional but more practical method for making an Egg Foo Yung *dish for the family. Instead of preparing several little egg "pancakes," one at a time, you make one big one in a skillet, cut it in quarters, and turn each section over to finish the cooking. Make the sauce first.*

Makes 4 servings at 179 calories each.

Foo Yung Sauce **5 eggs** **1 teaspoon vegetable oil** **1 can (1 pound)**	**Chinese or chop suey vegetables, well drained** **⅔ cup cubed cooked chicken**

 1. Prepare Foo Yung Sauce; keep warm.
 2. Beat eggs until fluffy. Heat oil in a 10-inch skillet over low heat; pour in eggs.

3. Spread vegetables and chicken evenly over eggs and continue cooking until egg edges are no longer liquid. Cut the "giant pancake" into 4 quarters; turn each quarter over with a large pancake turner.

4. Cook 2 to 3 minutes longer, or until the chicken and vegetables are heated through. Serve each section egg side up; spoon sauce over.

FOO YUNG SAUCE: Mix 1 envelope or teaspoon instant beef broth, 2 teaspoons cornstarch, 1 cup water and ¼ cup soy sauce in a small saucepan. Heat, stirring constantly, until sauce thickens and bubbles; cook 1 minute longer. Makes 1¼ cups of Foo Yung Sauce.

SWEET-AND-SOUR CABBAGE

Makes 8 servings at 44 calories each.

1 small head red cabbage (about 1 pound)	2 tablespoons wine vinegar
1 teaspoon vegetable oil	4 tablespoons lemon juice
1 medium-size onion, sliced	2 teaspoons salt
½ cup water	Pinch of pepper
2 large apples, pared and sliced thin	2 teaspoons liquid sugar substitute

1. Wash and shred cabbage.

2. Heat oil in a large skillet or Dutch oven. Add onion; sauté over low heat 10 minutes. Add the water, cabbage and apples. Cover; simmer 30 minutes.

3. Add vinegar, lemon juice, salt and pepper; simmer 10 minutes longer.

4. Stir in liquid sugar substitute and serve.

MUSHROOMS AND BEAN SPROUTS

Makes 6 servings at 67 calories each.

1 tablespoon vegetable oil	1 can (1 pound) bean sprouts, drained
2 stalks celery, diced	1 tablespoon soy sauce
1 medium-size onion, sliced in rings	1 tablespoon cornstarch
2 cans (4 ounces each) sliced mushrooms	1 envelope or teaspoon instant chicken broth

1. Heat oil in large (10-inch) skillet. Add celery and onions; sauté for 3 minutes.

2. Drain mushrooms; reserve liquid. Add mushrooms and bean sprouts to vegetables in skillet, heating and stirring gently 2 minutes.

3. Add enough water to mushroom liquid to make 1 cup. Blend with soy sauce and cornstarch; stir until cornstarch is dissolved. Add chicken broth. Mix sauce into the vegetables. Cook, stirring gently, about 5 minutes or until well-blended and thickened.

SWEET-AND-SOUR BEETS

Makes 4 servings at 65 calories each.

2 teaspoons cornstarch	1 can (16 ounces) sliced beets, drained
3 tablespoons cider vinegar	Sugar substitute to equal 4 tablespoons sugar
¼ cup water	
2 tablespoons sugar	Butter-flavored salt

1. Combine cornstarch, vinegar, water and sugar in a

medium-size saucepan. Cook, stirring occasionally, over moderate heat until simmering.

2. Add beets; simmer for 4 minutes. Stir in sugar substitute, season with butter-flavored salt; serve.

ORIENTAL "STIR-FRIED" BROCCOLI

To give frozen vegetables a Far-East flair, try this easy-to-do technique. Sliced defrosted asparagus spears or green beans would be equally interesting for you to try occasionally.

Makes 4 servings at 67 calories each.

1 package (10 ounces) frozen broccoli spears, partially thawed	1 small onion, sliced
	1 can (4 ounces) sliced mushrooms, drained
1 tablespoon vegetable oil	2 tablespoons soy sauce

1. Cut broccoli spears into 1- or 2-inch lengths.

2. Heat oil in nonstick skillet. Add broccoli, onion, mushrooms and soy sauce. Cook, stirring constantly, over high heat 2 to 3 minutes, or until broccoli is just tender. Serve at once.

SHRIMP SUKIYAKI

This Japanese main course of shrimp and vegetables is great for dinner in a hurry.

Makes 4 servings at 242 calories each.

3 tablespoons soy sauce
2 tablespoons dry
  sherry
½ teaspoon ground
  ginger
1 package (16 ounces)
  frozen shrimp, thawed
1 tablespoon vegetable
  oil
1 clove of garlic
1 medium-size onion,
  sliced (1 cup)
1 cup sliced celery

1 medium-size green
  pepper, cut into strips
1 envelope or teaspoon
  instant chicken broth
½ cup water
2 teaspoons cornstarch
1 can (8½ ounces)
  water chestnuts,
  sliced
1 can (16 ounces) bean
  sprouts, drained
  and rinsed

1. Combine the soy sauce, sherry and ginger in a large bowl. Add shrimp; marinate for 15 minutes.

2. Heat oil in a large (12-inch) skillet. Add garlic; sauté until brown. Remove garlic and discard.

3. Add onion, celery and pepper to the skillet. Sauté lightly, stirring frequently, for 3 minutes. Remove from skillet and reserve.

4. Pour shrimp and marinade into skillet. Cook 5 minutes. Remove and reserve.

5. Add chicken broth, water and cornstarch to the skillet. Heat, stirring constantly, over medium heat until broth dissolves and sauce becomes thickened and clear.

6. Return shrimp, marinade and vegetables to the skillet. Add the water chestnuts and bean sprouts. Heat and stir gently for 3 minutes. Serve immediately.

NOTE: This recipe is also very good using lean beef strips or cooked chicken instead of the shrimp, and is an excellent way to use leftover portions of meat.

Chapter 13

Wine Cookery

What wine can do to brighten bland food is nothing short of miraculous! But the real miracle occurs in the cooking; all of the alcohol calories evaporate, leaving nothing behind but a few calories' worth of sugar and flavor. What other delicious ingredient is so accommodating to calorie-counters!

Wine does wonders to spike the subtleties of chicken, fish and veal. It's unmatched as marinade—marvelously effective in tenderizing the least fattening cuts of beef, pork and lamb. Wine romanticizes salads and vegetables. And wine turns plain fruit into devilish desserts!

So there's no need to pass up the benefits of wine in the kitchen. Not even if you have a family of small-fry . . . because food cooked in wine is definitely nonalcoholic. Remember? The alcohol evaporates, along with the calories. Only the flavor is "intoxicating"!

Tips for New Wine Cooks

• The best wines to cook with are the dry ones: Red wines like Burgundy, claret and Chianti, or white wines like Chablis, Rhine wine, dry sherry or sauterne . . . or some dry vermouth from your martini-mixing stock!

• Don't spend a bundle on your kitchen wine shelf. Inexpensive "jug" wines will do very nicely.

• There's no hard-and-fast rule about which-wine-goes-in-what, but for starters you might prefer red wines in red meats, spicy dishes and robust sauces, and white for light sauces or poultry, seafood and veal courses. But not necessarily. Experimenting is half the fun!

• Wine cookery needn't be troublesome—try stirring a little sauterne into simmering chicken broth for a "Continental Consommé," or dashing Burgundy on burgers as they broil. Add a tablespoonful or two to transform canned tomato sauce (only 85 calories a cupful, compared with 200 or more for canned "spaghetti sauce").

• Wine is a terrific tenderizer, a natural marinade for those extra-lean cuts of meat, such as beef round, flank steak, leg of lamb or veal chops. These meats lack the fatty marbling that adds tenderness (and calories and cholesterol!).

• Spike your slow-simmer stews or ragouts with wine. Use it in place of water, stock, broth, bouillon, juice or whatever liquid your favorite recipe calls for. Or use it half-and-half.

• Put peaches, pears or any favored fruit in a party mood by poaching them in wine. Or marinate fresh fruit in wine while you're serving dinner. Uncooked wine desserts still contain the alcohol and calories, but "Tipsied Fruit" is a lot less fattening than layer cake . . . and just exotic enough to help you forget your apple-pie addiction!

Glamorous Main Dishes

FRENCH CHICKEN IN ORANGE SHERRY SAUCE

Chicken breasts are a dieter's delight! No need to strip the skin if you follow our fat-reducing technique for oven-browning. Add wine sauce for a quick main course that's s-o-o Continental!

Bake at 375° for 45 minutes.
Makes 6 servings at 217 calories each.

3 chicken breasts, split (about 2½ pounds)	1 tablespoon firmly packed brown sugar
½ teaspoon salt	1 teaspoon salt
1 medium-size onion, sliced	¼ teaspoon pepper
¼ cup chopped green pepper	1 teaspoon grated orange rind
1 cup sliced mushrooms	1 tablespoon flour
SAUCE	2 teaspoons chopped parsley
1 cup orange juice	Paprika
¼ cup dry sherry	1 orange, peeled and sliced
½ cup water	

1. Place the chicken breasts, skin side up, on a rack in broiler pan. Broil 2 inches from heat for 10 minutes, or until the skin is brown and crackly. Do not turn.

2. Place browned chicken breasts in a shallow 8-cup baking dish. Sprinkle with the ½ teaspoon salt. Add onion, green pepper and mushrooms.

3. Combine the orange juice, sherry, water, brown sugar, the 1 teaspoon salt, pepper, orange rind and flour in small saucepan. Blend well. Cook over medium heat, stirring constantly, until sauce thickens and bubbles; add parsley. Pour over chicken.

4. Bake in a moderate oven (375°) 45 minutes, or until the chicken is tender. Baste several times. Sprinkle with paprika and garnish with orange slices.

SKINNY SHISH KEBAB

Lean and lovely leg of lamb is the most calorie-wise buy for this dish. Carefully trimmed of fat, boneless lamb from the leg is less than 600 calories per pound. Prepackaged cubes of lamb can be double that.

Makes 8 three-ounce servings at 148 calories each.

2 pounds lean lamb (from leg)	2 teaspoons leaf basil, crumbled
1 cup dry white wine	3 tablespoons Worcestershire sauce
2 teaspoons garlic salt	
½ teaspoon pepper	

1. Trim all fat from lamb; cut into 2-inch cubes.
2. Place lamb cubes in glass or ceramic bowl. Combine the wine, garlic salt, pepper, basil and the Worcestershire sauce; pour over meat. Marinate 2 hours at room temperature; stir often.
3. Drain meat; reserve marinade. Thread the cubes on 8 skewers. Arrange on rack of broiler pan.
4. Broil, 2 inches from heat, for about 20 minutes, turning once. Brush with reserved marinade. Serve at once.

CANTONESE PORK STEAK

Well-trimmed boneless pork from the leg is under 700 calories per pound . . . fatty pork loin (as purchased) can be twice that.

Makes 6 three-ounce servings at 195 calories each.

1½ pounds fresh ham
  steak (1 inch thick)
½ teaspoon garlic
  powder

½ cup dry sherry
6 tablespoons soy sauce
2 tablespoons catsup
2 teaspoons cornstarch

1. Trim away all fat from the meat; sprinkle with garlic powder.

2. Place meat in plastic bag; add sherry and soy sauce. Close bag; place bag in a bowl. Refrigerate 2 hours or longer; turn the bag several times.

3. Drain the meat, reserving marinade. Place meat on a rack in broiler pan.

4. Broil, 4 inches from heat, 12 to 15 minutes per side, or until browned and cooked through.

5. Combine reserved marinade with water to make 1 cup; pour into medium-size saucepan. Stir in catsup and cornstarch. Cook over medium heat, stirring, until the sauce thickens and bubbles. Simmer 1 minute. Serve with meat.

STEAK UNO MOMENTO

A last-minute dinner dish made with "minute steaks" (machine-tenderized round steak cut into serving-size pieces). Try the same trick with extra lean ground round shaped into burgers.

Makes 6 servings at 188 calories each.

1 tablespoon vegetable
  oil
6 lean round "minute
  steaks" (1½ pounds)
½ teaspoon garlic salt
⅛ teaspoon pepper

1 can (8 ounces) sliced
  mushrooms
1 tablespoon flour
½ cup dry red wine
½ teaspoon leaf
  oregano, crumbled

1. Heat the oil in a nonstick skillet. Pan-fry steaks quickly on both sides over high heat. Sprinkle with garlic salt and pepper; remove from skillet.

2. Drain liquid from mushrooms into bowl; blend in flour. Pour into skillet; add wine and oregano. Cook over medium heat, stirring constantly, until sauce thickens and bubbles. Add the mushrooms. Simmer 5 minutes. Pour over steaks; serve.

SPEEDY SEAFOOD OMELET WITH WINE SAUCE

Who'd ever guess you forgot to defrost the roast when you can turn eggs and canned seafood into such an elegant spur-of-the-moment supper! The sauce is so slimming you'll want to try it again . . . on some cauliflower or broiled flounder.

Makes 2 servings at 298 calories each.

SAUCE

⅔ cup skim milk
1 tablespoon all-purpose flour
½ teaspoon salt
Pinch of cayenne
Dash of ground nutmeg
1 tablespoon dry white wine

OMELET

1 tablespoon diet margarine
3 eggs, slightly beaten
1 can (7 ounces) crabmeat, well drained, boned and flaked
2 teaspoons instant minced onion

1. Combine milk with flour, salt, cayenne and nutmeg in a small saucepan. Cook, stirring constantly, over moderate heat until mixture simmers and thickens. Remove from heat; stir in wine. Cover; reserve.
2. Melt margarine in a 10-inch nonstick skillet over moderate heat. Rotate the skillet so that the bottom and sides are completely coated.
3. When the moisture evaporates and margarine begins to sizzle, pour in eggs, all at once. Tilt pan so eggs

completely cover bottom. Sprinkle evenly with crab-meat and minced onion. Cook about 2 minutes, or until eggs are nearly set.

4. Fold omelet in half and lift out onto heated serving plate. Cut in half. Serve with sauce.

APPLE-WINE CHICKEN BAKE

Bake at 350° for 45 minutes.
Makes 4 servings at 189 calories each.

2 chicken breasts, split (about 1½ pounds)	**2 tablespoons chopped onion**
1 large apple, peeled and diced	**1 tablespoon dried parsley flakes**
½ cup dry white wine	**½ teaspoon salt**
2 tablespoons white raisins, chopped	**⅛ teaspoon pepper**

1. Place chicken, skin side up, on a rack in broiler pan. Broil, skin side only, 5 to 10 minutes, or until brown.

2. Place browned chicken, skin side up, in ovenproof baking dish. Surround with apples and raisins; pour in wine. Sprinkle with parsley, salt and pepper. Bake, covered, in moderate oven (350°) 35 minutes.

3. Uncover; continue baking 10 minutes longer, or until liquid reduces to a saucey thickness.

BEEF BURGUNDY

Here's a decalorized classic from lean, fat-trimmed beef round (only 612 calories per pound). Make it ahead of time . . . the waiting helps blend the flavors and allows the fat calories to surface for a pre warm-up skimming!

Makes 6 servings at 241 calories each.

1 tablespoon diet
  margarine
2 pounds extra lean
  beef round, trimmed
  of fat and cut in
  1½-inch cubes
1 clove of garlic, minced
1 cup Burgundy wine
½ teaspoon pepper

1 small bay leaf
Pinch of thyme
2 carrots, pared and
  sliced (about 1 cup)
½ pound mushroom
  caps (fresh or
  canned)
1 can (1 pound) small
  white onions, drained

1. Melt margarine in a heavy Dutch oven over moderate heat, until it sizzles. Add beef and garlic. Brown meat evenly on all sides.

2. Add wine, pepper, bay leaf and thyme. Cover; simmer over very low heat 1½ hours, or until meat is nearly tender.

3. Remove from heat; allow to cool. Chill several hours or overnight.

4. About 30 minutes before serving, remove meat from refrigerator and lift off hardened fat. Add carrots. Cover; simmer over moderate heat 15 minutes.

5. Uncover; stir in the mushrooms and onions. Continue to cook, uncovered, just until most of liquid evaporates.

ORIENTAL WINE MARINADE FOR MEAT, POULTRY AND FISH

Add a Far East flair to low-calorie food with the following marinade. The Chinese use a wine called "Shao Hsing" while the Japanese use Sake. Sherry is the closest Western substitute.

Makes 1⅓ cups at 3 calories per tablespoon.

⅓ cup soy sauce
½ cup dry sherry
½ cup water

1 teaspoon ground
  ginger
1 teaspoon garlic
  powder

Combine all ingredients and pour over meat, poultry or fish in a medium-size bowl. Let stand at room temperature 2 to 4 hours, or all day if marinating a solid roast.

EASY ORANGE BASTE FOR CHICKEN

Makes 1 cup at 14 calories per tablespoon.

½ cup dry white wine   2 tablespoons soy sauce
½ cup low-calorie
   orange marmalade

Combine all ingredients and brush on chicken as it bakes or broils.

WINE-GLAZED CHICKEN WINGS

Bake at 350° for 1 hour and 20 minutes.
Makes 32 bite-size servings at 18 calories each.

2½ pounds chicken   Thousand Island
   wings (about 16)   dressing
4 tablespoons low-   4 tablespoons orange
   calorie   juice
                   3 tablespoons sherry

1. Trim the tips from chicken wings. (Save for soup kettle.) Divide each wing in half by cutting through joint.

2. Combine remaining ingredients in large nonmetallic bowl. Add chicken wings and turn to coat evenly. Cover; marinate several hours or overnight in the refrigerator.

3. Place chicken, skin side down, in baking dish. Bake in moderate oven (350°) 30 minutes. Turn; baste

with remaining sauce; bake 50 minutes longer, basting occasionally with pan juices, until nicely browned and glazed.

Vegetables and Salads

CARROTS IN MARSALA

Makes 4 servings at 56 calories each.

1 pound fresh carrots
1 tablespoon diet
  margarine
¼ cup Marsala
1 teaspoon salt
⅛ teaspoon pepper
½ cup water
1 tablespoon chopped
  parsley

1. Wash and pare carrots; cut into 3-inch sticks.
2. Combine carrots, margarine, wine, salt, pepper and water in a large saucepan. Cover; bring to boiling. Lower heat; simmer 10 minutes, or until carrots are just tender.
3. Uncover saucepan; simmer until most of the liquid evaporates. Shake pan to glaze carrots evenly. Sprinkle with parsley.

CELERY AND PEAS, ORIENTAL STYLE

Makes 6 servings at 40 calories each.

½ cup water
4 cups sliced celery
½ cup frozen peas
1 teaspoon salt
Pinch of pepper
2 tablespoons soy sauce
3 tablespoons dry white
  wine
1 can (8½ ounces)
  water chestnuts,
  drained and sliced

1. Bring water to boiling in a large saucepan; add celery and peas. Cover; cook 5 minutes, or until celery is almost tender. Drain off any water, leaving vegetables in pan.

2. Add the salt, pepper, soy sauce, wine and water chestnuts to vegetables in saucepan. Toss together. Cook, stirring, 2 minutes longer.

WINE COLESLAW

Makes 6 servings at 37 calories each.

3 cups shredded
  cabbage
1 small onion, minced

½ cup Cooked Wine
  Dressing

Toss all ingredients together in large salad bowl to coat well. Chill; serve.

COOKED WINE SALAD DRESSING

Makes 1½ cups at 18 calories per tablespoon.

2 tablespoons all-
  purpose flour
1 tablespoon sugar
1 tablespoon vegetable
  oil
2 teaspoons salt

2 tablespoons prepared
  mustard
½ cup dry white wine
½ cup water
5 tablespoons wine
  vinegar
2 eggs, beaten

1. Combine flour, sugar, oil, salt, mustard, wine and water in a heavy nonstick saucepan or the top of a double boiler. Cook, stirring constantly, over very low heat until mixture thickens. Remove from heat.

2. Combine vinegar and eggs in a small bowl. Add a little of the hot mixture to the eggs, stirring constantly.

3. Pour egg mixture into remaining dressing, stirring rapidly. Cook, stirring constantly, over low heat until mixture thickens slightly. Remove from heat. Chill.

WHITE WINE SALAD DRESSING FOR TOSSED SALADS

Makes 1½ cups at 28 calories per tablespoon.

¾ cup dry white wine
4 tablespoons olive oil
2 tablespoons tarragon
  vinegar

4 tablespoons finely
  chopped onion
1 clove of garlic, minced
1 teaspoon salt
¼ teaspoon pepper

Combine all ingredients in a covered bottle; shake until thoroughly mixed. Chill.

TUNA-STUFFED MUSHROOMS

Bake at 425° for 10 minutes.
Makes about 24 mushrooms at 25 calories each.

2 pounds fresh
  mushrooms
1 tablespoon diet
  margarine
¼ cup white wine
¼ teaspoon salt

1 tablespoon onion
  flakes
1 teaspoon dried parsley
  flakes
1 can (7 ounces) tuna,
  packed-in-water

1. Wash and dry mushrooms. Remove and finely chop the stems.

2. Heat margarine in large nonstick skillet; add mushroom stems and all remaining ingredients. Cook and stir over moderate heat until wine is evaporated.

3. Pile mixture into mushroom caps. Bake in hot oven (425°) 10 to 12 minutes.

SAUTÉED MUSHROOMS AND WINE

Makes 4 servings at 40 calories each.

1 pound mushrooms, sliced	2 teaspoons vegetable oil
¼ cup dry white wine	½ teaspoon garlic salt

Combine all ingredients in a nonstick skillet. Cover; simmer 4 minutes. Uncover; continue simmering until all liquid evaporates and mushrooms are browned.

Desserts with Wine

PEACHES IN PORT

Makes 2 servings at 122 calories each.

Place 1 package (10 ounces) quick-thaw sliced peaches, thawed and drained in a shallow bowl with ¼ cup chilled port wine. Chill 30 minutes. At dessert time, spoon peaches into tall stemmed glasses.

ZABAGLIONE (ITALIAN WINE CUSTARD)

Makes 6 servings at 123 calories each.

6 egg yolks	⅓ cup dry sherry
6 tablespoons 10X (confectioners' powdered) sugar	6 egg whites
	Pinch of salt

1. Put egg yolks in top of a double-boiler over (but not touching) boiling water. Beat yolks, gradually adding sugar, until mixture is foamy.

2. Add the sherry; beat until mixture thickens slightly and is double in volume. Remove from heat.

3. Beat egg whites and salt in medium-size bowl. Fold into yolk mixture. Spoon into wine glasses; serve.

WINE-BAKED APPLES

Bake at 350° for 1 hour.
Makes 6 servings at 112 calories each.

8 medium-size baking apples
3 tablespoons brown sugar
3 tablespoons raisins
¾ cup dry white wine
½ cup boiling water

1. Core apples; pare skins half-way down. Arrange in a shallow 6-cup baking dish.

2. Fill apples with sugar and raisins; pour over wine and boiling water. Cover dish tightly with foil.

3. Bake in a moderate oven (350°) 30 minutes. Uncover; bake 30 minutes longer.

PEARS IN BURGUNDY

Makes 4 servings at 110 calories each (with sugar), 86 with sugar substitute.

1 can (16 ounces) diet-pack pear halves
½ cup dry red wine
½ cup orange juice
½ teaspoon cinnamon
¼ teaspoon ground cloves
¼ teaspoon grated lemon or orange rind
3 tablespoons sugar

1. Drain pear juice into a small saucepan; add the wine, orange juice, cinnamon, cloves, lemon or orange rind and sugar. Bring to boiling; lower heat. Simmer, uncovered, until liquid is reduced by half. Cool.

2. Arrange pear halves in 4 stemmed glasses. Pour warm liquid over pears; chill.

Chapter 14

Calorie-Shy Vegetables

Unfortunately for us could-be chubbies, the secret ingredient in our favorite vegetable dishes seems to be calories—melted butter, bubbling cheese, egg-rich sauce or syrupy bastes! If you've got a taste for rich foods and culinary extravagance, no plateful of greenery with a chaste squirt of lemon is going to satisfy you!

But you can duplicate the taste and texture of your favorite vegetable dishes if you're a Creative Low-Calorie Cook! You may even discover, for the first time in your life, that you're a vegetable fan. If you don't care for vegetables, chances are it's an "inherited" characteristic, passed on by a mother who didn't know how to cook them! Like overweight, vegetable-indifference can be cured by a little pinch of culinary imagination. As you read the recipes on the following pages, you'll see how far this imagination can take you.

Vegetable Pointers
for the Poundage Prone

• Try at least one "new" vegetable every week. Work your way through the alphabet, from artichokes to zucchini.

• Try a new technique! Stir-fry bite-size chunks of fresh vegetables, Oriental style. You can quick-cook enough vegetables to serve six in less than one table-spoon of oil. Douse well with soy sauce. A *wok* (Chinese fry pan) makes it fun!

• Cook vegetables normally served raw—try braised lettuce, simmered cucumbers, steamed celery, baked tomatoes. Then do the reverse—make a salad from raw spinach, green beans or sliced cauliflower.

• Simmer vegetables in fat-free broth or sugarless juice for a low-calorie flavor boost that needs no added butter or fat. Try broccoli in beef broth or green beans in chicken broth. Or how about summer squash in tomato juice, carrots in orange juice or cabbage in apple juice. One teaspoon of arrowroot or cornstarch (10 calories) will thicken it into a sauce! (Dissolve in a little cold juice before adding.)

• Treat yourself! Since you can't splurge on calories, indulge in an extravaganza of expensive or out-of-season vegetables—a whole pound of fresh mushrooms just for you, tiny Belgian carrots, asparagus flown in from the tropics.

• Combine vegetables creatively; never mind that it hasn't been done before. If the pairing sounds intriguing to you, you may become the inventor of a new succotash!

• Never, *never* overcook vegetables! Aside from the loss of nutritional value, overcooking creates flavorless pap that demands loads of calorific butter.

• If you have to count your calories, steer clear of any vegetables or combinations packed in their own sauce. Most include heavy concentrations of fats, starches or sugar. Some are as high as 300 calories a package or more . . . three or four times the calorie count of the same vegetable, unsauced!

Here are some "decalorized" favorites that are easy to prepare with the help of frozen or canned vegetables and calorie-safe convenience items.

WAIKIKI CARROTS WITH PINEAPPLE AND PEPPER

Low-calorie pineapple and frozen green pepper add an exotic Island touch to carrots. The bright colors make a particularly handsome vegetable dish to serve for company.

Makes 6 servings at 53 calories each.

1 envelope or teaspoon
   instant chicken broth
1 cup boiling water
¾ pound carrots, pared
   and sliced (about
   2 cups)
2 tablespoons instant
   minced onion

1 teaspoon parsley
   flakes
1 can (8 ounces) diet-
   pack pineapple tidbits
¼ cup chopped frozen
   green pepper
2 teaspoons cornstarch
½ teaspoon salt
Pinch pepper

1. Dissolve chicken broth in boiling water; add carrots. Cook 10 minutes, or until almost tender.
2. Add the onion and parsley flakes. Drain pineapple, reserving liquid. Stir pineapple and green pepper into carrots. Cook 1 minute longer.
3. Combine cornstarch with reserved pineapple juice; stir into simmering carrots. Add salt and pepper. Cook until sauce thickens and bubbles.

QUICK GREEN BEANS AMANDINE

Only half as fattening as butter or regular margarine . . . diet margarine and toasted almonds turn skinny "string beans" into a dieter's delight!

Makes 3 servings at 59 calories each.

1 tablespoon blanched
  slivered almonds
1 package (9 ounces)

frozen French-style
  green beans
1 tablespoon diet
  margarine

1. Spread almonds in shallow baking pan. Toast in a moderate oven (350°) for 10 minutes, or until almonds are lightly browned. Shake pan several times during toasting.

2. Cook green beans in a medium-size saucepan, following label directions. Drain. Toss beans with margarine and toasted almonds. Serve at once.

CHEESY ITALIAN GREEN BEANS

Fresh tomato slices topped with melting cheese add extra zest to this oven-easy green bean bake!

Bake at 325° for 30 minutes.
Makes 6 servings at 58 calories each.

1 envelope or teaspoon
  instant onion broth
½ cup boiling water
1 package (9 ounces)
  frozen Italian green
  beans
3 tomatoes, peeled and
  sliced

1 teaspoon instant
  minced onion
½ teaspoon salt
1 teaspoon leaf oregano,
  crumbled
2 ounces part-skim
  mozzarella cheese,
  shredded (about
  4 tablespoons)

1. Dissolve onion broth in boiling water; add the green beans. Cook 3 minutes.

2. Turn the beans and liquid into a shallow 6-cup baking dish. Top with tomato slices; sprinkle with minced onion, salt, oregano and cheese.

3. Bake in slow oven (325°) 30 minutes, or until

beans are bubbly and cheese is melted and lightly browned.

HUNGARIAN CAULIFLOWER IN "SOUR CREAM" SAUCE

Yogurt, at only 126 calories a cupful, serves as a stand-in for sour cream (close to 500 calories) in this paprika-powered vegetable dish.

Bake at 425° for 5 to 8 minutes.
Makes 6 servings at 57 calories each.

2 packages (10 ounces each) frozen cauliflower
1½ cups plain yogurt
1 teaspoon onion salt
1 teaspoon parsley flakes
2 tablespoons packaged bread crumbs
1 teaspoon paprika

1. Cook cauliflower in a large saucepan, following label directions. Drain and place in a shallow 6-cup baking dish.
2. Combine yogurt with onion salt and parsley flakes; spoon over the cauliflower. Sprinkle with bread crumbs and paprika.
3. Bake in a hot oven (425°) 5 to 8 minutes, or until bread crumbs are browned.

PARISIAN CARROTS, CELERY AND MUSHROOMS

A spoonful or orange breakfast drink concentrate adds citrus zing to this winning combination!

Makes 6 servings at 57 calories each.

¾ pound carrots, pared
and sliced (about
2 cups)

4 stalks of celery, thinly
sliced

1 cup boiling water

1 can (8 ounces) sliced
mushrooms

3 tablespoons instant
minced onion

2 teaspoons cornstarch

2 teaspoons orange-
flavored instant
breakfast drink

1 teaspoon salt

Pinch leaf rosemary,
crumbled

1. Cook carrots and celery in the boiling water in a
large saucepan 10 minutes, or until they are almost
tender.

2. Drain mushrooms, reserving liquid. Add mushrooms and onion to cooked vegetables.

3. Combine cornstarch and breakfast drink with reserved mushroom liquid; stir into vegetables. Add salt
and rosemary. Simmer until the sauce thickens and
bubbles.

ASPARAGUS IN MOCK BUTTER SAUCE

*Here's how to serve vegetables "swimming in butter,"
without using butter! If you like, add a few squirts of
lemon for a butterless "lemon butter"!*

Makes 2 servings at 39 calories each.

1 package (10 ounces)
frozen asparagus
spears

½ cup boiling water

1 teaspoon cornstarch

1 teaspoon imitation
butter-flavored salt

½ teaspoon parsley
flakes

2 tablespoons cold water

1. Cook asparagus spears in the boiling water in a
large saucepan 5 minutes, or until just tender.

2. Combine cornstarch, butter-flavored salt, the parsley flakes and cold water. Measure the asparagus cook-

ing liquid; there should be ½ cup (add water, if necessary). Return to saucepan with the asparagus. Stir the cornstarch mixture into cooking liquid. Simmer until sauce thickens and bubbles.

SQUASH ITALIANO

Green zucchini, simmered in tomato sauce and spicy Italian seasonings, topped with bread crumbs and cheese. At only 48 calories a serving, here's a treat that you can afford!

Makes 6 servings at 48 calories each.

1½ cups tomato sauce	each) frozen zucchini
1 teaspoon leaf oregano, crumbled	squash
1 teaspoon garlic salt	2 tablespoons grated Romano cheese
2 packages (10 ounces	1 tablespoon packaged bread crumbs

1. Combine tomato sauce, oregano and garlic salt in a large saucepan. Add the squash. Bring to boiling; cover. Lower heat; simmer for about 10 minutes, or until squash is tender.
2. Turn squash mixture into a shallow, 6-cup baking dish. Combine cheese and bread crumbs; sprinkle over squash.
3. Broil about 3 minutes, or until topping starts to brown.

QUICK ORANGE-GLAZED BEETS

This glaze is very good with canned or frozen carrots, too! The calorie content will be about the same for both of the vegetables.

Makes 4 servings at 63 calories each.

1 can (1 pound) sliced beets	marmalade (with sugar)
4 tablespoons low-calorie orange	1 tablespoon cider vinegar

1. Heat beets with their liquid in a medium-size saucepan; drain. Add marmalade and vinegar.

2. Cook, stirring gently, over low heat until the beets are glazed with sauce.

ASPARAGUS SESAME

Makes 4 servings at 35 calories each.

2 pounds asparagus or 1 package (10 ounces) frozen asparagus	2 tablespoons lemon juice
2 teaspoons sesame seeds	¼ teaspoon salt
2 teaspoons butter or margarine	¼ teaspoon liquid red-pepper seasoning

1. Wash asparagus; break off each stalk as far down as it snaps easily.

2. Cook, covered, in boiling salted water in a large skillet for 3 to 7 minutes, just until crisp-tender. Drain; remove to heated serving dish and keep warm. Brown sesame seeds in butter in skillet; add lemon juice, salt and red-pepper seasoning. Pour over cooked asparagus and garnish with lemon slices, if you wish.

BEEFY GREEN BEANS

Makes 3 servings at 25 calories each.

½ cup water
1 envelope or teaspoon
  instant beef broth

1 package (9 ounces)
frozen green beans

1. Bring water to boiling in medium-size saucepan.
Add beef broth and beans. Separate beans with a fork.
2. Heat to boiling. Reduce heat; simmer until tender.

ASPARAGUS MERINGUE

Bake at 325° for 40 minutes.
Makes 8 servings at 75 calories each.

2 packages (10 ounces
  each) frozen cut
  asparagus
1 teaspoon diet
  margarine
2 egg yolks
1 can (10½ ounces)
  condensed cream of
  asparagus soup
1 teaspoon salt

Generous dash of
  pepper
½ teaspoon dry
  mustard
Pinch of cayenne
  (*optional*)
1 tablespoon minced
  onion
3 tablespoons grated
  Parmesan cheese
3 egg whites

1. Cook asparagus according to package directions;
drain. Place in 1½-quart baking dish which has been
lightly greased with margarine.
2. Thoroughly mix yolks with the condensed soup,
salt, pepper, mustard, cayenne and onion. Pour over
asparagus; sprinkle with 2 tablespoons of the cheese.
3. Beat egg whites until stiff. Sprinkle remaining

tablespoon of cheese on top; fold in gently. Spoon over vegetable mixture.

4. Bake, uncovered, in a slow oven (325°) 40 minutes.

BROCCOLI BLUSH

Bake at 325° for 45 minutes.
Makes 8 servings at 57 calories each.

2 packages (10 ounces
 each) frozen cut
 broccoli
1 teaspoon diet
 margarine
1 container (4 ounces)
 cocktail onions,

drained *(optional)*
1 can (8 ounces)
 tomato sauce
4 tablespoons skim milk
2 eggs

1. Cook broccoli according to package directions; drain.

2. Lightly grease a shallow, 1½-quart baking dish with margarine. Add broccoli and onions.

3. Thoroughly blend tomato sauce, milk and eggs and pour over vegetables.

4. Place baking dish in a shallow pan of water. Bake in a slow oven (325°) 45 minutes, or until set.

TANGY BEET MOLD

Makes 6 servings at 35 calories each.

1 can (1 pound) sliced
 beets
1 envelope unflavored
 gelatin
½ cup water
3 tablespoons lemon
 juice

1 tablespoon wine
 vinegar
2 tablespoons minced
 onion
1 tablespoon
 horseradish
1 teaspoon salt

1. Drain beets; reserve liquid. Chop or slice beets into julienne strips.

2. Sprinkle gelatin over water in a small saucepan to soften. Add lemon juice, vinegar and ½ cup beet juice. Heat, stirring constantly, until gelatin is completely dissolved; cool.

3. Blend in onion, horseradish and salt. Chill until slightly thickened.

4. Fold in the drained beets. Pour into a 3-cup mold or individual salad molds. Chill several hours or overnight until set.

5. To unmold: Loosen salad around edge with a sharp knife. Dip mold very quickly in and out of hot water. Cover with serving plate; turn upside down; lift off mold. Garnish with lettuce leaves and cauliflowerettes.

PEAS WITH ARTICHOKE HEARTS AND MUSHROOMS

Sweet succulent peas don't have to be off limits when they share their calories with slimming artichokes and mushrooms!

Makes 8 servings at 68 calories each.

1 tablespoon vegetable oil
1 pound fresh mushrooms, sliced
2 tablespoons chopped onion
1 package (8 ounces) frozen artichoke hearts, partially thawed
1 package (10 ounces) frozen tiny green peas, partially thawed
1½ teaspoons garlic salt
Pinch pepper
1 envelope or teaspoon instant chicken broth
1 teaspoon parsley flakes
2 tablespoons water

1. Heat oil in a large, nonstick skillet; sauté the mushrooms 5 minutes. Remove mushrooms from skillet; reserve.

2. Add onion and artichoke hearts to same skillet. Sauté over high heat, stirring constantly. Add peas, garlic salt, pepper, chicken broth, parsley flakes and water; simmer 4 minutes.

3. Return mushrooms to skillet with peas and artichoke hearts; heat through. Serve at once.

BRUSSELS SPROUTS WITH YOGURT HOLLANDAISE

Here's a fuss-free Hollandaise that won't separate . . . and it's only a fraction as fattening as conventional recipes! Here it stars with tangy Brussels sprouts, but you'll enjoy it on any vegetable.

Makes 6 servings at 75 calories each.

2 packages (10 ounces each) frozen Brussels sprouts	1 tablespoon lemon juice
1 cup plain yogurt	½ teaspoon salt
2 large egg yolks	Pinch of paprika

1. Cook Brussels sprouts according to package directions, using a minimum amount of water. While vegetables cook, prepare the sauce.

2. Combine all remaining ingredients in a small saucepan (or the top of a double boiler). Cook, stirring constantly, over very low heat until thickened (do not boil). Pour sauce over hot sprouts.

APPLESAUCE-SAUERKRAUT BAKE

Here's a fragrant side dish for broiled franks or lean pork loin. If you like your sauerkraut mild, rinse it well before preparing this dish. The longer you bake it, the more un-sauer it is.

Bake at 350° for 40 minutes.
Makes 8 servings at 42 calories each.

1 can (1 pound, 11 ounces) sauerkraut, drained
1 envelope or teaspoon instant beef broth

3 tablespoons instant minced onion
1 cup unsweetened applesauce
2 teaspoons caraway seeds

1. Drain sauerkraut; rinse in cold water. Drain well.
2. Combine sauerkraut, beef broth, onion, applesauce and caraway seeds in 8-cup baking dish. Cover.
3. Bake in a moderate oven (350°) 40 minutes.

CARROT FLUFF

Bake at 350° for 45 minutes.
Makes 8 servings at 51 calories each.

3 cups cut-up carrots (about 1 pound)
3 eggs, separated
2 tablespoons snipped chives
⅛ teaspoon nutmeg

½ teaspoon salt
Generous dash of pepper
½ teaspoon diet margarine

1. Put carrots in large saucepan with water to cover. Bring to boiling over moderate heat; cook 20 minutes, or until tender; drain.

2. Combine carrots, egg yolks, chives, nutmeg, salt and pepper in container of electric blender. Whirl until well blended.

3. Beat egg white in small bowl with electric mixer, until stiff peaks form; fold into carrot mixture.

4. Lightly grease a 6-cup casserole or soufflé dish with margarine. Pile carrot mixture into casserole; set casserole in a pan of hot water. Bake in a moderate oven (350°) 45 minutes, or until thoroughly heated.

"BUTTER-BAKED" CORN ON THE COB

Bake at 350° for 20 minutes.
Makes 6 servings at 87 calories each.

6 ears of corn, shucked, or 3 packages frozen corn on the cob (2 ears to a package), thawed	6 teaspoons diet margarine ½ teaspoon butter-flavored salt ⅛ teaspoon coarse-grind pepper

1. Spread 1 teaspoon margarine on each ear; place ears on double thickness of aluminum foil. Season with salt and pepper.

2. Wrap securely; bake in moderate oven (350°) 20 minutes.

TIPSY CARROTS

Makes 8 servings at 49 calories each.

2 cans (1 pound each) small whole carrots, drained 2 tablespoons diet margarine 2 teaspoons lemon juice	1 tablespoon brown sugar substitute 4 tablespoons dry sherry 4 tablespoons sliced ripe olives

1. Combine margarine, lemon juice, brown sugar substitute and sherry in saucepan. Heat to boiling; add carrots. Cook gently 3 minutes.
2. Add olives; cook 2 minutes longer.

BARBECUED EGGPLANT

Makes 8 slices at 56 calories each.

1 large eggplant	¼ teaspoon liquid red-pepper seasoning
2 tablespoons oil	
2 tablespoons lemon juice	½ teaspoon salt
	2 tablespoons fine dry bread crumbs

1. Cut unpared eggplant into ¾-inch slices.
2. Combine oil, lemon juice, red-pepper seasoning and salt. Brush eggplant slices with mixture.
3. Place on grill 4 inches from charcoal briquets. Grill 5 to 7 minutes. Turn and brush with seasoning mixture. Grill 5 minutes. Sprinkle with crumbs; cook about 2 minutes.

CURRIED EGGPLANT

Makes 6 servings at 56 calories each.

3 tablespoons diet margarine	1 teaspoon curry powder
1 pound peeled, cubed eggplant (about 3 cups)	2 teaspoons garlic salt
	1 can (4 ounces) pimiento, drained and sliced
1 cup sliced onion	

1. Melt margarine in a large nonstick skillet over moderate heat. Add eggplant; coat thoroughly with

margarine and sauté lightly until just tender, about 8 minutes.

2. Add onions; cook until transparent but still crunchy. Stir in curry powder, garlic salt and pimiento. Cook a few minutes longer, just to heat thoroughly.

PINEAPPLE-GLAZED CARROTS

Makes 6 servings at 56 calories each.

1 pound carrots, pared and split lengthwise	Pinch of dried parsley flakes
1 can (8 ounces) crushed pineapple in juice, well drained	¼ teaspoon salt 1 teaspoon butter 1 teaspoon liquid
2 teaspoons cornstarch	sweetener

1. Place carrots in medium-size saucepan with water to cover. Bring to boiling over moderate heat; boil until tender, about 30 minutes. Drain; reserve cooking water.

2. Measure juice from pineapple; add water in which carrots were cooked to make ½ cup. Combine in saucepan with pineapple, cornstarch, parsley and salt. Heat, stirring constantly until sauce is thickened. Add butter and liquid sweetener; pour over carrots.

EASY "CANDIED" CARROTS

Makes 6 servings at 30 calories each.

2 tablespoons sugar-free maple syrup	Pinch of salt
1 teaspoon lemon juice	1 can (1 pound) sliced carrots
1 teaspoon butter	Parsley

Combine syrup, lemon juice, butter and salt in sauce-pan. Heat until butter melts. Add carrots; stir until carrots are hot and syrup is thick. Garnish with parsley.

SPINACH "CREAM CHEESE" CASSEROLE

Bake at 350° for 30 minutes.
Makes 14 servings at 73 calories each.

8 ounces Neufchâtel cheese	artichoke hearts (3 ounces)
½ cup skim milk	1 can (4 ounces) water chestnuts, sliced
4 packages (10 ounces each) frozen chopped spinach, thawed	2 tablespoons seasoned bread crumbs
6 frozen or canned	1 teaspoon salt
	⅛ teaspoon pepper

1. Soften cheese to room temperature. Add milk; whip until well blended.
2. Layer spinach, cheese-milk mixture, artichokes and water chestnuts in a 2-quart shallow casserole; sprinkle with salt and pepper; top with crumbs.
3. Bake in moderate oven (350°) 30 minutes.

BARBECUED VEGETABLE KABOBS

Makes 4 servings at 124 calories each.

2 tablespoons butter or margarine
4 tablespoons lemon juice
1 teaspoon leaf basil, crumbled
½ teaspoon ground marjoram
½ teaspoon salt
¼ teaspoon liquid red-pepper seasoning
1 medium-size cucumber, halved lengthwise, and cut into ½-inch slices

2 ribs celery cut in 8 one-inch chunks
1 can (8¼ ounces) whole beets, drained
½ pound mushrooms (cut in half if very large) or 1 can (8 ounces) whole mushrooms, drained
8 cherry tomatoes or 2 small tomatoes, quartered
4 large pitted ripe olives

1. Melt butter or margarine in a small saucepan. Add lemon juice, basil, marjoram, salt and red-pepper seasoning; reserve.

2. Thread the cucumbers on four 12-inch skewers, alternating with celery, beets and mushrooms. Place on grill 4 inches from charcoal briquets that have reached the light gray ash stage. Brush generously with butter sauce.

3. Grill 10 to 15 minutes, turning skewers occasionally and basting frequently with sauce. Just before vegetables are tender, add cherry tomatoes and olives to ends of skewers. Continue grilling until vegetables are tender.

Calorie-Wise Convenience Foods

1 tablespoon instant minced onion
  = 1 medium size onion
2 tablespoons onion flakes
  = 1 medium size onion
1 tablespoon celery flakes
  = ¼ cup fresh celery
1 tablespoon sweet pepper flakes
  = ¼ cup fresh bell peppers
⅛ teaspoon garlic powder
  = 1 clove of garlic

CHERRY TOMATOES AND ZUCCHINI

Makes 6 servings at 34 calories each.

2 medium-size zucchini
  (about 1 pound)
2 cups cherry tomatoes
1 tablespoon diet
  margarine

1 teaspoon lemon juice
¼ teaspoon basil
1 teaspoon salt
Dash of pepper

1. Scrub zucchini; slice ½ inch thick. Place in medium-size saucepan with water to cover; boil 6 minutes; drain.

2. Wash tomatoes, cut each in half. Add to zucchini.

3. Add all remaining ingredients. Cover; cook 2 minutes more. Toss thoroughly but gently.

OVEN "FRENCH-FRIED" POTATOES

Bake at 450° for 40 minutes.
Makes 8 servings at 101 calories each.

**4 large potatoes, peeled
 and cut in ¾-inch
 strips**

**2 tablespoons vegetable
 oil
2 teaspoons salt**

   1. Soak potatoes in cold water for 1 hour. Drain and
blot on paper toweling.

   2. Spread potatoes on a shallow nonstick baking pan
or cooky sheet; sprinkle with oil. Rotate potatoes to
distribute oil evenly.

   3. Bake in hot oven (450°) 40 minutes, or until
golden brown and tender. Turn frequently. Sprinkle
with salt before serving.

FLUFFY POTATOES

Makes eight ½-cup servings at 75 calories each.

**6 medium-size potatoes
 (2 pounds)
½ cup skim milk**

**1 teaspoon butter-
 flavored salt
Dash of pepper**

   1. Peel the potatoes; cut into chunks. Place in a large
saucepan with salted water to cover. Cover. Bring to
boiling over high heat. Reduce heat; cook 30 minutes,
or until tender; drain. Shake potatoes in pan over low
heat until fairly dry. Then mash thoroughly.

   2. Add milk, butter-flavored salt and pepper. Heat
gently while stirring together. Remove from heat and
whip vigorously.

POTATOES AND MUSHROOMS

Makes 10 servings at 67 calories each.

Fluffy Potatoes
**3 cans (4 ounces each)
 mushroom pieces,
 drained**

**2 tablespoons chopped
 chives**

1. After whipping potatoes, fold in the mushrooms and chives, mixing thoroughly.
2. Heat in slow oven (300°) 10 minutes.

POTATOES DUCHESSE

Bake at 450° for 10 minutes.
Makes 6 large puffs at 63 calories each.

**3 medium-size potatoes
 (1 pound)
1 teaspoon butter-
 flavored salt**

**1 egg
1 teaspoon diet
 margarine**

1. Peel potatoes; cut into chunks. Place in a large saucepan with salted water to cover. Cover; bring to boiling over high heat. Reduce heat to medium; cook 30 minutes, or until tender. Drain. Shake potatoes in pan over low heat until dry. Mash.
2. Add butter-flavored salt, milk and egg; whip thoroughly.
3. Lightly grease a baking sheet with margarine. Drop the potatoes by tablespoons onto baking sheet, making 6 large mounds; or pipe into decorative mounded swirls with a pastry tube.
4. Bake in a hot oven (450°) for 10 minutes, or until lightly browned.

BAKED STUFFED POTATOES

Bake at 450° for 1 hour.
Makes 8 servings at 95 calories each.

4 large, well-shaped
  baking potatoes
  (2 pounds)
½ cup warm skim milk
1 teaspoon dried onion
  flakes

1½ teaspoons butter-
  flavored salt
Pinch of pepper
3 tablespoons grated
  extra-sharp Cheddar
  cheese
⅛ teaspoon paprika

1. Scrub the potatoes; pierce lightly with fork. Bake
in hot oven (450°) 1 hour, or until tender. Remove;
cool.
2. Carefully slice potatoes in half; scoop out potato
pulp. Add milk, a little at a time, and whip until fluffy.
Beat in onion flakes, salt and pepper.
3. Pile into potato shells; sprinkle with cheese and
paprika. Bake in hot oven (425°) about 10 minutes to
heat.

CONFETTI SKILLET POTATOES

Makes 8 servings at 93 calories each.

6 medium-size potatoes
  (about 2 pounds)
1 medium-size onion,
  chopped (½ cup)
1 clove of garlic,
  minced
½ cup chopped parsley

1 tablespoon vegetable
  oil
1 envelope or teaspoon
  instant chicken broth
½ cup water
1 teaspoon salt

1. Pare potatoes; cut into ¼-inch slices. Place in

medium-size saucepan with water to cover. Bring to boiling; cook for 10 minutes.

2. Meanwhile, heat oil in a nonstick skillet. Add onion, garlic and parsley; sauté 2 minutes. Cover; cook over very low heat 10 minutes. Add chicken broth, water and salt. Bring to boiling.

3. Drain potatoes. Add to ingredients in skillet; toss gently together. Reduce heat; cover, and cook slowly 5 minutes longer.

Chapter 15

Party Foods

You don't have to be a social dropout just because you're watching your weight. Party foods, even the most terrifically calorific, can succumb to your special magic as a Creative Low-Calorie Cook.

Even dips! They can be incredibly poundage-potent, or so calorie-shy they barely count. Hostesses love them for their one-handed, fuss-free, help-yourself ease—and guests do, too. They're on hand everywhere, from the swankiest soiree to the most spontaneous, so it's really worthwhile becoming a skinny-dip expert. That way you can eliminate the extraneous calories at your own parties and be a more discriminate nibbler at somebody else's. And if it's an informal just-us-friends fete you're invited to, you can always help out with a pretty tray of your own special dips and dunkers . . . most harried hostesses will think you're simply a dear to offer!

How to "De-Calorize" Your Favorite Dips

Everyone has a favorite dip, either begged, borrowed or maybe even bungled into. The pinches of curry or sprinklings of soy that make your dip unique don't count for much, calorie-wise. It's the base that's usually frightfully fattening.

Most dips start out with sour cream at close to 500 calories a cupful or cream cheese at 850 per eight-ounce package. Sometimes mayonnaise is also larded in, something to really think twice about, at 1,600 calories a cupful! Your challenge is to duplicate these special flavors and textures with slimmer stand-ins. Here's how:

For a Sour-Cream-Flavored Dip Base

	Calories per	
	Tablespoon	Cup
Instead of sour cream USE:	25	485
Packaged sour cream mix blended with skim milk OR:	15	244
Mock Sour Cream (recipe follows) OR:	11	176
Unflavored yogurt	8	125

MOCK SOUR CREAM: A magic stand-in you whip up with your blender! Just add one quarter cupful of buttermilk to one cup low-fat creamed cottage cheese. Blend on high speed, scraping down the container sides often, until the mixture is smooth and creamy. So close in taste and texture you'll use it on fresh fruits or baked potatoes, or in any recipe that doesn't call for baking. (This "sour cream" can't take the heat!) Makes 1 cup at 176 calories.

Which is better? For the hostess in a hurry, yogurt can't be beat for a mix-it-up and dig-in dip, and it's the least caloried of all. The packaged sour-cream-sauce convenience mixes are great to have on hand for drop-in entertaining: You simply tear open a packet and mix it with skim milk, instead of the whole milk the directions call for. In your supermarket's gravy-mix section, sour cream comes in tear-open packets that need no refrigeration. (Packets make ⅔ cup. The calorie count for one cupful is given for comparison purposes.)

When nothing but the real thing will do, you may find sour half-and-half in some supermarkets. It's real sour cream with part of the butterfat removed, thus one third lower in calories! It's a much better choice for calorie-counters than the synthetic sour-cream substitutes. The synthetics have so much oil they're almost as fattening as the real thing (and the oil is often coconut oil, off limits for cholesterol watchers).

For a Creamy or Cream-Cheese-y Dip

For one without the tartness of sour cream, the most often used dip base is cream cheese mixed with milk. But two 3-ounce packages of cream cheese and four tablespoons of milk add up to a cupful of dip base that's 680 calories, or 43 calories a tablespoon! You can create an equally smooth nonsour dip base without all that softening and mixing, just by opening an 8-ounce container of part-skim ricotta. As is, ricotta has the perfect taste and texture for making a dip that's only 320 calories a cupful or 20 calories a tablespoon—hard to believe because ricotta has the velvety richness of a heavy cream that's thick enough to eat with a spoon! It's popular in Italian cuisine, but its cheesy flavor doesn't really develop until it is baked.

For a true cream-cheese flavor, use Neufchâtel, the part-skim twin sister of cream cheese. Just soften one 8-ounce package to room temperature, then blend in five tablespoons of skim milk for a Cream Cheese Dip that's only 606 calories a cupful or 31 calories per tablespoon. Not low-calories exactly, but lower than cream cheese.

For a Mayonnaise-Flavored Dip

It's easy to make any dip taste as if it's been dolloped with gobs of the rich stuff! Simply fork-mash a hard-cooked egg yolk and blend it in, along with a generous squirt of lemon juice and a pinch of celery salt. All that squanderously rich yolky flavor counts for only 60 calories, though it tastes like a whole 1,600-calorie-cupful of mayonnaise.

Easy-Do Dip Ideas

To make a variety of dips the easy way, simply mix up a whole blenderful of dip base, then measure out one-cup portions into several containers. Spice up each one differently, then refrigerate. Dips are best made well ahead of time so flavors can blend, and dry ingredients can soften. The crunchy add-ins, such as bacon bits, are best stirred in just before serving. Stage your dips dramatically in pretty bowls and dress them up with such eye-feasting garnishes as carrot curls and parsley fringes. Dips served with crunchy vegetables are particularly inviting in "greengrocer" bowls, the containers you fashion from the vegetables themselves—pepper cups, for example, or a bright purple hollowed eggplant half!

Try these delectable combinations. They're all based on one cupful of Mock Sour Cream, but they work equally well with any of the other dip-base suggestions. The calorie counts are for Mock Sour Cream unless otherwise specified.

Mock Sour Cream Variations

To one cup of Mock Sour Cream add your choice of the following:

CALIFORNIA DIP: 1 tablespoon dry onion flakes and 1 envelope or teaspoon instant beef broth. (The popular "onion soup dip," slimmed down. This combination adds only 35 calories, while the equivalent in onion soup mix weighs in at anywhere from 70 to 90 calories, depending on the brand.) Over 1 cup: 12 calories per tablespoon.

PIMIENTO DIP: 1 tablespoon chili sauce, 1 tablespoon chopped pimiento and ¼ teaspoon salt. Over 1 cup: 12 calories per tablespoon.

GARLIC DIP: 1/16 teaspoon garlic powder, 1 teaspoon salt and 1 tablespoon dried parsley flakes. Makes 1 cup: 11 calories per tablespoon.

ROQUEFORT DIP: 2 tablespoons crumbled Roquefort cheese, ½ teaspoon salt and ½ teaspoon Worcestershire sauce. Makes 1 cup: 15 calories per tablespoon.

CHEDDAR DIP: ¼ cup (2 ounces) shredded extra-sharp Cheddar, 1 tablespoon parsley flakes, ½ teaspoon salt. Makes 1¼ cups: 20 calories per tablespoon.

CRUNCHY BACON DIP: 1 teaspoon vinegar, 1 teaspoon garlic salt. Just before serving, stir in 2 tablespoons bacon-flavored vegetable protein product. Over 1 cup: 15 calories per tablespoon.

SEAFOOD DIP: 4 tablespoons of catsup, 2 tablespoons lemon juice, ¼ teaspoon liquid red-pepper seasoning, 1 teaspoon Worcestershire sauce, 2 teaspoons grated onion, 1 teaspoon of horseradish and ½ teaspoon salt. Makes 1½ cups: 11 calories per tablespoon.

DILLY DIP: 1 fork-mashed, hard-cooked egg yolk. Blend well and add ½ tablespoon lemon juice, 1 teaspoon dried dill weed, ¼ teaspoon celery salt and 1 teaspoon grated onion. Makes 1 cup: 15 calories per tablespoon.

CURRY DIP I: ½ teaspoon curry powder and 1 tablespoon chutney. Makes 1 cup: 12 calories per tablespoon.

CURRY DIP II: 1 teaspoon curry powder, ½ teaspoon prepared horseradish, ¼ teaspoon salt and 1 teaspoon sugar. Makes 1 cup: 12 calories per tablespoon.

DEVILED HAM DIP: One 2¼-ounce can deviled ham and 1 teaspoon prepared horseradish. Makes 1¼ cups: 18 calories per tablespoon.

Easy Low-Calorie Dips From Instant Mixes

Don't overlook packaged instant mixes for dip ease. Instant onion, horseradish, dill, Caesar, blue cheese—these are some of the intriguing possibilities. Most add only about 50 calories per cupful of dip base. With low-calorie MOCK SOUR CREAM, you create a dip that's only 12 calories instead of 23 calories (sour cream) or 30 calories (cream cheese) called for on the package directions. Salad dressing mixes vary your repertoire even further. Cheese Garlic, Green Goddess, Garlic, Caesar, Parmesan—a half-packet is just about right for a cupful of dip base and adds only 25 to 45 calories!

Chips and Dippers

Be sure to have lots of safe nibbles fresh from the greengrocer: Crunchy green pepper strips and carrot sticks; celery stalks in crunchy two-inch "scoopers," cucumbers in chips or strips, long white icicle radishes or red radish rosebuds, raw turnip fingers, raw mushroom slices, or snow-white cauliflowerettes.

Don't forget some dippers from a can: Crunchy water chestnuts sliced into chips, pickle slices, mini-pickles and other pickled vegetables on party picks. Fruit dippers, too: Pineapple fingers, either fresh or from a can; unpeeled apple or pear cubes (squirted with lemon to keep them white), mandarin orange sections or speared honeydew cubes.

OPEN CUCUMBER SANDWICHES

Makes 18 open sandwiches at 18 calories each.

4 slices diet white bread	½ teaspoon salt
1 medium-size cucumber	4 large radishes
	4 stuffed olives
1 tablespoon minced onion	1 ounce Neufchâtel cheese

1. Cut 4 circles from each slice of bread using a round cooky cutter or small juice glass. Stack rounds with wax paper between each; wrap securely and chill in freezer 30 minutes.

2. Pare cucumber, leaving some peel for color; cut into ⅛-inch slices. Layer in medium-size bowl; add onion and salt. Cover; chill until needed.

3. Cut radishes and olives into 4 slices each. Drain cucumber of any accumulated liquid.

4. Spread each bread round with a thin layer of the Neufchâtel cheese; add cucumber, radish and olive slices. Serve immediately or store in refrigerator until ready to use.

SHRIMP WITH DIPPING SAUCE

Make about 48 shrimp with sauce at 11 calories each.

1 package (16 ounces) frozen medium-size shrimp, peeled and deveined	1 teaspoon Worcestershire sauce
	Dash of liquid hot-pepper seasoning
1 tablespoon curry powder	2 cloves of garlic, crushed
1 tablespoon cornstarch	4 tablespoons dietetic catsup
1 tablespoon water	½ cup condensed beef broth
1 teaspoon soy sauce	
1 teaspoon prepared mustard	

1. Cook shrimp according to package directions; add curry powder to cooking water. Drain; chill.

2. Blend cornstarch and water; reserve. Combine soy sauce, mustard, Worcestershire sauce, hot-pepper seasoning, garlic, catsup and broth in saucepan. Bring to boiling; add cornstarch and water. Reduce heat to medium; cook and stir until sauce thickens. Cool.

3. Serve at room temperature as a dipping accompaniment to the cold shrimp.

Note: Sauce may be made ahead and stored for a day or two in refrigerator.

ASPARAGUS ROLL-UPS

Bake at 425° for 10 minutes.
Makes 16 roll-ups at 20 calories each.

1 package (10 ounces) frozen asparagus spears	¼ teaspoon salt
	⅛ teaspoon pepper
	¼ teaspoon paprika
4 slices diet-thin bread	1 teaspoon leaf basil,
2 tablespoons diet margarine	crumbled

1. Cook asparagus according to package directions; drain.

2. Remove crusts from the bread. Flatten slices with a rolling pin; cut each into 4 square quarters.

3. Melt margarine in small saucepan; add salt, pepper and paprika. Brush margarine on bread squares.

4. Stir basil into remaining margarine. Brush other side of bread squares.

5. Place 1 asparagus spear diagonally on each bread square. Roll up carefully; place seam-side down on baking sheet.

6. Bake in hot oven (425°) 10 minutes, or until bread is slightly toasty. Serve hot.

JOLLY WINE PUNCH

Makes 24 half-cup servings at 79 calories each.

5 cups freshly squeezed
  orange juice (10 to 12
  oranges)
¾ cup freshly squeezed
  lemon juice
2 bottles (12 ounces

each) low-calorie
lemon-lime
carbonated beverage
1 bottle (1 quart)
muscatel wine
Fresh mint sprigs

1. Chill all ingredients. Mix together and serve in large punch bowl.
2. Garnish with lemon and orange slices topped with mint sprigs, if you wish.

CLAM-STUFFED MUSHROOMS

Bake at 425° for 10 minutes.
Makes 16 stuffed mushrooms at 34 calories each.

1 can (about 8 ounces)
  minced clams
½ cup instant mashed
  potatoes
2 teaspoons oregano
2 teaspoons leaf basil,
  crumbled
½ teaspoon instant
  garlic powder

2 tablespoons chopped
parsley
1 tablespoon lemon
juice
1 tablespoon grated
Romano cheese
16 small mushroom
caps

1. Drain clams; pour juice into a small saucepan. Heat juice to boiling; remove from heat and stir in potatoes. Let stand 1 minute.
2. Add the clams, oregano, basil, garlic powder, parsley and lemon juice to potatoes. Mix thoroughly.

4. Spoon mixture into mushroom caps. Sprinkle top of each with cheese. Bake in hot oven (425°) 10 minutes.

PUNGENT CARROT AND BEAN STICKS

Makes about 100 sticks at 2 calories each.

4 medium-size carrots
½ pound fresh green
   beans
½ cup cider vinegar
1 cup water
½ teaspoon salt

1 teaspoon minced
   onion
1 teaspoon mustard
   seeds
1 clove of garlic,
   crushed
1 tablespoon dillweed

1. Pare and trim carrots. Put in water to cover in medium-size saucepan. Bring to boiling; cook 3 minutes. Remove from heat; cool and cut into 4-inch julienne strips.
2. Wash and trim green beans (leave whole).
3. Combine vinegar, water, salt, onion, mustard seeds, garlic and dillweed in a saucepan. Bring to boiling; add carrots and beans. Reduce heat; simmer 5 minutes. Remove from heat; cool.
4. Cover; chill 1 to 2 days. Serve cold as nibblers.

COTTAGE DEVILED EGGS

Makes 8 egg halves at 45 calories each.

4 hard-cooked eggs,
   shelled and halved
4 tablespoons low-fat
   cream-style cottage
   cheese
¼ teaspoon salt

Pinch of pepper
Pinch of dry mustard
½ teaspoon liquid
   red-pepper seasoning
1 tablespoon skim milk

Remove the yolks from eggs; mash with all remaining ingredients. Heap egg-yolk mixture into whites. Chill.

QUICK ONION TART

Makes 8 servings at 127 calories each.

2 medium-size onions, sliced
1 tablespoon butter or margarine
4 slices protein bread
1 cup low-fat cream-style cottage cheese

3 eggs
1 can (13 ounces) evaporated skimmed milk
1 teaspoon salt
⅛ teaspoon pepper

1. Heat butter or margarine in skillet. Add onions; sauté until lightly browned and soft. Remove from heat.
2. Stir onions into cottage cheese until well-blended.
3. Line 10-inch pie plate with bread. Spread cheese-onion mixture on top.
4. Slightly beat eggs, milk, salt and pepper in medium-size bowl; pour over bread, cheese and onions. Bake in a moderate oven (375°) 30 minutes, or until lightly brown.

RIBBON SANDWICHES

Makes 36 party sandwiches at 19 calories each.

2 hard-cooked eggs, shelled
Pinch of salt
Pinch of pepper
1 tablespoon sweet pickle relish

1 can (3¼ ounces) sockeye salmon
2 tablespoons low-calorie imitation mayonnaise
9 slices diet thin bread

1. Mash eggs with a fork and mix with salt, pepper, relish and 1 tablespoon of the mayonnaise.

2. Drain and flake salmon, removing any bones and skin. Combine with remaining mayonnaise.

3. Trim crusts from bread. Spread 3 slices with egg mixture and 3 with salmon mixture. Make 3 sandwich stacks as follows: Place egg mixture slice on top of salmon slice; top egg mixture with plain slice of bread. Repeat until you have 3 stacks of 3 layers each. Wrap; chill 2 hours.

4. Cut each sandwich in half with a sharp slicing knife or electric carving knife. Cut each half again, into thirds. Stack all on end. (If not served immediately, wrap securely and cover with a damp towel or wrap carefully in freezer wrap and freeze until ready to use.)

GINGER MELON BALLS

Makes four ½-cup servings at 47 calories each.

1 medium-size honeydew melon	2 tablespoons lemon juice
¼ teaspoon ground ginger	Dash of liquid sugar substitute

1. Halve melon; scoop out seeds. Cut out balls with a melon-ball cutter or ½ teaspoon of a measuring-spoon set.

2. Place melon balls in a medium-size serving bowl. Toss with ginger, lemon juice and sugar substitute. Chill until ready to serve.

MOCK GUACAMOLE DIP

Makes 1½ cups at 9 calories per tablespoon.

1 package (10 ounces) frozen broccoli in cheese sauce	2 tablespoons lemon juice
4 tablespoons plain yogurt	1 teaspoon minced onion
1 tablespoon grated Romano cheese	Pinch of curry powder Pinch of pepper

1. Prepare broccoli according to label directions.
2. Combine cooked broccoli with all remaining ingredients in the container of electric blender. Cover; blend for 30 seconds, or until smooth.
3. Chill. Serve with crackers or raw vegetables.
Note: Broccoli will not darken as avocado guacamole does.

LIVER PÂTÉ

Makes 2 cups at 22 calories per tablespoon.

1 teaspoon diet margarine	1 stalk of celery
1 pound calf's liver, cooked	1 clove of garlic
1 medium-size onion, peeled	2 tablespoons lemon juice
	½ teaspoon salt
	Pinch of pepper

1. Heat margarine in nonstick skillet; sauté liver about 5 minutes on each side or just until pink inside.
2. Put liver, onion, celery and the garlic through meat grinder.
3. Combine chopped ingredients with lemon juice, salt and pepper in a medium-size bowl. Blend until

smooth. Cover; chill thoroughly before serving. Garnish with fresh parsley.

CRAB-CHEESE DIP

Makes 4 cups at 24 calories per tablespoon.

2 cans (about 7½ ounces each) crab meat
1 carton (8 ounces) cream-style cottage cheese
2 tablespoons mayonnaise or salad dressing
1 tablespoon prepared mustard
1 tablespoon lemon juice
½ teaspoon salt
Parsley sprigs
Twisted lemon slices

1. Drain crab meat. Select reddest pieces for garnish; reserve.
2. Combine remaining crab meat with cottage cheese, mayonnaise, mustard, lemon juice and salt in container of electric blender. Cover; blend until mixture is smooth and creamy. Pour into a dipping bowl; chill at least half an hour before serving.
3. Garnish with the remaining crab meat, parsley sprigs and twisted lemon slices, if you wish.

Chapter 16

Decalorized Desserts

Wouldn't a slimming dinner seem more satisfying if you had a Grand Finale Dessert to look forward to? Like a Creamy Chocolate Angel Cake for example? For all its chocolate creaminess, it weighs in at a mere 124 calories a serving. If you're a Creative Low-Calorie Cook, you can trim down the calorie count of any cake you love . . . or any pie, pudding, parfait or plateful of cookies.

Of course, even slimmed-down cookies are fattening if eaten to excess. But a dessert to look forward to, even if only a cooky or two, can help keep you in line at dinnertime. All get-thin-and-stay-there programs work by eating fewer calories than you need to stay fat. The idea behind Creative Low-Calorie Cooking is to get more eating pleasure from fewer calories than you would with conventional cooking techniques. This chapter shows you how to do it without giving up the fun of making desserts.

Tips for Decalorizing
Your Favorite Desserts

• Experiment with cutting down on sugar . . . often by as much as one-half the amount called for in most standard recipes! If there are other sweet ingredients

276

(molasses, honey, raisins, fruit, etc.), you'll never miss the extra sugar calories!

• Heighten the impression of sweetness in low-sugar snacks by adding extra vanilla. Go light on sour or bitter ingredients such as lemon or chocolate . . . they need extra sugar to compensate.

• Add sweetness, without calories, by using sugar substitutes in place of part of the sugar. Replace one-third to one-half the sugar with liquid or granulated sugar substitute. (Check the label for equivalents.) When you use part-sugar and part-substitute there's no tip-off aftertaste!

• Diabetics and others on sugar-free diets can even experiment with totally sugar-free desserts, replacing all the sugar with sugar substitute. However, cakes, cookies and other baked goods won't be as large or as well-browned as in conventional recipes. For best results, experiment with recipes calling for other ingredients that give bulk (nuts, fruit, coconut, etc. . . . if permitted on your diet).

• Experiment by cutting down on the amount of shortening, butter, margarine or other fats—they cost you about 1,600 calories a cupful. Choose a low-fat recipe to begin with, or cut down by about one-third to one-half. To compensate, add a few tablespoons of water, if necessary.

• Diet margarine (half the calories and half the fat) will automatically slim down a dessert recipe. With cookies, it creates a delightfully soft, chewy, cakey texture because of the extra moisture. If you substitute diet margarine, cut down on the other liquids.

• Concentrate on desserts that couple their calories with nutritional plusses: protein-rich eggs, low-fat cheese and eggs for example or vitamin-happy fruits and juices.

• Naturally, if a recipe calls for milk you'll make it skim milk (half the calories). If a recipe calls for sour cream, use buttermilk or yogurt instead.

• Chocolate is fattening no matter what you do. But you can minimize the calorie cost by using cocoa in place of solid chocolate . . . 3 tablespoons (60 calories) equal one ounce (150 calories) but the less you use, the less sugar you'll need. Carob powder (found in health food stores) is a natural substitute that has chocolate's flavor but not its bitterness, so you need less sugar to sweeten a carob-chocolate cookie.

• Soy flour, also found in health food stores (or the health food section of your supermarket) can be used to replace up to one-third the flour in any recipe. (For example: ⅓ cup soy flour and ⅔ cup all-purpose flour in place of 1 cup regular flour.) Soy flour is slightly lower in calories and carbohydrates but much richer in protein. Soy protein-boosted baked goods are far more filling.

• Some desserts are so fattening that they defy de-calorization . . . pound cake, brownies, fudge bars, iced layer cakes, rich shortbread-type cookies and the like. With so many other low-calorie desserts to pick from, why concentrate on what you can't have!

APPLE-CHEESE BAKE

Bake at 350° for 30 minutes.
Makes 8 servings at 75 calories each.

1 can (1 pound, 4 ounces) unsweetened sliced apples, drained	½ teaspoon cinnamon
	Pinch of salt
3 tablespoons sugar	½ cup grated American cheese (2 ounces)
1½ tablespoons all-purpose flour	

1. Arrange apple slices in a shallow 6-cup baking dish. Combine sugar, flour, cinnamon and salt; sprinkle over apples.
2. Bake in moderate oven (350°) 25 minutes, or until apples are hot.

3. Top with cheese; continue baking, 5 minutes, or until the cheese is thoroughly melted.

CREAM PUFFS

Bake at 375° for 45 minutes.
Makes 9 pastry shells at 63 calories each.

½ cup water
2 tablespoons
  margarine

½ cup sifted all-
  purpose flour
½ teaspoon salt
2 eggs

1. Mix water and margarine in a medium-size saucepan; heat to boiling. Add flour and salt and beat together. Remove from heat; beat in eggs, one at a time, until all ingredients are blended.
2. Use a measuring tablespoon to drop heaping spoonfuls of dough onto nonstick cooky sheet. (Use 2 tablespoons for each puff.)
3. Bake in moderate oven (375°) for 45 minutes. Cool thoroughly before filling with 2½ tablespoons custard filling (see recipe below). Filled puff—108 calories.

CUSTARD FILLING

Makes 1½ cups at 22 calories per tablespoon.

1½ tablespoons
  cornstarch
¼ teaspoon salt
4 tablespoons sugar

2 egg yolks, beaten
1½ cups skim milk
½ teaspoon vanilla

1. Combine the cornstarch with the salt and sugar in a medium-size saucepan. Stir in the beaten egg yolks.

Gradually add the skim milk, stirring after each addition.

2. Cook, stirring constantly, over very low heat (or in a double boiler), until the mixture mounds slightly when dropped from a spoon.

3. Stir in vanilla; cool. Serve plain or use as filling for Cream Puffs (see recipe on page 279).

CHOCOLATE SOUFFLÉ

Bake at 350° for 45 minutes.
Makes 10 servings at 93 calories each.

4 whole eggs
1 egg white
1 container (8 ounces) vanilla yogurt
4 tablespoons dry cocoa powder
½ teaspoon vanilla

2 tablespoons Creme de Cacao
Pinch of salt
6 tablespoons sugar
½ teaspoon diet margarine

1. Separate the four eggs. Lightly beat the yolks; mix in yogurt, cocoa, vanilla and Creme de Cacao.

2. Beat 5 egg whites in bowl of electric mixer until frothy; add salt. Beat until stiff. Beat in 5 tablespoons of the sugar, 1 tablespoon at a time. Continue beating until stiff peaks form.

3. Gradually fold yolk mixture into egg whites.

4. Lightly grease a deep 2-quart casserole or soufflé dish with margarine; sprinkle greased dish with remaining 1 tablespoon of sugar. Spoon in the soufflé mixture. Place baking dish in a shallow pan of hot water; bake in moderate oven (350°) 45 minutes. Serve immediately.

"CREAM CHEESE" PASTRIES

Bake at 425° for 10 minutes.
Makes 30 pastries at 31 calories each.

2 tablespoons butter	¾ cup sifted all-purpose flour
2 tablespoons diet margarine	6 tablespoons low-calorie preserves
4 ounces imitation cream cheese or Neufchâtel cheese	

1. Have butter room temperature. Add margarine, cheese and flour; blend thoroughly until mixture forms a soft dough.

2. Place dough on a large sheet of wax paper; cover with second sheet of wax paper. Roll dough ⅛ inch thick between the 2 sheets. Chill in refrigerator 20 minutes.

3. Peel off wax paper. Cut dough into 2-inch squares. Spread ½ teaspoon of preserves on each square. Fold corners to middle to enclose the preserves; overlap ends and pinch together.

4. Place pastries on an ungreased baking sheet. Bake in hot oven (425°) 10 minutes, or until golden. Cool slightly before removing from baking sheet.

Cakes

CREAMY CHOCOLATE ANGEL CAKE

Bake at 350° for 40 minutes.
Makes 16 servings at 124 calories each.

¾ cup sifted cake flour
¼ cup unsweetened
    cocoa
½ cup sugar
10 egg whites
    (1¼ cups)
¼ teaspoon salt
1 teaspoon cream of
    tartar

½ cup sugar
½ teaspoon vanilla
1½ tablespoons liquid
    sugar substitute
3 envelopes (1¼ ounces
    each) low-calorie
    whipped topping mix
Green grapes
Strawberries

1. Sift flour, cocoa and ½ cup of the sugar onto wax paper.
2. Beat egg whites with the salt and cream of tartar in large bowl of electric mixer until they are very foamy and begin to hold a shape. Gradually beat in remaining ½ cup sugar. Continue beating until stiff peaks form. Beat in the vanilla and liquid sugar substitute.
3. Gently fold the flour mixture into the egg whites, a few tablespoons at a time. Turn into an ungreased 9-inch spring form pan. Carefully cut through batter with a spatula to avoid air pockets.
4. Bake in moderate oven (350°) 40 minutes, or until surface of cake is dry and center springs back when lightly pressed with fingertip. Invert cake in pan on wire rack. Let stand until cold.
5. Carefully loosen cake from side of pan; remove side. Loosen from bottom of pan; split crosswise into 3 layers.
6. Prepare whipped topping mix following label direc-

tions. Spread topping between layers and on top of cake. Leave sides unfrosted. Garnish top of cake with grape and strawberry halves.

QUICK GINGERBREAD WITH ORANGE ICING

Makes 12 servings at 185 calories each.

1 package gingerbread cake mix

2 packages (3 ounces each) Neufchâtel cheese

1 tablespoon warm water or orange juice

4 tablespoons 10X (confectioners' powdered) sugar

3 teaspoons liquid sweetener

1 teaspoon grated orange or lemon rind

1. Prepare gingerbread according to package directions. When cool, split crosswise into 2 layers.
2. Cream the cheese with water or juice. Blend in sugar, liquid sweetener and orange or lemon rind.
3. Spread top of 1 gingerbread layer with frosting; assemble the layers; frost the top.

GOLD AND WHITE ANGEL CAKE

Bake at 300° for 1¼ hours.
Makes 12 servings at 76 calories each.

6 egg whites
½ teaspoon cream
   of tartar
Dash of salt
½ cup granulated sugar
Granulated sugar
   substitute to equal
   4 tablespoons sugar
3 egg yolks

1 teaspoon orange juice
½ teaspoon lemon juice
½ teaspoon grated
   lemon peel
   (optional)
⅔ cup sifted cake flour
¼ teaspoon almond
   extract
¼ teaspoon vanilla
   extract

1. Beat egg whites, cream of tartar and salt in a large nonplastic bowl, until stiff peaks form. Combine the sugar and sugar substitute; sprinkle over the beaten whites gradually, beating well after each addition.

2. In another large bowl beat egg yolks until thick and light-colored. Mix in orange juice, lemon juice and peel.

3. Fold half of the egg whites into the yolk mixture.

4. Sprinkle ⅓ cup of the cake flour over the top of the remaining egg white mixture and fold in gently but thoroughly. Fold in extracts.

5. Sprinkle the remaining ⅓ cup of flour over the egg yolk mixture; fold in.

6. Alternately transfer the 2 mixtures to an ungreased angel cake tube pan (10-inch size), for a marbled effect. Tap the filled pan sharply once or twice on a countertop to settle the batter. Bake in a slow oven (300°) 1¼ hours. Invert cake in pan on wire rack; cool. Remove pan.

Cookies

27-CALORIE PROTEIN-RAISIN GEMS

Bake at 375° for 8 minutes.
Makes 5 dozen cookies at 27 calories each.

¾ cup sifted all-
    purpose flour
⅓ cup sifted low-fat
    soy flour
½ teaspoon baking
    soda
½ teaspoon salt
½ cup (½ an 8-ounce
    container) diet
    margarine

5 tablespoons firmly
    packed brown sugar
Sugar substitute to
    equal 8 tablespoons
    sugar
1 teaspoon vanilla
1 egg
1 cup raisins

1. Sift the flours, baking soda and salt onto wax paper.

2. Beat the diet margarine, brown sugar, sugar substitute vanilla and eggs until blended.

3. Add sifted dry ingredients to margarine mixture; mix well. Stir in raisins.

4. Use a measuring teaspoon to drop level spoonfuls of the dough on a cooky sheet.

5. Bake in a moderate oven (375°) for 8 minutes. Remove from cooky sheets; cool on paper toweling.

32-CALORIE APRICOT PINWHEELS

Bake at 375° for 12 minutes.
Makes 7 dozen cookies at 32 calories each.

1 cup dried apricots,
  finely chopped
½ cup boiling water
2½ cups sifted all-
  purpose flour
½ teaspoon baking
  powder
10 tablespoons butter

or margarine,
  softened
¼ cup firmly packed
  brown sugar
Sugar substitute to
  equal 4 tablespoons
  sugar
6 tablespoons cold water

1. Combine the apricots and boiling water in small bowl; allow to stand until most of water is absorbed. Drain.

2. Sift flour and baking powder into mixing bowl.

3. Beat butter or margarine, brown sugar, sugar substitute and water until well blended; add to flour mixture. Blend with a fork until the dough forms a ball.

4. Place the dough on wax paper; flatten slightly. Wrap in the wax paper; chill in freezer 20 minutes.

5. Roll out the dough on a floured surface to form 10x24-inch rectangle. Spread drained apricots over dough. Roll up the dough from the longer side to form a 24-inch-long roll; cut in half. Wrap each roll tightly in wax paper. Chill in refrigerator 3 hours or overnight.

6. Cut the rolls into ⅜-inch-thick slices. Place on nonstick cooky sheets.

7. Bake in a moderate oven (375°) for 12 minutes. Let the cookies cool on paper toweling.

21-CALORIE PEANUT BUTTER COOKIES

Bake at 375° for 8 minutes.
Makes 5 dozen cookies at 21 calories each.

⅔ cup sifted all-
    purpose flour
½ teaspoon baking
    soda
½ teaspoon baking
    powder
3 tablespoons butter
  or margarine,
  softened

4 tablespoons peanut
    butter
2 tablespoons firmly
    packed brown sugar
Sugar substitute to
    equal 4 tablespoons
    sugar
1 teaspoon vanilla
2 eggs, beaten

1. Sift flour, baking soda and the baking powder onto wax paper.

2. Beat butter or margarine, peanut butter, brown sugar and sugar substitute together. Add vanilla and eggs; beat until fluffy.

3. Add sifted dry ingredients to peanut butter mixture; mix well.

4. Use a measuring teaspoon to drop level spoonfuls of cooky dough on nonstick cooky sheets.

5. Bake in a moderate oven (375°) for 8 minutes. Let the cookies cool on paper toweling.

33-CALORIE TOLL HOUSE COOKIES

Bake at 375° for 8 minutes.
Makes about 100 cookies at 33 calories each.

2¼ cups sifted all-
    purpose flour
1 teaspoon baking soda
1 teaspoon salt
1 cup (8-ounce
    container) diet
    margarine
⅔ cup firmly packed
    brown sugar

Sugar substitute to
    equal ¾ cup sugar
2½ teaspoons vanilla
2 eggs
½ cup (½ a 6-ounce
    package) semisweet
    chocolate pieces
½ cup chopped walnuts

1. Sift flour, baking soda and salt onto wax paper.
2. Beat the diet margarine, brown sugar, sugar substitute, vanilla and eggs until blended.
3. Add sifted dry ingredients to margarine mixture. Stir in chocolate pieces and walnuts.
4. Use a measuring teaspoon to drop level spoonfuls of the dough on a cooky sheet.
5. Bake in a moderate oven (375°) for 8 minutes, or until cookies are golden brown. Remove from cooky sheets; cool on paper toweling.

28-CALORIE BUTTERSCOTCH COOKIES

Bake at 375° for 8 minutes.
Makes 3 dozen cookies at 28 calories each.

1 cup sifted all-purpose
flour
½ teaspoon baking
powder
½ teaspoon salt
3 tablespoons butter or
margarine, softened
2 tablespoons firmly
packed brown sugar

1 envelope (½ a 2⅛-
ounce package) low-
calorie butterscotch
pudding and pie
filling mix
1 egg
½ teaspoon vanilla

1. Sift flour, baking powder and salt onto wax paper.
2. Beat together butter or margarine and sugar. Add pudding mix; blend well. Add egg and vanilla; beat until fluffy. Blend in sifted dry ingredients.
3. Shape dough into a roll 1½ inches in diameter on wax paper. Wrap tightly in the wax paper. Chill in the freezer 30 minutes, or until firm enough to slice.
4. Cut roll into ⅛-inch slices. Place on nonstick cooky sheets.
5. Bake in a moderate oven (375°) 8 minutes, or until cookies are browned on the edges. Cool on some paper toweling.

Pies

Pie-making Tips

• Piecrust pastry is the most calorific part of any pie; have it well-chilled so you can roll it out extra thin. Discard the surplus—the calories you don't bake won't count! Deep-dish and single-crust pies are much lower in calories, too!

• Fruit is the least fattening part of a pie, so be super-generous with the filling. A pie that towers with apples looks extra luxurious, but it's actually less fattening.

• Sugar substitutes also can really help to rescue a pie from the forbidden list. You may not care for a completely sugarless pie, unless dictated by a no-sugar diet, but the trick of using part sugar and part substitute can drastically alter the calorie count without affecting the flavor. Half-and-half is a good base for experimenting—for dieters and nondieters!

• Unlike sugar, spice adds everything nice but practically no calories, so spice up a pie to suit yourself. A touch of vanilla can heighten the impression of sugar-sweetness while such extracts and flavorings as orange, lemon, brandy or rum can really turn on the flavor.

• Do watch out for gratuitous dabs of butter or margarine stuck into pies for no good reason. A tablespoon is 100 calories, and it's easy to add many times that amount with no noticeable flavor effect.

• Well-fruited pie needs less thickener. Flour is 28 calories per tablespoon and cornstarch 29, but cornstarch is a better choice because you need only half as much.

CHOCOLATE SWIRL PIE

Thaw-and-serve whipped topping doubles for calorific heavy cream in this well-marbled pie.

Makes 8 servings at 151 calories each or 10 servings at 120 calories each.

1 envelope (1 ounce) low-calorie chocolate pudding and pie filling	2 cups skim milk
	1½ cups thawed, frozen nondairy whipped topping
1 envelope unflavored gelatin	Low-Calorie Graham Cracker Pie Shell
Pinch of salt	

1. Combine the pudding mix, gelatin and salt in a medium-size saucepan. Add the skim milk; stir until mixture is well blended.

2. Cook over medium heat, stirring constantly, until mixture thickens and bubbles. Remove from heat; cover surface with wax paper. Cool.

3. Remove wax paper; stir pudding until smooth. Swirl in whipped topping; turn into pie shell. Refrigerate about 3 hours, or until set.

LOW-CALORIE GRAHAM CRACKER PIE SHELL

Bake at 400° for 5 minutes.
Makes 1 nine-inch pie shell.
Total calories: 524.

3 tablespoons *soft* diet margarine	1 cup packaged graham cracker crumbs

1. Blend margarine and crumbs thoroughly, using a fork. Press onto bottom and sides of a 9-inch pie plate.

2. Bake in hot oven (400°) 5 minutes. Cool before filling.

EASY LOW-CALORIE BANANA PIE

Here's a blender-easy dessert that's made in minutes with the aid of instant pudding mix.

Makes 8 servings at 173 calories each or 10 servings at 138 calories each.

2 envelopes unflavored
  gelatin
½ cup boiling water
3½ cups skim milk
½ teaspoon cinnamon

1 package (3¾ ounces)
  vanilla instant
  pudding mix
1 ripe banana
Low-Calorie Graham
  Cracker Pie Shell

1. Place gelatin in container of electric blender; add boiling water. Blend at high speed, scraping sides of container several times, until the gelatin is dissolved.

2. Add about 2 cups of the skim milk (do not overfill container); blend briefly. Pour about half of mixture into bowl; add remaining milk and cinnamon to mixture in container; blend briefly.

3. Add pudding mix to milk mixture in container; blend until smooth. Add to blended mixture in bowl; mix well. Refrigerate a few minutes until mixture thickens.

4. Slice banana into bottom of pie shell; fill with chilled filling. Refrigerate about 3 hours, or until set.

NEW-FASHIONED LOW-CALORIE PUMPKIN PIE

Makes 8 servings at 121 calories each.
Conventional recipe is 240 calories per serving.

1 cup canned pumpkin
2 eggs
1¼ cups liquid
    skimmed milk
½ tablespoon
    cornstarch
¼ cup firmly packed
    brown sugar
Sugar substitute to
    equal ¼ cup sugar

¼ teaspoon salt
½ teaspoon ground
    cinnamon
⅛ teaspoon ground
    allspice
⅛ teaspoon ground
    ginger
⅛ teaspoon ground
    nutmeg

1. Prepare a pastry. Roll out to an 11-inch round on a lightly floured board. Fit into an 8-inch pie plate; turn edge under; flute.

2. Put all the remaining ingredients in your blender or in electric-mixer bowl and beat on high speed until smooth. Pour into prepared piecrust; bake in a moderate oven (350°) for 60 minutes, until crust is lightly browned.

3. Roll out pastry trimmings; cut into leaves or other fancy shapes with a cooky cutter; place on cooky sheet. Bake cutouts with pie, or after pie is out of oven and you have room, just until golden. Arrange on top of pie.

"MOM'S APPLE PIE," DECALORIZED

Makes 8 servings at 151 calories each.
Conventional recipe is 306 calories per serving.

Skinny Piecrust
6 cups thinly sliced
 apples
½ cup sugar
Sugar substitute to
 equal ½ cup sugar

1 tablespoon cornstarch
¼ teaspoon salt
½ teaspoon ground
 cinnamon
¼ teaspoon ground
 nutmeg

1. Prepare pastry; roll out to an 11-inch round on a lightly floured board. Fit into 8-inch pie plate; turn edge under; flute. Sprinkle apples with sugar, sugar substitute, cornstarch, salt, cinnamon and nutmeg and turn into pastry-lined pie plate. Cut a piece of foil into round to cover apples, but not pastry. The foil will keep the apple filling juicy and flavorful, just as in a conventional pie with a top crust. Bake in a moderate oven (375°) 1 hour, or until apples are tender.

2. Roll out pastry trimmings; cut into leaves or other fancy shapes with a cooky cutter; place on cooky sheet. Bake cutouts with pie, or after pie is out of oven and you have room, just until golden. Then arrange on top of the pie.

SKINNY PIECRUST

429 calories (single 8″ piecrust with pastry cutouts).
Conventional recipe is 1,045 calories.

½ cup sifted all-
 purpose flour
¼ cup diet margarine

¼ teaspoon salt
¼ teaspoon baking
 powder

1. Have diet margarine *room temperature* (this is important).

2. Sift flour, salt and baking powder together in a deep bowl.

3. Add margarine all at once. Cut in with fork or pastry blender and continue mixing until no pastry sticks to the sides of the bowl.

4. Shape into a ball. Wrap in wax paper and refrigerate until *thoroughly chilled* (one hour or more).

Cheesecakes

Rich as heavy cream, crowned in a ruby glaze of ripened fruit, cheesecake is the royalty of desserts—it's hard to imagine anything more fattening! Be a Creative Low-Calorie Cook and you can cut the calorie-count in half, or even in thirds, without ever having to skimp a single whit on flavor!

As an example: Cream cheese is the business end of some of the world's best-known cheesecakes (Lindy's, for one), but you can duplicate its flavor by substituting Neufchâtel cheese, the low-fat slim relative of cream cheese. Neufchâtel cheese weighs in at 584 calories per eight-ounce package (compared with 848 for cream cheese), yet it's such a taste-twin, you can use it in any recipe calling for cream cheese, even such earthy stuff as a cream-cheese-and-jelly sandwich (spread on diet bread with low-sugar jam, quite naturally).

Skinny-down your cheesecake even further by using one of the other even-lower-calorie soft cheeses; they're all pretty much interchangeable. Cottage cheese is a trim 200 calories per cupful, more or less, depending on whether it's skim or creamed. Or make a cake with farmer cheese, 310 calories per eight-ounce package. Farmer cheese is midway between cottage cheese and cream cheese in taste and texture. Or try a cheesecake with part-skim ricotta, 320 calories per cupful. A favorite in Italian cuisine, ricotta's velvety texture and mild flavor make for a cheesecake that's more creamy and less cheese-y.

STRAWBERRY GLAZED CHEESE PIE

Makes 10 servings at 177 calories each.

Graham-Cracker Crust	1 tablespoon lemon
½ cup water	juice
½ cup instant nonfat	1 teaspoon vanilla
dry milk (powder)	¼ cup flour
½ cup sugar	1 pound cottage cheese
4 eggs	(any kind)
¼ teaspoon salt	Jeweled Fruit Glaze

1. Prepare a 9-inch pie plate, using Graham-Cracker Crust.

2. Combine water, dry milk powder, sugar, eggs, salt, lemon juice, vanilla, flour and cottage cheese in container of an electric blender; whirl until smooth. (Or you may sieve cheese into a bowl, add remaining ingredients, then beat with a rotary beater until smooth.) Pour into prepared crust.

3. Bake in very slow oven (250°) for 1 hour. Turn oven off and leave pie in oven for 1 hour longer, then remove from oven; cool.

4. Top the cooled pie with Jeweled Fruit Glaze. Chill until glaze is set.

GRAHAM-CRACKER CRUST: Grease sides and bottom of pan recommended in recipe with 1 tablespoon butter or margarine (or 2 tablespoons diet margarine). Sprinkle with ½ cup of graham-cracker crumbs; press firmly into place. Chill 1 hour, or until firm.

JEWELED FRUIT GLAZE: Wash and hull 1 pint of strawberries. Leave whole or cut in half lengthwise. Arrange on top of pie, cut-side down. Blend 1 tablespoon cornstarch with 1 cup of water in a small saucepan. Cook over low heat, stirring constantly, until clear and thickened. Add enough liquid sweetener to equal ½ cup sugar. Stir in a few drops red food coloring. Cool slightly. Spoon over strawberries.

VARIATIONS: Canned water-pack pitted red cherries, frozen or fresh blueberries, or canned pineapple chunks packed in juice may be glazed the same way.

SKINNY NO-BAKE CHEESECAKE

This is a trimmed-down traditional refrigerator cheese-cake, only one third as fattening as it would be with whole milk, all sugar, some whipped cream and a conventional graham-cracker crust.

Makes 12 servings at 103 calories each.

Graham-Cracker Crust	2 teaspoons lemon juice
1 pound cottage cheese (any kind)	1 teaspoon grated orange rind
2 envelopes unflavored gelatin	1 teaspoon vanilla
1 cup water	Liquid or granulated no-calorie sweetener to equal ½ cup sugar
2 eggs, separated	
¾ cup liquid skim milk	½ cup nonfat dry milk (powder)
2 tablespoons sugar	
¼ teaspoon salt	

1. Prepare an 8-inch spring-form pan, using the Graham-Cracker Crust.

2. Press cheese through a sieve or food mill into a large bowl.

3. Sprinkle gelatin over ½ cup of the water in a small bowl. Let stand 5 minutes to soften.

4. Beat egg yolks in the top of a double boiler until fluffy; add skim milk, sugar and salt. Place over hot, not boiling water. Cook, stirring constantly, until thickened. Add gelatin; stir until dissolved. Remove from heat; stir into cheese in large bowl.

5. Add lemon juice, orange rind, vanilla and sweetener to cheese mixture; chill until as thick as unbeaten egg white.

6. Beat egg whites until stiff but not dry in a small

bowl. Beat nonfat dry milk with remaining ½ cup water until almost creamy in a second small bowl. Fold egg whites, then milk into cheese mixture until no streaks of white remain. Spoon into prepared pan. Chill until set, about 4 hours.

Gelatin Desserts

ORANGE WHIP

Makes 8 servings at 20 calories each.

1 envelope low-calorie
  orange-flavor gelatin
  (2 to a package)
1 cup boiling water
¾ cup cold water
1 teaspoon grated
  orange peel
1 teaspoon grated
  lemon peel

1 tablespoon lemon
  juice
1 egg white
1 tablespoon sugar
1 medium-size orange,
  peeled and cut into
  bite-size pieces

1. Thoroughly dissolve gelatin in boiling water in large bowl of electric mixer. Add cold water, grated peels and lemon juice. Chill until partially set and very thick.

2. Beat egg white to soft peak stage; gradually add sugar and continue beating until stiff.

3. Beat thickened gelatin at high speed until foamy and double in volume. Continue beating; add beaten white in 2 or 3 additions.

4. When well blended, fold in orange pieces. Spoon into 6-cup mold; chill until set before turning out onto serving plate.

APRICOT WHIP

Makes 6 servings at 25 calories each.

1 envelope low-calorie
  orange-flavor gelatin
  (2 to a package)
½ cup boiling water

1 can (8½ ounces)
  dietetic apricot halves
1½ teaspoons lemon
  juice
¼ teaspoon rum

1. Dissolve the gelatin in the boiling water in a saucepan.

2. Drain the apricots, reserving the juice. Add juice and water to make ½ cup to the hot gelatin mixture; add the lemon juice and rum. Chill until slightly thickened.

3. Place saucepan in a bowl of ice and water. Beat with a chilled rotary beater until fluffy.

4. Chop the apricots fine and fold in. Chill in individual molds until firm.

GEL COOKERY TIP: When recipe directions call for heating the gelatin in liquid "until the gelatin is dissolved," make sure all the granules have disappeared. A rubber spatula is a convenient utensil to use for stirring. When the gelatin seems dissolved, tilt the pan to make sure no undissolved granules remain.

STRAWBERRY MOUSSE

Makes 8 servings at 38 calories each.

1 envelope unflavored
   gelatin
½ cup water
1½ cups fresh or
   frozen sliced
   strawberries
   (unsweetened),
   thawed and crushed

2 egg whites
⅛ teaspoon salt
2 tablespoons sugar
½ cup evaporated
   skimmed milk,
   whipped

1. Sprinkle gelatin over water in medium-size sauce-pan; let stand to soften. Place over low heat; stir constantly until gelatin dissolves.
2. Remove from heat; stir in strawberries. Cool.
3. Beat egg whites with salt until stiff but not dry.
4. Gradually add sugar and beat until very stiff.
5. Fold in strawberry mixture. Fold in whipped cream.
6. Turn into 6-cup mold or serving bowl. Chill until firm.

LEMON SNOW

Makes 8 servings at 66 calories each.

2 envelopes unflavored
   gelatin
1 cup cold water
1 can (6 ounces) frozen
   lemonade concentrate,

kept frozen
½ cup ice water
3 egg whites

1. Sprinkle gelatin over water in medium-size sauce-pan. Place over low heat; stir constantly until gelatin dissolves, about 3 minutes.

2. Remove from heat. Add frozen concentrate; stir until melted. Add ice water. Chill until slightly thick.

3. Combine with egg whites in large bowl; beat on high speed of electric mixer until mixture begins to hold its shape. Turn into 8-cup mold or serving bowl, or into individual serving dishes. Chill until firm.

SUGARLESS CHOCOLATE CHIFFON

Makes 6 servings at 82 calories each.

1 envelope unflavored
   gelatin
1½ cups skim milk,
   divided
3 eggs, separated
¼ cup plain cocoa

⅛ teaspoon salt
Sugar substitute to
   equal ⅔ cup sugar
2 teaspoons vanilla
¼ teaspoon cream of
   tartar

1. Sprinkle gelatin over ½ cup cold milk in saucepan.

2. Beat egg yolks with remaining 1 cup milk; add to saucepan.

3. Add cocoa and salt. Place over low heat or hot water; stir constantly until gelatin dissolves and mixture thickens slightly, about 5 minutes.

4. Remove from heat; stir in sugar substitute and vanilla.

5. Chill, stirring occasionally, until mixture mounds slightly when dropped from spoon.

6. Beat egg whites with cream of tartar until very stiff. Fold into the gelatin mixture. Turn into 4-cup mold. Chill until firm. Unmold.

Fast and Fancy Fruit Desserts

STRAWBERRIES ROMANOFF

Makes 6 servings at 66 calories each (with sugar); without sugar, 53 calories per serving.

3 cups fresh
  strawberries
½ cup orange juice
2 tablespoons orange
  liqueur

2 tablespoons sugar or
  sugar substitute to
  equal 2 tablespoons
  sugar
Low-calorie whipped
  topping

1. Wash and hull the berries. Leave whole. Combine them in a bowl with orange juice, liqueur and sugar or sugar substitute. Refrigerate.

2. At serving time, spoon the berries and liquid into six champagne glasses.

3. Top each with 1 tablespoon of the whipped cream topping or prepared low-calorie topping mix.

CHERRIES JUBILEE

Makes 8 servings at 139 calories each. (If made with sugar substitute, 129 calories.)

1 quart vanilla ice
  milk (97 percent
  fat-free)
1 can (16 ounces) red
  pitted cherries,
  packed in water
½ teaspoon almond
  extract

1 tablespoon cornstarch
2 tablespoons sugar (or
  equivalent sugar
  substitute)
3 or 4 drops of red food
  coloring
¼ cup brandy

1. Pile half-cup servings of ice milk into eight stemmed sherbet glasses.

2. In a chafing dish or saucepan, combine the cherries, almond extract, cornstarch, sugar and food coloring. Cook and stir over moderate heat until sauce simmers and clears.

3. Pour brandy on the surface of the sauce. Ignite the brandy vapors. Spoon flaming cherries over ice milk and serve immediately.

Frozen Desserts

VANILLA ICE CREAM

Makes 8 servings at 58 calories each.

1 envelope unflavored gelatin	3 tablespoons sugar, divided
1 cup cold water, divided	1 tablespoon liquid sweetener
¾ cup instant nonfat dry milk, divided	1 tablespoon vanilla
1½ cups skim milk	1 tablespoon lemon juice

1. Soften the gelatin in one-half cup of the cold water.

2. Mix 4 tablespoons of the milk powder into the liquid skim milk and heat in a saucepan until milk bubbles around edges. Dissolve gelatin mixture in milk. Stir in 2 tablespoons of the sugar, the liquid sweetener and the vanilla. Chill until slightly thickened.

3. Beat the remaining ½ cup of the milk powder with the remaining ½ cup of the cold water until it begins to thicken slightly. Add the lemon juice and remaining 1 tablespoon of sugar and beat until almost the consistency of whipped cream. (This takes a while, 5 minutes or more.)

4. Fold in the chilled gelatin mixture and spoon into 2 aluminum refrigerator trays. Freeze until the edges are set; beat until fluffy, then freeze until firm.

QUICK ORANGE ICE

Makes 3 servings at 50 calories each.

1 envelope low-calorie
  orange-flavor gelatin
  (2 to a package)
½ cup hot water
1 cup orange juice
	Pinch of grated orange
	  rind
	½ teaspoon liquid
	  sweetener

1. Dissolve the gelatin in the hot water.
2. Add the orange juice, rind and sweetener.
3. Freeze almost firm; then beat until creamy. Return to the freezer until firm.

FOR THE KIDS: Make popsicles by freezing in an ice cube tray and inserting a stick in each cube.

QUICK CHOCOLATE SAUCE

Makes 2⅓ cups at 11 calories per tablespoon.

2½ cups skim milk
1 envelope (1 ounce)
  low-calorie chocolate
	pudding and pie
	  filling mix
	Pinch of salt

1. Gradually add the milk to pudding mix in a saucepan.
2. Cook over low heat, stirring constantly, until the mixture comes to a boil. Add the salt.
3. Cool; cover top to keep a skin from forming, or use hot over dietetic ice cream.

Chapter 17

Slimming Sauces

There's no secret to making tasty sauces. But sauces are the secret to making many of the world's most famous gourmet dishes. For the Creative Low-Calorie Cook, the trick is to slim down the classics—rich, calorie-laden Hollandaise, creamy, diet-breaking white sauce and poundage-prone gravies from roasts and slow-simmered stews.

In this chapter we show you how to make skinnies out of these and all your other favorites—fruit sauces for poultry, meat sauces for pasta, wine, vegetable and barbecue sauces, plus a dozen well-seasoned variations for basic white sauce.

Making your own sauces is a rewarding yet very simple part of creating memorable dining moments. Making slim sauces is just as easy.

And the results? No one will ever know the difference between these sauces and their original high-calorie relatives. But everyone will see the difference in you!

SUGARLESS RAISIN SAUCE

(For poultry or ham.)

Makes 1⅔ cups at 10 calories per tablespoon.

1 tablespoon cornstarch
1½ cups cold water
¼ teaspoon cinnamon
Pinch of ground cloves

1 tablespoon cider
  vinegar
½ cup seedless raisins
2 teaspoons liquid
  sweetener

1. Combine all ingredients except the sweetener in a medium-size saucepan.
2. Cook, stirring constantly, over low heat until sauce is thickened. Remove from heat; stir in sweetener.

WHOLE-BERRY CRANBERRY SAUCE

Bake at 300° for 45 minutes.
Makes 3 cups at 13 calories per tablespoon.

1 quart fresh
  cranberries
½ cup sugar

4 tablespoons water
3 tablespoons liquid
  sweetener

1. Wash and drain cranberries. Pour into an oven-proof casserole. Sprinkle with sugar; add water; cover.
2. Bake in a slow oven (300°) for 45 minutes; add more water if necessary.
3. Remove from oven; stir in sugar substitute.
SUGARLESS CRANBERRY SAUCE: Bake the berries without any sugar and substitute ¼ cup orange juice for the water. When cooked, stir in no-calorie sugar substitute to taste, equal to 2 cups of sugar. Makes 3 cups at 5 calories per tablespoon.

EGGLESS MOCK HOLLANDAISE

Makes 1 cup at 9 calories per tablespoon.

1 envelope or teaspoon
  instant chicken broth
1 cup boiling water
1 tablespoon cornstarch

1 tablespoon lemon
  juice
1 tablespoon butter or
  margarine

  1. Dissolve broth in water. Combine with cornstarch, lemon juice and butter in a small saucepan.
  2. Cook, stirring constantly, over low heat until thickened.

YOGURT HOLLANDAISE

Makes 1 cup at 13 calories per tablespoon.

2 egg yolks
¾ cup plain yogurt
1½ teaspoons lemon
  juice

⅛ teaspoon salt
Pinch of paprika

  1. Beat egg yolks until frothy; add yogurt and lemon juice.
  2. Pour into top of double boiler over hot water. Cook, stirring constantly, until thick and smooth. Add seasonings.

MEAT SAUCE FOR PASTA

Makes 6 cups at 169 calories each.

1½ pounds lean ground round
2 small onions, chopped (¾ cup)
2 cloves of garlic, minced
2 cans (1 pound, 12 ounces each) tomatoes
½ cup red wine or water
4 tablespoons dried parsley flakes
2 teaspoons salt
1 teaspoon sugar
½ teaspoon paprika
½ teaspoon oregano
2 bay leaves

1. Spread meat on foil over broiler tray. Broil until brown, about 10 minutes.
2. Combine meat and remaining ingredients in a heavy skillet or Dutch oven.
3. Cover; bring to boiling. Reduce heat; simmer 1½ hours, stirring occasionally. Uncover last 10 minutes to reduce liquid. Skim off fat.

EASY CURRY SAUCE

Makes 2 cups at 9 calories per tablespoon.

2 envelopes or teaspoons instant chicken broth
2 cups skim milk
¼ cup sifted flour
¾ teaspoon curry powder

Combine chicken broth, flour and curry powder in a medium-size saucepan. Gradually add milk. Cook, stirring constantly, over medium heat until mixture thickens and boils. Serve over hot, cooked vegetables or fish.

EASY TOMATO SAUCE

Makes 1½ cups at 7 calories per tablespoon.

1 tablespoon diet margarine	1 can (1 pound) tomatoes
¼ cup finely chopped onion	2 envelopes or teaspoons instant beef broth

1. Heat margarine in a large skillet. Add onions; sauté until tender.

2. Stir in tomatoes and beef broth. Simmer, uncovered, 15 minutes, or until sauce is thick and well blended. Serve over hamburger patties, meat loaf or fish cakes.

FAT-FREE GRAVY

1. Pour all the pan drippings into a tall, narrow glass or container; add ice cubes. Wait 5 minutes. Lift off hardened fat. (If you can't wait, use a bulb-type baster to siphon off the fat that rises to the surface.) Return the liquid to the roasting pan and heat over moderate heat. With a fork, scrape up any particles that adhere to the bottom of the pan.

2. To thicken the gravy, combine 2 tablespoons flour and ¼ cup cold water for each cupful of drippings. Stir into simmering liquid and continue to simmer until thickened. Salt and pepper to taste.

FRENCH WINE AND CHEESE SAUCE

Makes 2½ cups at 11 calories per tablespoon.

2 cups skim milk
1 teaspoon butter-
   flavored salt
Pinch of nutmeg
½ teaspoon dry
   mustard
Pinch of cayenne

2 tablespoons
   cornstarch
4 tablespoons dry
   sherry or vermouth
3 ounces Swiss or
   Gruyère cheese,
   shredded

1. Combine milk, salt, nutmeg, mustard and cayenne in a nonstick saucepan; bring to boiling over high heat.

2. Mix cornstarch and wine together; stir into sauce. Reduce heat; cook, stirring constantly, until slightly thickened.

3. Remove from heat; add cheese. Stir until cheese is melted.

CUCUMBER SAUCE
(For seafood specialties!)

Makes ¾ cup at 14 calories per tablespoon.

1 large cucumber, pared
   and seeded
4 tablespoons imitation
   sour cream
1 tablespoon minced
   onion
½ teaspoon salt

½ teaspoon grated
   lemon peel
1½ teaspoons lemon
   juice
3 tablespoons snipped
   fresh parsley

Grate cucumber; drain thoroughly. Combine with remaining ingredients in medium-size bowl. Cover; chill.

RANCHHOUSE BARBECUE SAUCE

Makes 2⅔ cups at 8 calories per tablespoon.

1½ cups boiling water
3 envelopes or
  teaspoons instant
  broth
1 cup catsup
2 teaspoons cornstarch
3 tablespoons cider
  vinegar

1 tablespoon
  Worcestershire sauce
¼ teaspoon oregano
¼ teaspoon ground
  marjoram
⅛ teaspoon thyme
Dash of garlic salt

1. Dissolve beef broth in boiling water. Stir in catsup and cornstarch.
2. Add all remaining ingredients; blend thoroughly.
3. Spread on the meat while broiling or barbecuing.

SALSA VERDE (GREEN SAUCE)

Makes 1 cup at 17 calories per tablespoon.

½ cup low-calorie
  Italian salad dressing
1 small bunch parsley
2 tablespoons capers,
  washed and drained
1 slice dry protein
  bread, crumbled

½ teaspoon salt
4 drops liquid red-
  pepper seasoning
1 clove of garlic
1 unstuffed green olive

Combine all ingredients in a container of electric blender. Cover; blend on high speed 30 seconds, or until puréed. Serve with hot or cold meats.

BASIC "WHITE SAUCE"

Makes 1 cup at 11 calories per tablespoon.

½ cup instant nonfat
  dry milk
1 cup water
1 tablespoon flour

1 tablespoon cornstarch
½ teaspoon salt
Pinch of white pepper

Combine all ingredients in a medium-size saucepan; beat until smooth. Cook, stirring constantly, over low heat until thickened. Simmer for 1 or 2 minutes longer.

"WHITE SAUCE" VARIATIONS

For "Thin White Sauce," use only ½ tablespoon each of flour and cornstarch. For "Heavy White Sauce," increase the flour and cornstarch to 1½ tablespoons. For creamed fish, vegetables or other bland dishes, add a few drops of butter flavoring.

CHEESE SAUCE—Stir in 4 tablespoons grated Cheddar cheese until melted. (8 calories per tablespoon)

EGG SAUCE—Mix in 1 grated hard-cooked egg before serving. (12 calories)

WHITE MUSHROOM SAUCE—Add a dash of Worcestershire sauce and the contents of one 4-ounce can of mushroom stems and pieces, drained and chopped. (12 calories per tablespoon)

WHITE ONION SAUCE—Add a dash of garlic powder and 2 tablespoons of dried onion flakes to "Thin White Sauce." (7 calories)

HERB SAUCE—Add 2 teaspoons chopped chives, 2 teaspoons minced parsley and a pinch of thyme. (11 calories per tablespoon)

HOT HORSERADISH SAUCE—Add 3 tablespoons horseradish. (12 calories)

QUICK BECHAMEL SAUCE—Omit salt and add

one envelope or teaspoon instant chicken broth, one finely minced hard-cooked egg and a generous shake of paprika. Whirl in your blender. (17 calories per tablespoon)

PICKLE SAUCE—Add 3 tablespoons of chopped dill pickles. (12 calories)

PIMIENTO SAUCE—Add 2 tablespoons of chopped pimiento. (12 calories)

CURRY SAUCE—Add ½ teaspoon curry powder. (11 calories)

Chapter 18

Calorie Guide

A

Almonds, shelled,	850	1 cup
salted	83	10 nuts
Anchovies, canned fillets	28	4
Apple	70	1 med.
Apple butter	33	1 tbsp.
Apple juice	120	1 cup
Applesauce, canned,		
sweetened	230	1 cup
diet-pack	100	1 cup
Apricots		
fresh	55	3
canned in heavy syrup	110	½ cup
canned, diet-pack	56	½ cup
dried	90	10
Apricot nectar, canned	140	1 cup
Artichokes, fresh, cooked	30	1 med.
frozen, hearts, cooked	22	½ cup
Asparagus, fresh, cooked	20	6 spears
canned	20	6 spears
frozen, spears, cooked	23	5
Avocado	245	½ med.
	186	½ cup

B

Bacon, broiled or fried	100	2 slices
Canadian, lean, broiled	50	3 slices
Bamboo shoots, canned	41	1 cup
Banana	85	1
Barley, pearl, cooked	142	1 cup
Bean sprouts, canned	20	½ cup
Beans, baked, with pork		
and molasses	325	1 cup

314

with pork in tomato sauce	295	1 cup
Beans, green or wax		
fresh cut, cooked	15	½ cup
canned, cut	14	½ cup
frozen, cut, cooked	18	½ cup
kidney, canned	230	1 cup
lima, fresh, cooked	180	1 cup
frozen, cooked	94	½ cup
dried, large, cooked	260	1 cup
Beef, brisket, fresh	266	1 slice
corned	266	1 slice
pot roast, blade	506	1 slice
rib roast	243	1 slice
rump	235	1 slice
sirloin	186	1 slice
steak, cubed, raw	793	12 oz.
steak, club, raw	305	6 oz.
steak, flank	200	3 slices
porterhouse	412	1 piece
round	406	1 piece
ground, round, raw	271	6 oz.
sirloin	353	1 piece
stew meat, chuck, boneless, raw	421	4 oz.
Beef and vegetable stew canned	210	1 cup
Beef broth canned, condensed	66	1 can
cubes instant	8	1 env.
canned corned beef	185	3 oz.
canned corned beef hash	155	3 oz.
Beef potpie, frozen	436	8 oz.
Beef TV Dinner	350	1
Beer	100	1 cup
Beets, fresh, cooked, diced	50	1 cup
Biscuits, baking powder	129	1
Blackberries, fresh	43	½ cup
frozen, unsweetened	55	½ cup
Blueberries, fresh	43	½ cup
frozen, sweetened	129	½ cup
frozen, unsweetened	45	½ cup
Bologna	87	1 slice
Bran flakes, 40%	95	¾ cup
Brandy	100	2 oz.
Brazil nuts, shelled	100	4
Bread		
Boston brown	100	1 slice
cracked-wheat	60	1 slice

French	108	1 piece
Italian	108	1 piece
pumpernickel	65	1 slice
raisin, unfrosted	60	1 slice
rye	55	1 slice
white, enriched	60	1 slice
whole-wheat	55	1 slice
Bread crumbs, dry	345	1 cup
soft	120	1 cup
Broccoli, fresh, spears, cooked	40	4
frozen, chopped, cooked	25	½ cup
frozen, spears, cooked	26	3
Brownies	120	1
Brussels sprouts, fresh, cooked	45	1 cup
frozen, cooked	29	½ cup
Butter	100	1 tbsp.
Buttermilk	90	1 cup

C

Cabbage, raw, finely shredded	25	1 cup
cooked, finely shredded	35	1 cup
Cabbage, Chinese, raw, chopped	15	1 cup
cooked, chopped	20	1 cup
Cakes		
angel	110	1 wedge
chocolate with icing	445	1 wedge
cupcake with icing	185	1
plain cake, without icing	200	1 slice
poundcake	140	1 slice
spongecake	120	1 wedge
Candy		
caramels	42	1
chocolate creams	47	1
chocolate fudge	66	1
chocolate-mint patty	40	1
marshmallows	26	1 large
peanut brittle	125	1
Cantaloupe	60	½ med.
balls	20	½ cup
Carbonated beverages	90	8 oz.
Carrots, raw, whole	20	1
raw, grated	45	1 cup
cooked, diced	45	1 cup
Cashew nuts, roasted	164	8

Catsup	15	1 tbsp.
Cauliflower, raw		
flowerettes	25	1 cup
cooked, flowerettes	25	1 cup
frozen, flowerettes, cooked	15	½ cup
Celery, raw, diced	15	1 cup
raw, stalk	5	1
Cheese		
blue or Roquefort	105	1 oz.
Camembert	86	1 oz.
Cheddar or American,		
grated	445	1 cup
grated	30	1 tbsp.
process	105	1 oz.
cottage, skim milk		
cream-style	240	1 cup
cottage, dry	195	1 cup
cream	55	1 tbsp.
Parmesan, grated	31	1 tbsp.
Swiss, natural	120	1 oz.
Swiss, process	105	1 oz.
Cheese foods, Cheddar	90	1 oz.
Cheese spreads	35	1 tbsp.
Cherries, sour, red, canned	230	1 cup
Cherries, sweet, fresh	80	1 cup
canned, sweetened	112	½ cup
canned, diet-pack	57	½ cup
Chicken, broiled,		
quartered	248	1 piece
roast	200	3 slices
roast	101	1 leg
roast	147	1 thigh
Chicken broth, canned		
condensed	74	10 oz.
cubes	6	1
instant	10	1 env.
Chicken livers	146	¼ lb.
Chicken potpie, frozen	482	8 oz.
Chicken TV Dinner	489	1
Chili con carne, canned		
without beans	335	1 cup
with beans	510	1 cup
Chili sauce	17	1 tbsp.
Chocolate, unsweetened	145	1 oz.
semisweet pieces	906	6 oz.
Chocolate bar, milk, plain	150	1 oz.
Chocolate malted milk		
shake with ice cream	500	1½ cups
Chocolate milk	205	1 cup

Chocolate syrup, thin	50	1 tbsp.
Clams, raw	65	6 large
canned, clams and liquid	45	½ cup
Clam juice	35	1 cup
Cocoa, with whole milk	235	1 cup
Cocoa powder	21	1 tbsp.
Coconut, shredded	335	1 cup
Cod, fresh, poached	84	4 oz.
frozen, fillets, poached	84	4 oz.
frozen, sticks, breaded	276	5
Cola	95	8 oz.
Cookies		
chocolate wafer	36	1
creme sandwich, chocolate	54	1
fig bars, small	55	1
gingersnaps	52	1
sugar wafer	10	1
vanilla wafer	18	1
Corn flakes, plain	100	1 cup
presweetened	110	¾ cup
Corn, sweet		
fresh, cooked	70	1 ear
canned, cream-style	92	½ cup
canned, whole-kernel	70	½ cup
frozen, whole-kernel	73	½ cup
Corn meal, dry	420	1 cup
Corn muffins	150	1
Corn oil	125	1 tbsp.
Corn syrup, light or dark	60	1 tbsp.
Cornstarch	30	1 tbsp.
Cornstarch pudding with		
whole milk chocolate	67	½ cup
vanilla or butterscotch	72	½ cup
low-calorie, with skim		
milk chocolate	57	½ cup
vanilla or butterscotch	55	½ cup
instant chocolate	183	½ cup
vanilla or butterscotch	170	½ cup
Cottonseed oil	125	1 tbsp.
Crab meat	89	3 oz.
Cracker meal	45	1 tbsp.
Crackers		
cheese	34	10
graham, plain	30	1
chocolate graham	56	1
oyster	60	20
peanut-butter sandwich	45	1
pretzels	7	5 sticks
rye wafers	21	1

saltines	14	1
soda	23	1
Cranberry juice, bottled	160	1 cup
Cranberry sauce, sweetened, canned, jellied or whole-berry	26	1 tbsp.
Cream, half-and-half	20	1 tbsp.
heavy or whipping	55	1 tbsp.
light, coffee, or table	30	1 tbsp.
sour, dairy	29	1 tbsp.
Cucumber, raw, whole	30	1
raw, sliced	5	6 slices
Custard baked with whole milk	285	1 cup

D

Dates, dry, whole	100	5
Doughnuts. cake type	125	1
Duck, roast	165	3 slices

E

Egg, whole	80	1
white	15	1
yolk	60	1
Eggplant, fried	139	1 slice
Endive, Belgian	10	1 stalk
curly or chickory, broken	5	1 cup
Escarole	5	2 leaves

F

Farina, cooked	100	1 cup
Figs, fresh	90	3 small
canned, in syrup	150	½ cup
canned, diet-pack	68	½ cup
dried	100	2 med.
Flounder, fillet, fresh, poached	170	8 oz.
frozen, poached	76	4 oz.
Flour, all-purpose	400	1 cup
cake or pastry, sifted	365	1 cup
self-rising, enriched	385	1 cup
whole-wheat	400	1 cup
Frankfurter (10 per lb.)	120	1
French dressing, low-calorie	9	1 tbsp.
regular	65	1 tbsp.
Fruitcake, dark	115	1 sliver

Fruit cocktail canned, in syrup	195	1 cup
canned, diet-pack	60	½ cup

G

Gelatin, unflavored		
Gelatin dessert, flavored	35	1 tbsp.
ready-to-eat, regular		
low-calorie	81	½ cup
Gin	9	½ cup
Ginger ale	105	2 oz.
Gingerbread	80	8 oz.
Grapefruit, fresh	175	1 piece
fresh sections	55	½ med.
canned, sections	75	1 cup
canned, diet-pack	175	1 cup
Grapefruit juice, fresh	70	1 cup
canned, sweetened	95	1 cup
canned, unsweetened	130	1 cup
frozen concentrate,	100	1 cup
sweetened reconstituted		
unsweetened reconstituted	115	1 cup
Grapes, fresh, Niagara,	100	1 cup
Concord, Delaware,		
Catawba, Scuppernong	65	1 cup
Malaga, Muscat,		
Thompson seedless,		
Emperor, Flame, Tokay	95	1 cup
Grape juice, bottled		
or canned	165	1 cup

H

Haddock, fresh, broiled	100	6 oz.
frozen, broiled	88	4 oz.
frozen, fish-sticks,		
breaded	280	5
Halibut, fresh, broiled	217	8 oz.
frozen, broiled	144	4 oz.
Ham, baked	253	1 slice
boiled, sliced	135	2 oz.
Herring, pickled	127	2 oz.
Hominy grits, cooked	120	1 cup
Honey, strained	65	1 tbsp.
Honeydew melon	73	⅛ med.
cubes	58	1 cup

I

Ice cream, commercial		
chocolate	200	⅔ cup

vanilla	193	⅔ cup
Ice cream, brick	145	1 slice
Ice milk, chocolate	144	⅔ cup
vanilla	136	⅔ cup

J and K

Jams, jellies, preserves	55	1 tbsp.
Kale, cooked	30	1 cup
Kidney, cooked, beef	118	3 oz.
lamb	111	3 oz.
pork	130	3 oz.

L

Lamb chop, loin, raw	223	6 oz.
rib, raw	240	5 oz.
shoulder, raw	252	5 oz.
Lamb roast, leg	165	1 slice
Lamb shank, raw	275	10 oz.
Lard	125	1 tbsp.
Leeks, chopped, cooked	25	½ cup
Lettuce, head	47	1 lb.
Lemon	20	1 med.
Lemonade concentrate, reconstituted	110	1 cup
Lemon juice, fresh	5	1 tbsp.
	60	1 cup
Limeade concentrate, reconstituted	105	1 cup
Lime juice, fresh	4	1 tbsp.
	65	1 cup
Liqueurs	165	1 oz.
Liver, cooked beef	117	3 oz.
calf's	136	3 oz.
lamb	171	3 oz.
pork	115	3 oz.
Liverwurst	100	1 slice
Lobster, fresh, boiled	108	¾ lb.
canned, meat	80	½ cup
frozen tails, boiled	81	3 small

M

Macaroni, cooked	155	1 cup
Macaroni and cheese, baked	470	1 cup
Mandarin oranges canned, in syrup	55	⅓ cup
canned, diet-pack	29	⅓ cup

Mango	133	1 med.
Manhattan	165	2½ oz.
Margarine	100	1 tbsp.
Martini	145	2½ oz.
Mayonnaise	100	1 tbsp.
imitation	55	1 tbsp.
Melba toast	17	1 slice
Milk,		
buttermilk	90	1 cup
condensed, sweetened	980	1 cup
dry, instant nonfat	250	1 cup
evaporated	345	1 cup
skim	90	1 cup
whole	160	1 cup
Mixed vegetables,		
frozen, cooked	55	½ cup
Molasses	50	1 tbsp.
Muffins, plain	140	1
Mushrooms, fresh	14	6
canned, with liquid	40	1 cup
Mustard, prepared	4	1 tsp.

N

Nectarines	50	1 med.
Noodles, egg, cooked	200	1 cup

O

Oat cereal, ready-to-eat	100	1 cup
Oatmeal	130	1 cup
Okra, fresh, cooked	25	8 pods
frozen, sliced, cooked	26	½ cup
Olives, green unpitted	15	4 med.
ripe, unpitted	15	2 large
Olive oil	125	1 tbsp.
Onion, green	20	6 small
raw, whole	40	1 med.
raw, chopped	60	1 cup
Onion soup mix, dry	150	1 env.
Orange, fresh	70	1 med.
sections	50	½ cup
Orange juice, fresh	110	1 cup
canned, unsweetened	120	1 cup
frozen concentrate,		
reconstituted	110	1 cup
Oysters, raw	160	15 med.
Oyster stew	200	1 cup

P

Pancakes, buckwheat	55	1 cake
plain, home recipe	60	1 cake
Papaya, fresh, cubed	70	1 cup
Parsley, fresh, chopped	1	1 tbsp.
Parsnips, cooked, diced	100	1 cup
Peaches, fresh, whole	35	1 med.
fresh, sliced	65	1 cup
canned, in syrup	90	2 halves
canned, diet-pack	54	2 halves
dried, uncooked	420	1 cup
cooked, unsweetened	220	1 cup
frozen, sweetened	99	⅓ cup
Peach nectar, canned	120	1 cup
Peanuts, roasted, salted	100	20 med.
chopped	55	1 tbsp.
dry-roasted	170	¼ cup
Peanut butter	95	1 tbsp.
Pears, fresh, whole	100	1 med.
canned, in syrup	58	2 halves
canned, diet-pack	62	2 halves
Pear nectar, canned	130	1 cup
Peas, blackeye, frozen, cooked	95	½ cup
Peas, green, fresh, cooked	115	1 cup
canned	146	1 cup
frozen, cooked	60	½ cup
Pecans, halves	100	12
	376	½ cup
Peppers, sweet, green, raw	15	1 med.
green, raw, diced	16	½ cup
red, raw	20	1 med.
Persimmons	75	1 med.
Pickles, dill	15	1 (5")
sweet	30	1 (3")
Pies,		
apple	290	⅛
blueberry	255	⅛
cherry	299	⅛
custard	233	⅛
lemon meringue	264	⅛
mince	298	⅛
pecan	479	⅛
pumpkin	230	⅛
Pimientos, canned	10	1 med.
Pine nuts (pignolias)	671	½ cup

Pineapple, fresh, diced	75	1 cup
canned, crushed, in syrup	195	1 cup
canned, sliced, in syrup	90	2 slices
canned, cubes, juice-pack	57	½ cup
Pineapple juice, canned	135	1 cup
frozen, reconstituted	125	1 cup
Plums, fresh, whole	25	1 med.
canned, in syrup	100	3 plums
canned, diet-pack	75	3 plums
Pork, chop, rib, raw	250	6 oz.
chop, loin, raw	283	6 oz.
roast, loin	330	1 chop
luncheon meat	165	2 oz.
Popcorn, popped, with		
oil and salt	40	1 cup
plain	24	1 cup
sugar-coated	135	1 cup
Potatoes, baked,		
without skin	90	1 med.
boiled, without skin	80	1 med.
French fried, frozen	125	10 pcs.
mashed, with milk only	70	½ cup
Potato chips	115	10
Pretzels, small sticks	10	10
Prunes	70	4 med.
cooked, unsweetened	295	18 med.
Prune juice	200	1 cup
Pumpkin, canned	75	1 cup

R

Radishes	5	4
Raisins	460	1 cup
Raspberries, red, fresh	70	1 cup
canned, in syrup	100	½ cup
frozen, sweetened	115	½ cup
Rhubarb, cooked with		
sugar	385	1 cup
Rice, cooked, brown	100	⅔ cup
precooked, cooked	140	⅔ cup
long-grain, white	185	1 cup
wild	73	½ cup
Rice cereal, ready to eat	115	1 cup
puffed	55	1 cup
Rolls,		
frankfurter	120	1
French	118	1
hamburger	123	1
Parker house	114	1
Rum	105	2 oz.

Rutabagas, cubed, cooked	25	½ cup
Rye wafers	63	3

S

Salad dressings,		
blue cheese, low-calorie	15	1 tbsp.
regular	65	1 tbsp.
French, low-calorie	9	1 tbsp.
regular	65	1 tbsp.
mayonnaise, imitation	55	1 tbsp.
regular	100	1 tbsp.
salad dressing	65	1 tbsp.
Thousand Island,		
low-calorie	33	1 tbsp.
regular	75	1 tbsp.
Salad oil	125	1 tbsp.
Salami	130	3 slices
Salmon, fresh, steak,		
broiled	430	6 oz.
canned	120	½ cup
Sardines, canned, in oil	100	4
Sauerkraut, canned	32	1 cup
Scallops, sea, fresh,		
steamed	105	6 med.
frozen, steamed	210	1 cup
Sesame seeds	10	1 tbsp.
Sherbet, orange, milk	260	1 cup
Shortening, vegetable	110	1 tbsp.
Shredded wheat biscuit	94	1
Shrimps, fresh, poached	100	7 med.
canned	167	5 oz.
frozen, poached	100	9 med.
cocktail, tiny, canned	33	15
Sole, fillet, fresh,		
poached	177	1 piece
Sole, fillet, frozen,		
poached	88	4 oz.
Soups, canned condensed,		
prepared with water,		
following label directions,		
asparagus, cream of	51	1 cup
bean with bacon	130	1 cup
beef broth	22	1 cup
beef noodle	55	1 cup
black bean	80	1 cup
celery, cream of	75	1 cup
cheese	142	1 cup
chicken broth	85	1 cup
chicken, cream of	85	1 cup

chicken gumbo	48	1 cup
chicken noodle	54	1 cup
chicken vegetable	60	1 cup
chicken with rice	44	1 cup
chili beef	133	1 cup
clam chowder	60	1 cup
consommé	25	1 cup
green pea, cream of	110	1 cup
madrilene	27	1 cup
minestrone	85	1 cup
mushroom, cream of	113	1 cup
onion	52	1 cup
pepper pot	83	1 cup
potato, cream of	59	1 cup
Scotch broth	74	1 cup
split pea	130	1 cup
tomato	73	1 cup
tomato rice	82	1 cup
turkey noodle	65	1 cup
turkey vegetable	58	1 cup
vegetable	63	1 cup
vegetable beef	61	1 cup
Soups, packaged mix prepared with water, following label directions, beef	87	1 cup
chicken noodle	60	1 cup
chicken rice	55	1 cup
green pea	128	1 cup
mushroom, cream of	46	1 cup
onion	40	1 cup
potato, cream of	90	1 cup
tomato vegetable	69	1 cup
vegetable	69	1 cup
Soy sauce	10	1 tbsp.
Soybean oil	125	1 tbsp.
Spaghetti, cooked	155	1 cup
Spinach, fresh, cooked	40	1 cup
canned	45	1 cup
frozen	24	½ cup
Squash, yellow, zucchini, crookneck, patty pan, sliced, cooked	30	1 cup
frozen, cooked	20	½ cup
Squash, acorn, banana, hubbard, baked, mashed	130	1 cup
frozen, cooked	50	½ cup
Strawberries, fresh	55	1 cup

Strawberries, frozen,		
whole, unsweetened	55	1 cup
sliced, sweetened	140	½ cup
Succotash, frozen, cooked	87	½ cup
Sugars, brown, firmly		
packed	820	1 cup
	51	1 tbsp.
granulated	770	1 cup
	45	1 tbsp.
lump	25	1
10X (confectioners'		
powdered)	495	1 cup
	30	1 tbsp.
Sweet potatoes, baked		
or boiled	170	1 med.
canned, without syrup	235	1 cup
Syrup,		
corn, light, or dark	60	1 tbsp.
maple	61	1 tbsp.
maple-blended,		
low-calorie	21	1 tbsp.
maple-blended, regular	54	1 tbsp.
pancake	55	1 tbsp.
sorghum	55	1 tbsp.

T

Tangerine	40	1 large
Tangerine juice, canned		
unsweetened	105	1 cup
Tapioca, quick-cooking,		
uncooked	35	1 tbsp.
Tomatoes, fresh	35	1 med.
canned	50	1 cup
Tomato juice, canned	45	1 cup
Tuna, canned, in oil,		
drained	170	½ cup
canned, in water	109	½ cup
Turnips, yellow, cooked,		
diced	50	1 cup
white, cooked, diced	35	1 cup
Turkey, roast	134	1 slice
Turkey potpie, frozen	429	8 oz.
Turkey TV dinner	325	1 pkg.

V

Veal, chop, loin, raw	251	8 oz.
chop, rib, raw	240	6 oz.
roast, leg	159	1 slice

scallopini, sautéed	172	3 pieces
Vinegar	2	1 tbsp.

W

Walnuts, chopped	50	1 tbsp.
halves	650	1 cup
Watermelon, fresh	115	1 wedge
cubed	40	1 cup
Wheat cereal, cooked	175	1 cup
flakes, ready-to-eat	100	1 cup
puffed	83	1 cup
puffed, presweetened	105	¾ cup
shredded	94	1 biscuit
Wheat germ	27	1 tbsp.
Whiskey	105	2 oz.
Wine, dry	85	3 oz.
sweet	160	3 oz.

Y and Z

Yams, pared, cubed, cooked	90	½ cup
Yogurt, skim milk	120	1 cup
whole milk	176	1 cup
Zwieback	31	1 slice

Index

Index